MASTERING

GERMAN

Linda Maine
September 27/83
Highbridge.

MASTERING
GERMAN

ANTONY J. PECK

EDITORIAL CONSULTANT
BETTY PARR

First edition 1982
Reprinted 1983

Published by
THE MACMILLAN PRESS LTD
London and Basingstoke
Companies and representatives throughout
the world

Filmset in 10/12pt Compugraphic English
Times and Univers
by Reproduction Drawings Ltd, Sutton,
Surrey

Printed in Hong Kong

ISBN 0 333 32587 7 (hard cover)
     0 333 32588 5 (paper cover-home)
     0 333 35464 8 (paper cover-export)

Cassette ISBN 0 333 34059 0

For
D.K.M.P.

CONTENTS

II REFERENCE MATERIAL

SERIES EDITOR'S PREFACE

The first language books in the Master Series, which are intended primarily for adult beginners without a teacher, should fill a notable gap in an otherwise well-cultivated field. The publishers make no promises of instant mastery, and recognise that no one slim volume can contain more than the basic essentials of any living language. We believe, however, that these books provide a carefully planned introduction to the language as well as a secure foundation for further study.

Existing publications seem either to concentrate on teaching 'how to survive abroad' or else to adopt a mainly academic approach. In these new books, our aim is to assist not only those studying a language for practical – generally touristic or commercial – purposes, but also those wishing to acquire a more formal knowledge of the grammar and structures of the language, with the intention of extending their skills of reading and writing by subsequent study. The dual aims of these books are made clear from the start, so that students may determine their own learning procedures and work through the material in ways best suited to their needs and capacity. The main emphasis is placed on understanding and speaking the language, but due attention has been paid to the importance of reading, especially for interpreting instructions and seeking information, and of writing, for such practical tasks as filling in forms, making reservations and writing simple letters.

The author's introduction clearly explains the content and presentation of the teaching material. The table of contents is specific and informative and the student may see at a glance the ground to be covered. It is advisable to study the introduction very closely, in order to make the best use of this carefully structured course. The presentation of each chapter is consistent, and the dialogues which form the basis of the teaching are followed by a list of new German words in order of their appearance; this vocabulary list provides the English meaning and appropriate grammatical clues, as well as stress marks to help solve one of the major problems of German pronunciation.

Mastery of the spoken language presents one of the greatest difficulties to the student working alone; without considerable linguistic experience, it is impossible to develop an ear for the sounds and intonation of a language by reading the printed page. In *Mastering German* there is a detailed guide to pronunciation, in addition to the indications of stress given in the vocabulary lists; but these alone could not convey the true nature of the spoken language. It is true that German has so much in common with English that it is relatively easy at first to make encouraging progress in acquiring a reasonably satisfactory pronunciation. However, the similarity between the two languages will become a decoy unless care is taken to listen to the finer differences and to discriminate between similar but not identical sounds. To this end, there is a most useful 'optional extra' in the form of a cassette, on which the pronunciation key and all the dialogues in the book are recorded by native speakers.

The authors of the language books in the Master Series, who are all gifted teachers of individuality and experience, have tried to ensure that those who use these books thoughtfully may experience the pleasure of successful language study without the direct intervention of a teacher. All concerned with the project hope that the books will establish for the learner a continuing involvement with the infinite variety and endless fascination of languages.

BETTY PARR
Editorial Consultant

INTRODUCTION:
HOW TO USE THIS BOOK

LEARNING AIMS

1. The first aim of *Mastering German* is to enable students to acquire the ability to take part in every-day communication with native speakers of German. This means being able to take part in the following two sorts of language exchange:

   (a) You need to be able to 'survive' in the language, and that means being able to take part in a number of transactions which are necessary for your health and comfort. This includes such things as going shopping, ordering meals, reserving rooms in hotels and finding your way around by public transport.

   (b) The other sort of language which you need is the language for making social contact with speakers of German. This social language is particularly important for those students who are likely to meet German speakers either at home or abroad, and will need to spend some time with them in a social setting. Businessmen, in particular, may find this sort of language of great use for helping to create a suitable social atmosphere in which business can be done.

2. The other aim of *Mastering German* is to give students a solid foundation of German grammar as a base for further learning at a higher level. Students preparing for public examinations will benefit from the clear explanations of points of grammar and from the exercises on them, which can be corrected by the student working alone, using the answers at the back of the book.

THE MATERIALS

Mastering German consists of a book and a sound recording. Students who are beginning the study of German will find the recording of particular use in helping them to acquire good pronunciation, intonation and stress. A guide to pronunciation is included in the book, and has been recorded. It will be found on the cassette after the dialogues. Students who already have some mastery of the pronunciation of German may still find that the dialogues, using native speakers, will help them to speak not only with clarity, but with a good range of expression.

HOW TO FIND YOUR WAY ABOUT THE BOOK

When you look at the table of contents, you will see that each chapter is presented under two headings:

1. *Topic* This expresses the main communicative aim of the chapter. It describes what you will be able to do with the language you have learned.
2. *Grammar* Here the main elements of formal grammar are listed.

Students who wish to 'cash in' their study as soon as possible should concentrate first on mastering the topics. The most important parts of the book for them are the dialogues, the notes on the dialogues and the vocabulary, the structures to learn and Section A of the exercises. These are the communicative parts of the book, and will help you learn how to make an arrangement or meet somebody, how to request a service, how to make a suggestion or proposal, etc.

Other students, who wish alternatively, or additionally, to acquire a grasp of German grammar, should pay particular attention to Section B of the structural explanations which takes a point of grammar arising in the dialogue, and gives it thorough and systematic treatment, and also Section B of the exercises, which concentrates on these grammatical points.

LANGUAGE FOR SPEAKING AND LANGUAGE FOR UNDERSTANDING

The main emphasis in this book is on the skills of speaking and under-standing. Some parts of the language presented will consist of things students will want to *say*, and others will consist of things students want to *understand*. Each student will have a good idea of those things he or she is most likely to want to say, and should consequently concentrate on practising these parts of the language aloud. It is necessary to remember, however, that the better you become at speaking the language, the freer natives will feel in replying to you. In choosing the topics to include in this book, the proposals of the

Threshold Level for Language Learning, published by the Council of Europe, has provided a most useful point of reference.

STRUCTURE OF THE CHAPTERS

Each chapter begins with a number of dialogues, which give examples of speakers using the language for the purpose indicated in the table of contents. These dialogues are recorded on tape by native speakers of German. The dialogues are translated into English and printed in Part II. They have been set out on a line-for-line basis, so that students can instantly understand them. The dialogues are followed by explanatory notes and a vocabulary list.

After the dialogues and the notes on them, comes a section of the chapter called Structural Explanations. In part (a) of this section, you will find a number of phrases and structural patterns, which will help you to use and build on the language of the dialogues, in order to use German freely and cope with the topic of that particular chapter.

In part (b) you will find some points of grammar which are explained fully and clearly, and which will help you to build up a systematic knowledge of German, based on the points of grammar which arise in the dialogue.

Part 4 of the chapter consists of Exercises. These are divided into two sections. The exercises in Section A correspond to the communicative aims of the chapter, while Section B contains exercises of a more grammatical nature, which will help you to master the grammatical rules which arise from the dialogue.

Students should note that the German alphabet coincides with the English alphabet, except in one case. The symbol ß is the equivalent of 'ss'. The rule concerning the use of ß and ss is a complicated one, and may safely be left until a more advanced stage in learning German. Students simply need to note at this stage that the two symbols are pronounced identically. Students who wish to learn the rule for using ß should consult *German Grammar and Usage* by A. E. Hammer, page 409 (see bibliography).

HOW TO GET THE BEST OUT OF MASTERING GERMAN

1. All students

Every student should be able to derive benefit from studying the dialogues which are written in good, colloquial German and recorded on tape by native speakers. The following procedure is recommended.

(a) Study the aims of the chapter. In particular, look at the *topic* of a chapter to see how it sets out to teach you to use German. This will inform you of what you should be able to do by the time you have got to the end of the chapter, and this in turn will help you to evaluate your own progress.

(b) Read through the German text of the dialogue and listen to it simultaneously on tape. Try to work out the meaning of each sentence as it occurs. Very often the common linguistic ancestry of English and German will help you to find out the meaning. These similarities between English and German will sometimes be more apparent when looking at the spelling of words, and sometimes when listening to the way they are spoken. When you have predicted the meaning as far as you can, refer to the translation at the back of the book, so as to be quite sure that you understand the dialogue thoroughly before proceeding.

(c) If you are working with a book alone, work out the pronunciation of the sentences in the dialogue, using the pronunciation guide. If you are working with a tape-recording, speak the dialogue quietly while listening to the tape-recording. By degrees increase the volume of your own voice, and decrease the volume of the recording. After two or three times, it should be possible to pronounce the dialogue accurately and with good expression. When you are beginning to establish a correct pronunciation of the sentences, it will probably help to stop the tape-recording after each sentence, and to repeat it aloud several times before continuing to the next sentence. Probably all students will be able to derive some benefit from working with the dialogues in this way.

2. **For students with little language learning experience**

(a) Having worked through the dialogues in the way described above, go on to the section labelled *Structures to learn*. With the help of the pronunciation key, speak the sentences aloud, noting carefully which uses of language they help you to master.

(b) For those with little linguistic experience it is probably advisable to omit the study of the grammatical section, and go straight to those exercises which are based on the objectives stated at the beginning of the chapter. Do the exercises as best you can without referring to the answers at the back of the book. Only when you have really thought about what you want to say, and tried hard to get it right, should you check with the answers.

(c) Beginners may well find that the best way of using *Mastering German* is to work their way through the book as indicated above, concentrating on:

    (i) The Dialogues,
    (ii) The Structures to learn,
    (iii) The Exercises (Section A).

When the whole book has been worked through in this way, it would be appropriate to return to Chapter 1, and go through the book again as indicated below.

3. Intermediate students

Intermediate students who have already mastered the rudiments of German should work first through the dialogues as indicated above, and run through the *Structures to learn* and the communicative exercises as indicated for beginners. In this way, intermediate students will derive considerable benefit from putting to practical use elements of the language which they may previously have learned.

Intermediate students would then be well advised to proceed directly to the grammar section, in order to give the language of the dialogues and the structures to learn a firm grammatical foundation.

The structural exercises (Section B) based on the grammar section should then be gone through carefully, checking answers with the answer key at the back of the book.

STUDENTS WISHING TO USE MASTERING GERMAN TO REVISE FOR PUBLIC EXAMINATIONS

These students should consult the table of contents, looking particularly at the second entry for each chapter, in order to find the particular point of grammar which they wish to study. These students should read and study very carefully the grammar section, and should not forget that there are exercises on it, which can be checked by referring to the answer key at the back.

VOCABULARY LEARNING

Section 2 of each chapter contains a list of the most important words which have occurred in the chapter. It is not a complete list of all the new words which have occurred, since these are given by the translation of the dialogues. The word list gives a basic vocabulary which you should be able to use actively.

Here are some suggestions, intended to help you to learn new vocabulary items:

1. Cover up the English translation, and try to use your existing knowledge and your increasing knowledge of German to guess the meaning of the German word. Then check whether you are right or wrong by uncovering the English version. Continue in this way until you can recognise all the new words.

2. Then go on to the more difficult way of learning vocabulary, and cover up the German version and try to remember the equivalent for each English word. You should try to remember whether nouns are masculine, feminine or neuter, and how they make their plurals. If possible, work with a friend who can ask you the English words and check whether you have succeeded in remembering the German equivalent.

REVISION TESTS

Chapter 10 and Chapter 20 consist of tests on the earlier chapters in the book and are intended to help you gauge your own progress.

Alles Gute!!

I TEACHING UNITS

CHAPTER 1

GREETINGS AND INTRODUCTIONS

1.1 DIALOGUES 📼

Dialogue 1

Professor Hecht has called to return a catalogue which he borrowed from a business acquaintance, Herr Kirchhof.

1 *Sekretärin*: Ach, Herr Professor. Guten Tag!
  Prof. Hecht: Guten Tag, Frau Hausmann.
    Ist Herr Kirchhof da?
  Sekretärin: Ja, Moment bitte.
5 Herr Kirchhof ...
  Professor Hecht ist da.

  ...

  Herr Kirchhof: (at door) Guten Tag, Herr Professor!
  Prof. Hecht: Guten Tag, Herr Kirchhof!
  Herr Kirchhof: Bitte, kommen Sie herein.
10 *Prof. Hecht*: Danke.
  Wie geht es Ihnen?
  Herr Kirchhof: Sehr gut, danke.
  Bitte, nehmen Sie Platz.
  Prof. Hecht: Danke.
15 *Herr Kirchhof*: Eine Tasse Kaffee?
  Prof. Hecht: Oh ja, bitte sehr.
  Herr Kirchhof: Frau Hausmann, zwei Tassen
  Kaffee, bitte.
  Frau Hausmann: Ja, gern.
20 *Herr Kirchhof*: Nun, wie geht es Ihrer Frau?
  Prof. Hecht: Ausgezeichnet!
  Herr Kirchhof: Und Andreas und Daniella?

4

Wie geht es Ihnen?

Photograph: Bavaria-Verlag/Oscar Poss

Prof. Hecht: Auch sehr gut.
25 *Herr Kirchhof*: Und hier ist der Katalog.
Prof. Hecht: Ja, der Katalog.

Dialogue 2
Elke Kustmann is having a party at her flat in the Fürstenstraße in Munich. She works at a smart dress shop in Munich and is cele-

brating having sold a very expensive fur coat to the wife of a businessman. She has been rewarded with a handsome commission. Amongst her guests is her current admirer, Fritz Löb.

(Front door bell rings)

1 *Elke*: Herr Doktor! Guten Abend!

Doktor Neumann: Elke! Guten Abend!

Elke: Wie schön.

Kommen Sie herein.

5 *Doktor Neumann*: Danke.

Darf ich meine Frau vorstellen?

Elke: Guten Abend, Frau Neumann.

Willkommen!

Frau Neumann: Guten Abend!

10 Danke schön für die Einladung.

Elke: Bitte, bitte.

Das ist Fritz.

Fritz: Guten Abend!

Löb ist mein Name.

(Front door bell rings again)

15 *Elke*: Eckhard!

Eckhard: Elke!

Elke: Du hier!

Das ist fantastisch!

Eckhard: Elke, du bist noch immer so schön.

20 *Elke*: Ach, nein.

Eckhard: Doch. Doch.

Fritz: (Clears his throat)

Elke: Ach, ja.

Das ist Fritz.

Eckhard: Becker.

25 *Fritz*: Angenehm.

Fritz: Löb.

Eckhard: Angenehm.

(Front door bell rings again)

Elke: Entschuldigen Sie!

. . .

(Some hours later)

Prof. Hecht: Auf Wiedersehen!

30 Vielen Dank.

Elke: Nichts zu danken.

Auf Wiedersehen!

1.2 INFORMATION

(a) Notes on Dialogue 1

| 1. | Herr Professor | When you speak to a person with a title, such as 'Professor' or 'Doctor', you address them in German as Herr Professor or Herr Doktor. |

Other titles are: Herr: 'Mr',
                   Frau: 'Mrs',
                   Fräulein: 'Miss'

| 1. | Guten Tag | The greeting Guten Tag applies to the whole day, where in English we would say 'Good morning' or 'Good afternoon'. |
| 15. | Eine Tasse Kaffee? | This is short for '(Would you like) a cup of coffee?' |

(b) Notes on Dialogue 2

1.	Guten Abend	This greeting is used from about 6 pm onwards.
11.	Bitte, bitte	This emphatic repetition of the word bitte is best translated as 'don't mention it'.
14.	Löb ist mein Name	If you wish to state your name, you can begin by stating it in order to give it emphasis, but it would also be quite possible to say Mein Name ist Löb.
18.	Fantastisch	Here are some other words which you might find useful for expressing enthusiasm: wunderbar großartig klasse Note that you can use the first two in any society, but klasse is slightly more colloquial.
21.	Doch	This word means 'yes' when spoken emphatically, because

the previous sentence has been
in the negative. If, therefore,
the previous speaker says e.g.
'no it isn't' and you wish to
reply emphatically 'oh yes it is',
you would use the word doch.

24. Becker — Adults who introduce
themselves to other adults do so
by stating their family name.

25. Angenehm — This word literally means
'pleasant' and is best translated
by the conventional English
phrase 'pleased to meet you'.

31. Nichts zu danken — 'Don't mention it' is clearly not
a literal translation, but is a
good rendering of the meaning.

(c) Word list

Here is a list of the most important words in this chapter. They should
be learnt by heart. They are given here in the order in which they occur
in the chapter. After each noun, the plural ending is given in brackets.
For more information on the plural of nouns, see the Grammar
section of Chapter 14. In German, certain syllables of words are
stressed. This is shown in bold type.

die Sekret**ä**rin (-nen)	secretary
der Herr (-en)	man; husband
Frau	Mrs
da	there
bitte	please
kommen	to come
danke	thank you
sehr	very
gut	good
nehmen	to take
der **Kaff**ee	coffee
die **Tass**e (-n)	cup
ausge**zeich**net	splendid
und	and
auch	also/too
hier	here
der Kata**log** (-e)	catalogue

die Frau (-en)	wife; woman
vorstellen	to introduce
will**komm**en	welcome
danke schön	thank you very much
die **Ein**ladung (-en)	invitation
fan**tas**tisch	fabulous
der **Name** (-n)	name
noch **imm**er	still
schön	beautiful
doch	yes (after a negative)
der Mann (¨er)	husband; man
das **Auto** (-s)	car
der Schuh (-e)	shoe

(d) Some phrases

Moment bitte	Just a moment, please
Kommen Sie her**ein**	Do come in
Wie geht es **Ihn**en?	How are you?
Bitte, nehmen Sie Platz	Please sit down
Bitte sehr	yes please
Wie schön!	How nice!
Noch **imm**er	Still
Ent**schuld**igen Sie	Excuse me
Auf **Wie**dersehen	Goodbye
Vielen Dank	Thank you very much

1.3 STRUCTURAL EXPLANATIONS

(a) Structures to learn

  (i) How to greet people

Guten { Tag / Morgen / Abend

Good { morning; afternoon / morning / evening

Gute { Nacht / Besserung / Reise

Goodnight
Get better soon
Have a good journey

  (ii) Other frequently used greetings

Guten Appetit!	Enjoy your meal. (Nearly always said by people sitting at the same table, before they begin to eat.)

Alles Gute!	All the best
Prost! Prosit! Zum Wohl! }	Cheers! Good health!
Viel Glück	Good luck!
Viel Spaß! Viel Vergnügen! }	Have a good time!

(iii) How to be polite

Bitte Bitte schön Bitte sehr	These phrases are used when you offer somebody something, e.g. when you tender a salesperson some money, or when you hand somebody an object, or when a waiter places a dish of food on the table. It is a rather more polite equivalent of 'Here you are'.
Bitte Bitte schön Bitte sehr }	The same expression means 'please'. Bitte schön and Bitte sehr are slightly more emphatic.
Danke Danke schön Danke vielmals }	All these expressions mean 'thank you'. They are arranged in order of degree of emphasis.
Bitte	Bitte can also mean 'don't mention it'. It is used when somebody has thanked you for something. Here is a possible exchange: Er: (offering something) Bitte sehr! Sie: (thanking him emphatically) Danke vielmals. Er: Bitte, bitte (don't mention it).
Grüß Gott	This means the same as Guten Tag, but is used in the south of Germany and Austria.

N.B. The letter ß is pronounced as if it were 'ss'.

(iv) **How to introduce yourself**

1. State your family name e.g. Freeman!
                                 Hardy!
                                 Willis!
   If somebody introduces himself to you by stating his or her
   family name, shake hands and say Angenehm.

2. Johnson ⎫
   Peterson ⎬ ist mein Name
   Davidson ⎭

3.
   Mein Name ist ⎧ Jones
                  ⎨ Smith
                  ⎩ Robinson

(v) **How to introduce somebody else**

1.
   Hier ist ⎧ Mr Smith
            ⎨ Dr Jones
            ⎩ Prof. Pike

2.
   Darf ich ⎧ meinen Mann ⎫
            ⎪ meine Frau   ⎪
            ⎨ Herrn Schmidt ⎬ vorstellen?
            ⎩ Dr Jones   ⎭

3. If you wish to make it known that you are about to introduce
   people to each other, you can use the phrase Darf ich vorstellen?
   to indicate your intention, and then continue with:

   Hier ist ⎧ Mr Jones
            ⎨ Herr Schmidt

(vi) **How to take your leave**

Auf Wiedersehen   This can be used on most
                         occasions.

Auf Wiederhören   Reserved exclusively for ending a
                         telephone conversation.

Kommen Sie gut heim ⎫   An expression of the wish that the
Kommen Sie gut nach ⎬   person concerned will reach
   Hause   ⎭   home safely.

(b) Grammar
   (i) Verbs and pronouns
Verbs are words, or combinations of words, which express states,

actions or events. In the following sentences, the verbs are printed in italics.

He *is* ill	They both *jumped* for the ball
She *lives* in Manchester	She *gets* a cheque every month
I *like* beer	They *are going* on holiday soon
He *has* a bad cold	I *buy* my shirts at Harrods

Each verb in German has six forms, three in the singular and three in the plural. These forms tell you who performs the action or event of the verb, or to whom or to what the state expressed by the verb refers.
Here is a table showing corresponding English forms.

Singular		**Plural**	
ich	I	wir	we
du	you (familiar form)	ihr	you (familiar form)
er	he	Sie	you (formal or polite form)
sie	she	sie	they
es	it		

The above forms are called *pronouns*. They are words used instead of nouns. All the above pronouns are known as *personal pronouns* because they refer to people. Here, you see them together with the verb 'to be'.

The verb SEIN – to be

ich	bin	I am
du	bist	you are (familiar form)
er	ist	he is
sie	ist	she is
es	ist	it is
wir	sind	we are
ihr	seid	you are (familiar form)
Sie	sind	you are (formal or polite form)
sie	sind	they are

N.B. The familiar forms du bist and ihr seid are used amongst members of the family, and when addressing children up to the age of about 12 or 13.

(ii) **Adjectives**

An *adjective* is a word which *describes* someone or something. In the following sentences, the adjectives are printed in italics.

That is a *fat* man	*My* son is thirteen
This car is *old*	Beer is *best*

Possessive adjectives indicate to whom something belongs. They correspond to the *personal pronouns* given above.

> Mein Name   –   my name
> Meine Frau   –   my wife

You will find a complete list of *possessive adjectives* in the appendix.

(iii) Nouns

The names of people, things and places are *nouns*. In the following sentences, the nouns are printed in italics. Note that some nouns can be abstract.

> The *man* was drowning   We're going to *town*
> She made some *coffee*   He felt great *happiness*

(iv) Gender

All nouns in German are categorised in three genders: masculine, feminine, neuter. Gender only *partly* corresponds to male and female, and you should consequently learn the gender of each noun as you meet it.

> Mann (man or husband) is masculine, shown in the vocabulary list thus: der Mann.
> Frau ('Mrs' as a title, or wife) is feminine, shown in the vocabulary list thus: die Frau.
> Auto (car) is neuter, shown in the vocabulary list thus: das Auto.

(v) Singular and plural

A singular noun is *one* person, thing or place. A plural noun is *more than one* person, thing or place.

(vi) Agreement

Agreement means that two words, e.g. a noun and an adjective, are both masculine, or both plural.

Possessive adjectives, as all adjectives, must agree with the noun they describe.

mein Mann	my husband	dein Mann	your husband
meine Frau	my wife	deine Frau	your wife
mein Auto	my car	dein Auto	your car
meine Schuhe	my shoes	deine Schuhe	your shoes

You will find a complete list of *adjective agreements* in the appendix.

(vii) **Capital letters**
a) Capital letters are used at the beginning of sentences.
b) They are also used for all nouns.
c) They are used for 'you' in the polite form and also for possessive adjectives in the polite form.

1.4 EXERCISES

Exercise 1
1. What would you say to somebody who is just going to bed?
2. What would you say to somebody who is just going to take her driving test?
3. What would you say to somebody for whom you have just poured out a drink?
4. What would you say to your secretary first thing in the morning?
5. What would you say to your aged mother as she gets into the train to go home?
6. What would you say to your friend when you visit him in hospital?
7. What would you say to the head waiter as you go into a restaurant one evening?
8. What would you say to a friend who is just going off on holiday?
9. What would you say to an acquaintance you met on the street during the lunch hour?

Exercise 2
You are giving a party to celebrate your birthday. The frontdoor bell rings, Dr Schmidt and his wife are there.
1. What do you say to him?
2. He introduces his wife to you. What does he say?
3. You are very pleased to meet her.
4. Ask them to come in.
5. Ask them to sit down.
6. Frau Schmidt wants to thank you for the invitation. What does she say?
7. Ask them if they would like a cup of coffee.
8. He would like a cup. What does he say?
9. She doesn't like coffee.
10. The frontdoor bell rings again.

Exercise 3
You have been corresponding with Herr Kunze of Siemens for some time. You have an appointment to see him in Düsseldorf, and he has

invited you to his home for dinner. How would you reply to the things he says to you?

1. Guten Abend!
2. Kommen Sie herein.
3. Wie geht es Ihnen?
4. Darf ich meine Frau vorstellen?
5. Bitte, nehmen Sie Platz.
6. Whisky?

CHAPTER 2

GETTING ABOUT

2.1 DIALOGUES 📼

Dialogue 1

Frau Meyer is a widowed lady of 75. She has gone on a special cheap day-return train journey to Regensburg. She wants to revisit the house where she was born. She is looking for the post office in the Amalienstraße, where her parents used to have a flat on the third floor. However, everything has changed since she was a girl.

1   *Frau Meyer*: Entschuldigen Sie!
    Wie komme ich zur Amalienstraße, bitte?
  Fußgänger: Wie bitte?
  Frau Meyer: Die Amalienstraße.
5   Wie komme ich zur Amalienstraße?
  Fußgänger: Ja ... die Amalienstraße ...
  Frau Meyer: (interrupting) Furchtbar!
    Ganz furchtbar!
  Fußgänger: Wie bitte?
10 *Frau Meyer*: Hier ist alles neu.
  Fußgänger: Ja, das stimmt.
    Zur Adriastraße, nicht wahr?
  Frau Meyer: Nein, nicht zur Adriastraße, zur Amalienstraße.
    Wie komme ich zur Amalienstraße?
15 *Fußgänger*: Ach, ja.
    Gehen Sie hier geradeaus, nehmen Sie dann die erste Straße
    links.
  Frau Meyer: Die erste Straße links.
  Fußgänger: Das ist die Marktstraße.
20   Gehen Sie die Marktstraße hoch, dann kommen Sie zur
    Amalienstraße.

Regensburg – hier ist alles neu . . .

Photograph: J. Allan Cash Ltd

Frau Meyer:　Danke.
Fußgänger:　Bitte.

Dialogue 2

Fritz Löb teaches English at a Munich school. He is an expert on romanesque churches. He is separated from his wife, but has no children. He is friendly with Elke but can't really afford her tastes. Elke is driving Fritz to see a very beautiful baroque church in a small Alpine town called Mittenwald.

(Elke hoots her horn)

1　*Elke*:　Entschuldigen Sie!
　　Wie kommen wir nach Mittenwald?
　Junge:　Wie bitte?
　Elke:　Nach Mittenwald
5　*Junge*:　Ich weiß es nicht.
　Elke:　Danke.
　(Under breath)
　　Blöder Kerl!
　　Du Fritz, frag' doch das Mädchen dort drüben.
　Fritz:　Entschuldigen Sie!
10　Wie kommen wir nach Mittenwald?
　Mädchen:　Nach Mittenwald?
　　Fahren Sie hier geradeaus.

Fritz: Geradeaus.
Mädchen: Nach Garmisch.
15   Dort biegen Sie nach links ab.
      Das ist die B28.
Fritz: Ist das weit?
Mädchen: Nein.
      Zwanzig Kilometer ungefähr.
20 *Fritz*:   Danke.
Mädchen: Fahren Sie Richtung Innsbruck.
Fritz: Richtung Innsbruck.
      Danke.
Mädchen: Bitte.

2.2 INFORMATION

(a) Notes on Dialogue 1

4. Wie bitte?

You can say wie bitte? or just bitte? if you do not understand what somebody says and you want them to repeat it.

7. Ja ... die Amalienstraße

Note that it is very typically German, when people ask you a direct question, to begin the answer with the word ja. It is really just a way of getting time to think, but if you learn to use it, you will sound immensely typical.

12. Das stimmt

This is a very useful phrase for conveying your agreement with what somebody else has just said.

(b) Notes on Dialogue 2

7. Blöder Kerl!

We know it's nice to know how to be rude to people, but beware! In Germany you may have to pay a fine for saying something like this.

| 16. Die B28 | The letter 'B' stands for Bundesstraße. This is the equivalent of an 'A' road. |

(c) Word list

Here is a list of the most important words in this chapter. They should be learnt by heart. They are given here in the order in which they occur in the chapter.

der Fußgänger	pedestrian
wie?	how?
kommen	to come
furchtbar	terrible
ganz	quite
hier	here
alles	everything
neu	new
nein	no
nicht	not
gehen	to go
ge**rad**eaus	straight on
nehmen	to take
dann	then
die **Straß**e (-n)	street
links	left
rechts	right
fragen	to ask
das **Mäd**chen (-)	girl
dort **drüb**en	over there
fahren	to go (by car)
biegen	to turn
weit	far
zwanzig	twenty
unge**fähr**	approximately
die **Rich**tung (-en)	direction
das **Krank**enhaus (¨er)	hospital
das **Kur**hotel (-s)	spa hotel
der **Bahn**hof (¨e)	station
der **Sport**platz (-e)	sports ground
die **Spar**kasse (-n)	savings bank
nächst-	next
erst-	first
zweit-	second
dritt-	third
das **Hallen**bad (¨er)	indoor swimming pool
das **Frei**bad (¨er)	open-air swimming pool

die **Grund**schule (-n)	primary school
der **Camping**platz (¨e)	camping ground
der **Kinder**garten (¨)	nursery school
die **Reit**halle (-n)	riding hall
das **Restaur**ant (-s)	restaurant
der **Markt**platz (¨e)	market place
die **Post**	post office
das **Rat**haus	town hall
der **Dom**	cathedral
der **Park**platz (¨e)	car park
die **Werk**statt (¨e)	service station

(d) Some phrases

Nicht wahr?	Isn't it? etc.
Gehen Sie die **Markt**straße hoch	Go up Market Street
Ich weiß es nicht	I don't know

2.3 STRUCTURAL EXPLANATIONS

(a) Structures to learn

  (i) How to find your way in town

Wie komme ich   How do I get to

zum
- Krankenhaus (*n*)
- Kurhotel (*n*)
- Bahnhof (*m*)
- Sportplatz (*m*)

the
- hospital
- Spa Hotel
- station
- sports ground ?

zur
- Sparkasse (*f*)
- Amalienstraße (*f*)

- savings bank
- Amalienstraße

Note that you use zum with all masculine and neuter words, and zur with all feminine words.

  (ii) How to understand some of the directions which people may give

(a) Gehen Sie (hier):
    geradeaus
    links
    rechts
    die Marktstraße { hoch / entlang

(a) You go:
    straight on
    to the left
    to the right
    up / along { Market Street

(b) Nehmen Sie die:

nächste erste zweite dritte	} Straße {	rechts links

(b) You take the:

next first second third	} street {	on the right on the left

(iii) How to find your way when driving

When you are driving the places you want to get to are usually some distance away, and you must use the word nach.

Wie	{ komme ich kommen wir	How do I/we get to
nach	{ Perlach Rothenburg ? Dasburg	Perlach Rothenburg ? Dasburg

(iv) How to understand some of the directions you may hear

Fahren Sie (hier)	{ links geradeaus rechts	Go	{ left straight on right
Biegen Sie nach	{ rechts links } ab	Turn	{ right left

(b) Grammar
(i) Cardinal numbers

The numbers 1 – 30 are as follows:

1	eins	11	elf	21	einundzwanzig
2	zwei	12	zwölf	22	zweiundzwanzig
3	drei	13	dreizehn	23	dreiundzwanzig
4	vier	14	vierzehn	24	vierundzwanzig
5	fünf	15	fünfzehn	25	fünfundzwanzig
6	sechs	16	sechzehn	26	sechsundzwanzig
7	sieben	17	siebzehn	27	siebenundzwanzig
8	acht	18	achtzehn	28	achtundzwanzig
9	neun	19	neunzehn	29	neunundzwanzig
10	zehn	20	zwanzig	30	dreißig

N.B. There is no 's' in 16. There is no 'en' in 17.

You will find further numbers in the appendix.

(ii) **Ordinal numbers**
Numbers indicating the chronological order in which things occur.

1st (first)	der, die, das erste
2nd (second)	der, die, das zweite
3rd (third)	der, die, das dritte
4th (fourth)	der, die, das vierte
5th (fifth)	der, die, das fünfte

You will find further such numbers in the appendix.

(iii) **Fahren and gehen**
The words fahren and gehen both mean 'to go'. You use fahren when you are mobile with a car or a motorbicycle, and you use gehen when you are on foot.

(iv) **Zu and nach**
You use zu for the names of streets, or places or buildings in town which are a comparatively short distance away. You use nach for greater distances, for the names of suburbs of towns, e.g. Perlach, or when asking how to get to other towns, e.g. Mittenwald.

(v) **Verbs**
The most frequently used parts of verbs are:

I	–	e.g.	I go, I have
he	–	e.g.	he goes, he has
she	–	e.g.	she goes, she has
we	–	e.g.	we go, we have
you	–	e.g.	you go, you have

In German, verb forms have endings which agree with the personal pronouns they accompany.

Regular verbs follow a regular pattern of agreement which, once learned, can be applied to other regular verbs of the same type.

Here are two examples of *regular* verbs:

The verb GEHEN – to go

Personal pronoun	Stem	Ending
ich (I)		e
er (he)		t
sie (she)	GEH-	t
wir (we)		en
Sie (you)		en

The verb KOMMEN – to come

Personal pronoun	Stem	Ending
ich (I)		e
er (he)		t
sie (she)	KOMM-	t
wir (we)		en
Sie (you)		en

ich	gehe	I go		ich	komme	I come
er	geht	he goes		er	kommt	he comes
sie	geht	she goes		sie	kommt	she comes
wir	gehen	we go		wir	kommen	we come
Sie	gehen	you go (formal or polite)		Sie	kommen	you come (formal or polite)

The verbs GEHEN and KOMMEN are *regular* in the sense that:
a) the stem is unchanged for each part of the verb,
b) the endings are identical for each verb.

Note that the *polite* or *formal* 'you' has a personal pronoun Sie with a capital 'S'.

The verb FAHREN – to go, or to travel (by car or public transport).

This verb is *irregular*, because the spelling and pronunciation of its stem changes from one person to another.

	ich	fahre	I go
Vowel ⟶	er	fährt	he goes
changes here ⟶	sie	fährt	she goes
	wir	fahren	we go
	Sie	fahren	you go (formal or polite)

You will find tables of the most common German verbs in the appendix.

(vi) Accents

The only accent in German is called the Umlaut. It is written with two small dots. They occur from time to time above the letters 'a', 'o' and 'u'. The Umlaut has the effect of changing the sound of the vowel beneath it. Whenever you see a word with an Umlaut in one of the dialogues, you should pay particular attention to the pronunciation.

2.4 EXERCISES

Exercise 1
Imagine that you are in the small town of Brakel and really want to find out what it has to offer. How would you ask the way to the following places?

1. The hospital   Krankenhaus (*n*)
2. Savings bank   Sparkasse (*f*)
3. Station   Bahnhof (*m*)

4. The sports ground	Sportplatz (*m*)
5. The indoor swimming-pool	Hallenbad (*n*)
6. The open-air swimming-pool	Freibad (*n*)
7. The primary school	Grundschule (*f*)
8. The old-people's home	Altenheim (*n*)
9. The Capuchin church	Kapuzinerkirche (*f*)
10. The camping ground	Campingplatz (*m*)
11. The nursery school	Kindergarten (*m*)
12. The riding hall	Reithalle (*f*)
13. The mini golf course	Minigolfplatz (*m*)
14. The Forest restaurant	Waldrestaurant (*n*)
15. The market place	Marktplatz (*m*)
16. The post office	Post (*f*)
17. The town hall	Rathaus (*n*)
18. The cathedral	Dom (*m*)
19. The car park	Parkplatz (*m*)

m – masculine
f – feminine
n – neuter

Exercise 2

Suppose your exhaust-pipe has gone while you have been bombing down the Autobahn. How are you going to find your way to the following service stations?

1. The Audi service station	Audi-Werkstatt (*f*)
2. The Volkswagen service station	Volkswagen-Werkstatt (*f*)
3. The Opel service station	Opel-Werkstatt (*f*)
4. The Ford service station	Ford-Werkstatt (*f*)
5. The Rolls-Royce service station	Rolls-Royce-Werkstatt (*f*)

Exercise 3

You are on holiday travelling by car in Germany (possibly in your Rolls-Royce). You are by yourself and you want to find the way to the following places:

1. Warburg
2. Brakel
3. Eissen
4. Manrode
5. Offendorf

By now you've picked up a hitch-hiker.

6. Paderborn
7. Detmold
8. Peckelsheim
9. Steinheim
10. Holzminden

Exercise 4
Learn the following dialogue. Take it in turns to play the parts, if you are learning with a partner.

| SALZBURG   6km |

A: Wie weit ist es nach   How far is it to Salzburg,
      Salzburg, bitte?   please?
B: Sechs Kilometer ungefähr. About 6 km.

1. | DESSAU   21 km | 6. | KUFSTEIN   9 km |

2. | HALLE   52 km | 7. | ZÜRICH   56 km |

3. | JENA   101 km | 8. | TÜBINGEN   71 km |

4. | LINZ   23 km | 9. | ANSBACH   56 km |

5. | KITZBÜHEL   39 km | 10. | FULDA   45 km |

CHAPTER 3

STAYING IN HOTELS

3.1 DIALOGUES 📼

Dialogue 1

Antonio Santos came from Naples when he was 5 years old, went
to school in Germany, and consequently speaks perfect German.
He studies at a fashion school in Munich and is currently doing
some practical work in the business where Elke works. Antonio's
Uncle and Aunt have written from Naples to say that they want to
come and see him in Munich. They have asked him to book a
room for them.

1   *Antonio*:   Guten Abend!
    Empfang: Guten Abend!
    Antonio: Ich möchte ein Zimmer reservieren.
    Empfang: Ja, für wie lange?
5   *Antonio*:   Für fünf Nächte.
      Von Montag bis Samstag.
    Empfang: Ja. Ein Einzelzimmer oder ein Doppelzimmer?
    Antonio: Ein Doppelzimmer.
    Empfang: Mit Bad oder Dusche?
10 *Antonio*:   Mit Dusche.
      Ein ruhiges Zimmer bitte.
    Empfang: Ja, ja. Das Zimmer ist schön ruhig.
    Antonio: Gut.
    Empfang: Auf welchen Namen bitte?
15 *Antonio*:   Santos. S-A-N-T-O-S.
    Empfang: Vielen Dank.
    Antonio: Was kostet das Zimmer?
    Empfang: Es kostet 60 Mark.
    Antonio: Ist das mit Frühstück?

20 *Empfang*:   Ja, das ist mit Frühstück und Mehrwertsteuer.
    Antonio: Danke.
    Empfang: Bitte.

Dialogue 2

Elke has decided to go north to Hamburg for the weekend, and
try to see an old boyfriend of hers. She hopes that if she sees him
again, it may help her to get her emotions sorted out with respect
to Fritz.

1 *Elke*:   Guten Tag!
   Empfang: Guten Tag?
   Elke: Haben Sie ein Zimmer frei bitte?
   Empfang: Jawohl.
5   Was für ein Zimmer?
   Elke: Ein Einzelzimmer.
      Mit Bad.
   Empfang: Für wieviele Nächte, bitte schön?
   Elke: Ich bleibe zwei Nächte.
10 *Empfang*:   Ein Einzelzimmer mit Bad.
      Ja, das ist möglich.
   Elke: Was kostet das Zimmer?

Ihr Zimmer ist im fünften Stock . . .

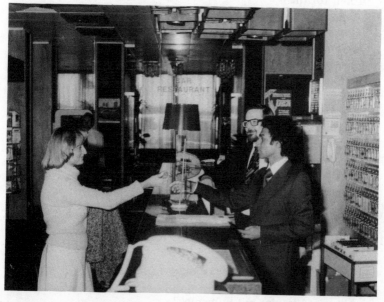

Photograph: Bavaria-Verlag/Ulrike Kment

Empfang: Das kostet pro Nacht 95 Mark mit Frühstück.
Elke: Ich nehme es.
15 *Empfang*: Bitte, tragen Sie sich ein.

   . . .

Ihr Zimmer ist im fünften Stock.
Elke: Hat das Zimmer einen Ausblick?
Empfang: Jawohl, es hat einen schönen Ausblick.
Über die Alster.
20 *Elke*: Wie schön.
Empfang: Haben Sie Gepäck?
Elke: Ja, mein Gepäck ist hier.
Empfang: Portier!

Dialogue 3

Fritz has been wanting to see the Petrikirche in Bad Reichenhall for ages. Elke won't be in Munich next weekend, so that will give him just the opportunity he needs. Anyway, Elke is not so interested in churches.

(On the telephone)

1 *Empfang*: Hotel Bayerischer Hof.
Fritz: Guten Tag!
Haben Sie ein Zimmer für nächsten Samstag, bitte?
Empfang: Für den zwölften?
5 *Fritz*: Ja, für Samstag den zwölften.
Empfang: Nein, es tut mir leid, wir sind völlig ausgebucht.
Fritz: Danke schön.
Empfang: Bitte sehr.

3.2 INFORMATION

(a) Notes on Dialogue 1

6. Samstag	There are two words for 'Saturday' in German, Samstag, which is used predominantly in the south of Germany, that is to say south of the river Main. The other word is Sonnabend, which is used more frequently in the north.
20. Mehrwertsteuer	You have to pay VAT in Germany, just as you do in

England. Usually, however, the VAT is already included in the price.

(b) Notes on Dialogue 2

7. Mit Bad

Although only a bath is mentioned, this nearly always means that you have a private bathroom.

15. Bitte, tragen Sie sich ein

'Please sign the register' is naturally not a word-for-word translation of the German, but it does give the meaning.

20. Die Alster

The Alster is a lake in the centre of Hamburg, which is one of the main attractions of the city. There are several steamer routes which criss-cross the lake, and which many workers use to travel to and from work. In the winter the Alster often freezes over, and becomes a vast skating rink.

(c) Word list

Here is a list of the most important words in this chapter. They should be learnt by heart. They are given here in the order in which they occur in the chapter.

gut	good
der **A**bend (-e)	evening
das **Z**immer (-)	room
re**ser**vie**ren**	to reserve
die Nacht (¨e)	night
von	from
bis	to
Montag	Monday
Samstag	Saturday
das **Ei**nzelzimmer (-)	single room
oder	or
das **Do**ppelzimmer (-)	double room
mit	with

das Bad (¨er)	bath
die **Dusche** (-n)	shower
ruhig	quiet
das **Früh**stück	breakfast
kosten	to cost
frei	free; available
wie**viel**?	how many?
bleiben	to stay
möglich	possible
was?	what?
nehmen	to take
der Stock (¨e)	floor (of a building)
der **Aus**blick (-e)	view
schön	beautiful
das Ge**päck**	luggage
völlig	completely
ausgebucht	booked up
leider	unfortunately
mit	with
ohne	without
das **Zwei**bettzimmer (-)	twin bedroom
die **Wo**che (-n)	week
heute	today
von	from
bis	until
wann?	when?
morgen	tomorrow
ein **biß**chen	a bit

(d) Some phrases

Für wie **lang**e?	For how long?
Schön **ruh**ig	Nice and quiet
Auf **wel**chen **Na**men, bitte?	What name, please?
Vielen Dank	Thank you very much
Was **kos**tet ... ?	What does ... cost?
Was für ein ... ?	What sort of a ... ?
Im **fünf**ten Stock	On the fifth floor
Es tut mir leid	I'm sorry
Das geht in **Ord**nung	That's all right

3.3 STRUCTURAL EXPLANATIONS

(a) Structures to learn

(i) How to establish whether there is a room available

What you need to *say*	What you need to *understand*
Ich möchte ein Zimmer reservieren	1. Ja, das ist möglich
I should like to reserve a room	Ja, das geht
	Ja, ein Zimmer habe ich noch
Haben Sie ein Zimmer frei?	There is a room available
Have you got a room available?	2. Nein, leider, alles ist ausgebucht
Haben Sie ein Zimmer für heute abend?	Nein, wir sind völlig ausgebucht
Have you got a room for tonight?	Nein, es tut mir leid
	There is no room available

(ii) How to describe the sort of room you want

What you need to *say*

(Ich möchte)	ein Einzelzimmer	a single room
	ein Doppelzimmer	a double room
	ein Zweibettzimmer	a twin bedroom
	mit/ohne Dusche	with/without shower
	mit/ohne Bad	with/without bath

(iii) How to say how long you want it for

What you need to *understand*

Für wie lange, bitte?	For how long?
Für wieviele Nächte?	For how many nights?
Von wann bis wann?	From when to when?

What you need to *say*

Für eine Nacht	For one night
Für zwei Nächte	For two nights
Für eine Woche	For a week

Von heute bis Montag	From today until Monday
Von Montag bis Samstag	From Monday until Saturday

What you need to *understand*

1. Ja, das ist möglich
   Ja, das geht in Ordnung
   You're in luck

2. Nein, es tut mir leid
   Nein, das ist nicht möglich
   You'd better try somewhere else!

(iv) How to confirm the booking

Gut, ich nehme das Zimmer	Bitte, tragen Sie sich ein
Good, I'll take the room	Please sign the register

(b) Grammar

(i) Days of the week

You will find a complete list in the appendix.

(ii) Months of the year

These are in the appendix, too.

(iii) Dates

When you want to say '*On* a certain date', the ordinal number for the date ends in -en. The English word 'of' is not translated.

Am ersten Januar	On the first of January
Am zweiten Februar	On the second of February
Am dritten März	On the third of March
Am vierten April	On the fourth of April

See Chapter 2 for information on ordinal numbers.

When you want to say '*For the* (a certain date)', the ordinal number for the date ends in -en.

Haben Sie ein Zimmer
{
Für den ersten Januar
Für den zweiten Februar
Für den dritten März   ?
Für den vierten April
Für den fünften Mai
}

$$
\text{Have you got a room}
\left\{
\begin{array}{l}
\text{For the 1st January} \\
\text{For the 2nd February} \\
\text{For the 3rd March} \qquad ? \\
\text{For the 4th April} \\
\text{For the 5th May}
\end{array}
\right.
$$

(iv) Dates continued

Der wievielte ist heute?   What is the date today?

When you want to say '*It is* (a certain date)', the ordinal number for the date ends in -e.

$$
\text{Es ist}
\left\{
\begin{array}{l}
\text{der erste Januar} \\
\text{der zweite Februar} \\
\text{der dritte März} \\
\text{der vierte April} \\
\text{der fünfte Mai}
\end{array}
\right.
\quad \text{It is}
\left\{
\begin{array}{l}
\text{the 1st of January} \\
\text{the 2nd of February} \\
\text{the 3rd of March} \\
\text{the 4th of April} \\
\text{the 5th of May}
\end{array}
\right.
$$

(v) More verbs
The verb BLEIBEN – to stay or remain

This is a *regular* verb. Its stem is unchanged throughout and its endings are also regular.

ich		e	ich	bleibe	I stay
er		t	er	bleibt	he stays
sie	BLEIB-	t	sie	bleibt	she stays
wir		en	wir	bleiben	we stay
Sie		en	Sie	bleiben	you stay (formal or polite)

The verb HABEN – to have

This is unfortunately *irregular*, but it is one of the most important and frequent verbs in the whole language, so you had better learn it.

ich	habe	I have
er	hat	he has
sie	hat	she has
wir	haben	we have
Sie	haben	you have (formal or polite)

The verb NEHMEN – to take

This is *irregular*, too. Notice how the spelling of the stem changes.

ich	NEHM-	e		ich	nehme	I take
er				er	nimmt	he takes
sie	NIMM-	t		sie	nimmt	she takes
wir				wir	nehmen	we take
Sie	NEHM-	en		Sie	nehmen	you take
						(formal or
						polite)

You will find a table of the most common verbs in the appendix.

(vi) How to express duration

Questions about duration	Statements about duration
Wie lange? – How long?	O lange! – For a long time
Für wie lange? – For how long?	Nicht lange – Not for long
Wie lange bleiben Sie? – How long will you be staying?	Von Dienstag bis Freitag – From Tuesday until Friday
	Bis morgen – Until tomorrow
	Bis Dienstag – Until Tuesday
	Nur bis Mittwoch – Only until Wednesday
	Ein bißchen – For a little while
	Noch ein bißchen – For a little while longer

3.4 EXERCISES

Section A

Exercise 1
Ask for the following types of hotel room for the length of time indicated. The first one is done for you. If you are studying with a partner, take it in turns to provide both roles.

Guest:	Haben Sie ein Zimmer frei?
Hotel:	Jawohl. Was für ein Zimmer?
Guest:	Ein Einzelzimmer.
Hotel:	Für wie lange?
Guest:	Für eine Nacht.

34

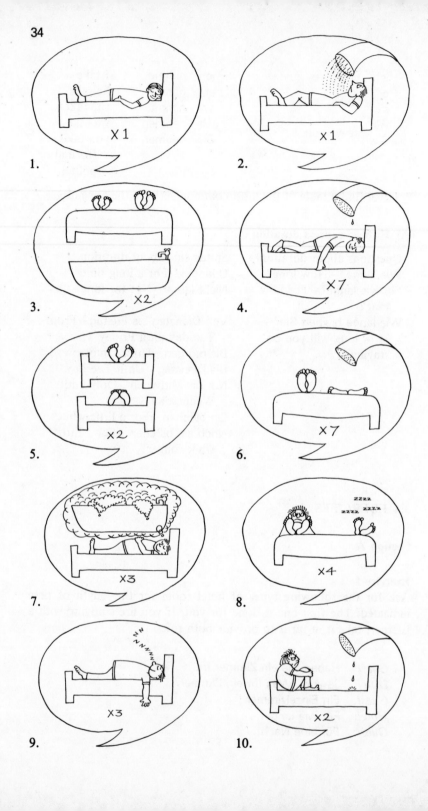

1.

2.

3.

4.

5.

6.

7.

8.

9.

10.

Exercise 2

Provide the role of Herr Schmidt. If you are studying with a partner, take it in turns to provide both roles. You will find the complete dialogue with the answers to the exercises in the appendix.

Schmidt	*Empfang*
1. Greet the receptionist.	
	2. Guten Tag, der Herr!
3. Ask if there is a room available.	
	4. Ja, ein Zimmer habe ich.
5. Ask whether there is a single room available.	
	6. Für wie lange, bitte?
7. Say you want it for one night.	
	8. Für eine Nacht. Das geht in Ordnung.
9. Say you'll take the room.	
	10. Tragen Sie sich bitte ein!

Exercise 3

Provide the role of Herr Müller. If you are studying with a partner, take turns to provide both roles. You will find the complete dialogue with the answers to the exercises.

Müller	*Rezeption*
1. Greet the receptionist.	
	2. Grüß Gott!
3. Ask whether there is a room available.	
	4. Ja, das ist möglich.
5. Ask whether there is a double room available with a private bathroom.	
	6. Ja, ein Doppelzimmer habe ich noch. Für wieviele Nächte bitte?
7. Say you want it from today till Sunday.	
	8. Ja, das geht.
9. Say you'll take the room.	
	10. Bitte, tragen Sie sich ein.

Section B

Exercise 4

Note the endings of the verb BLEIBEN. Most German verbs in the present tense have the same endings.

ich	bleibe	-e
du	bleibst	-st
er	bleibt	-t
sie	bleibt	-t
wir	bleiben	-en
ihr	bleibt	-t
Sie	bleiben	-en
sie	bleiben	-en

Complete the verbs with the correct endings:
1. Hab– Sie ein Einzelzimmer?
2. Wie lange bleib– Sie?
3. Ich nehm– das Zimmer.
4. Entschuldig– Sie, bitte.
5. Wie komm– ich nach Stauting?
6. Fahr– Sie hier geradeaus.
7. Er bieg– hier nach links ab.
8. Nehm– Sie dann die erste Straße links.
9. Geh– Sie die Marktstraße hoch.
10. Hab– Sie einen Tisch für zwei?
11. Ich hab– einen Tisch um 8 Uhr.
12. Sie bleib– eine Nacht.
13. Sie komm– zur Adriastraße.

Exercise 5

This is how to express the year

1933 – neunzehnhundertdreiunddreißig
1956 – neunzehnhundertsechsundfünfzig
1981 – neunzehnhunderteinundachtzig

Now state the following dates (c.f. ordinal numbers in Chapter 2):
1. 2.5.1978.
2. 16.6.1982.
3. 31.12.1979.
4. 11.8.1982.
5. 27.3.1983.
6. 17.5.1985.

CHAPTER 4

TRAVELLING BY TRAIN

4.1 DIALOGUES 📼

Dialogue 1

Frau Meyer is going to see her great friend Mitzi, who lives in Augsburg, about 50 km from Munich.

1 *Frau Meyer*: Grüß Gott!
    Angestellte: Grüß Gott!
    Frau Meyer: Einmal zweiter Klasse nach Augsburg, bitte.
    Angestellte: Einfach oder hin und zurück?
5 *Frau Meyer*: Hin und zurück , bitte.
    Was kostet das?
    Angestellte: Zweiunddreißig Mark, bitte sehr.
    Frau Meyer: Was? So viel?
    Angestellte: Tut mir leid.
10 *Frau Meyer*: Das ist ja unerhört!
    Angestellte: Ich kann nichts dafür.
    Frau Meyer: Vierzig Mark.
    Angestellte: (counts) 33, 34, 35, 40, bitte.
    Frau Meyer: Danke.
15 (still grumbling) Zweiunddreißig Mark.
    Das ist ja unerhört.

    Frau Meyer: Entschuldigen Sie, bitte!
    Information: Ja, bitte?
    Frau Meyer: Wann fährt der Zug nach Augsburg?
20 *Information*: Augsburg ... Augsburg ....
    Der Zug fährt um 9 Uhr 27.
    Und kommt um 10 Uhr 13 an.
    Frau Meyer: Danke.
    Muß ich umsteigen?

Einmal zweiter Klasse, bitte

Photograph: J. Allan Cash Ltd

25   *Information*:   Nein. Der Zug fährt direkt.
      Frau Meyer: Danke.
      Information: Bitte.

Dialogue 2

Antonio wants to go with his uncle and aunt as far as Innsbruck.
They will go on to Rome, and he will return alone to Munich.

1   *Antonio*:   Guten Tag!
    Angestellte: Guten Tag!
    Antonio: Zweimal zweiter Klasse nach Innsbruck, bitte.
    Angestellte: Einfach oder hin und zurück?
5   *Antonio*:   Einfach, bitte.

Angestellte: Zweimal einfach nach Innsbruck.
Achtundneunzig Mark, bitte schön.
Antonio: Moment.
Dann auch einmal nach Innsbruck.
10 *Angestellte*: Einfach?
Antonio: Nein.
Hin und zurück.
Angestellte: Zweimal einfach.
Einmal hin und zurück.
15 Stimmt's?
Antonio: Ja, das stimmt.
Angestellte: Das macht 196 Mark, bitte schön.
Antonio: Um wieviel Uhr fährt der Zug nach Innsbruck?
Information: Um neun Uhr einunddreißig.
20 *Antonio*: Danke.
Auf welchem Gleis?
Information: Auf Gleis 3.
Antonio: Danke.
Information: Bitte.

4.2 INFORMATION

(a) Notes on Dialogue 1

3. Einmal	In German you draw attention linguistically to the fact that there is only one person travelling. Compare with line 3 of Dialogue 2.
4. Einfach	Literally this means 'simple', but in this context means 'a single'.
5. Hin und zurück	This means literally 'there and back'.
9. Tut mir leid (Es) tut mir leid	Es tut mir leid is the fuller form of this expression, and is slightly more formal.
19. Wann fährt der Zug ... ?	Note that the word 'does' does not exist in German. The question form is made by

	making the subject and the verb change places in the sentence.
22. Und kommt ... an	The English verb 'to arrive' is rendered in this sentence in German by a verb which has two parts to it.

(b) Notes on Dialogue 2

3. Zweimal	This indicates that there are two people travelling.
15. Stimmt's?	Literally stimmt es?. This more colloquial form is usually used.

(c) Word list

Here is a list of the most important words in this chapter. They should be learnt by heart. They are given here in the order in which they occur in the chapter. N.B. Verbs with separable affixes are shown thus: an_kommen.

einfach	single
oder	or
hin und **zurück**	return
was?	what?
uner**hört**	terrible
der Zug (¨e)	train
umsteigen	to change (trains)
di**rekt**	straight through
einmal	one (i.e. person travelling)
zweimal	two (i.e. people travelling)
dann	then
auch	also/too
der Gleis (-e)	platform
an_kommen	to arrive
ab_fahren	to leave
ab_waschen	to wash up
ab_trocknen	to dry up
auf_räumen	to tidy up
an_rufen	to ring up (i.e. telephone)
ein_kaufen	to do the shopping
ab_schließen	to lock up

ab_geben	to give up
aus_gehen	to go out
der **Teller** (-)	plate
das **Spiel**zeug (-e)	toy
die **Lebensmitt**el (plural only)	provisions
der **La**den (⸚)	shop
die **Arbeit**	work
wieder**hol**en	to repeat
der Chef	boss
die **Mut**ter (⸚)	mother
das Kind (-er)	child

(d) Some phrases

So viel?	As much as that?
Ich kann nichts da**für**	There's nothing I can do about it
Das stimmt	That's right
Um **wie**viel Uhr?	At what time?
Muß ich ... ?	Must I ... ?
Um 9 Uhr	At nine o'clock

Special note

Eine Angestellte	A female employee
Ein Angestellter	A male employee
Eine Reisende	A female traveller
Ein Reisender	A male traveller

4.3 STRUCTURAL EXPLANATIONS

(a) Structures to learn

(i) How to state how many tickets you want
(in other words how many people are travelling)

Einmal	–	one person is travelling
Zweimal	–	two people are travelling
Dreimal	–	three people are travelling

(ii) How to state the class you are travelling

Erster Klasse	–	1st class
Zweiter Klasse	–	2nd class

(iii) **How to state your destination**
nach Augsburg
nach Innsbruck

(iv) **Single or return?**
Einfach
Hin und zurück

Note the similar construction of the following sentences:
1. Einmal erster Klasse nach München, hin und zurück.
2. Zweimal zweiter Klasse nach Bremen, einfach.
3. Dreimal erster Klasse nach Regensburg, hin und zurück.
4. Einmal zweiter Klasse nach Reutlingen, einfach.
5. Zweimal erster Klasse nach Fürth, hin und zurück.
6. Zweimal erster Klasse nach Feuchtwangen, einfach.

If you miss out any of these elements when you ask for your ticket, you will be asked about it.

(v) **How to ask what time a train leaves**

Wann fährt der Zug nach
{
Hamm
Münster
Höxter ?
Bielefeld
München
}

(vi) **How to ask what time the train arrives**

Wann kommt der Zug in
{
Hamm
Münster
Höxter
Bielefeld
München
}
an?

(vi) **How to ask if and where you have to change trains**

(Wo) muß ich umsteigen?
(Where) do I have to change?

(b) Grammar

(i) Observe how these sentences are formed:

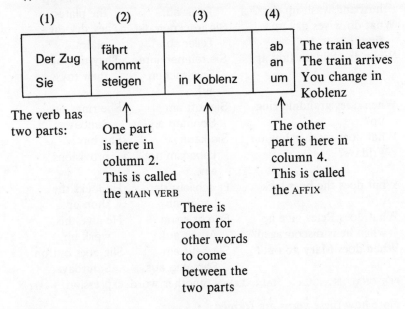

(1)	(2)	(3)	(4)	
Der Zug	fährt		ab	The train leaves
	kommt		an	The train arrives
Sie	steigen	in Koblenz	um	You change in Koblenz

The verb has two parts:

One part is here in column 2. This is called the MAIN VERB

The other part is here in column 4. This is called the AFFIX

There is room for other words to come between the two parts

(ii) Observe how these sentences are similar:

What do all good husbands do?	Sie waschen ab.	They do the washing up.
What do wives do afterwards?	Sie trocknen ab.	They do the drying up.
What do (some) children do before they go to bed?	Sie räumen auf.	They tidy up.
What does grandma do on Sunday?	Sie ruft an.	She rings up.
What does mother do on Friday afternoon?	Sie kauft ein.	She goes shopping.
What does the boss do before going home?	Er schließt ab.	He locks up.
What does Peter do if he is very discouraged?	Er gibt auf.	He gives up.
What does Mary do every Saturday night?	Sie geht aus.	She goes out.

PERSONAL PRONOUN + MAIN VERB + AFFIX

(iii) And these:

What does the good husband wash up first?	Er wäscht die Teller ab.	He washes up the plates.
What do wives dry up first?	Sie trocknen die Teller ab.	They dry the plates.
What do children tidy up?	Sie räumen ihre Spielsachen auf.	They tidy up their toys.
When does grandma ring up?	Sie ruft am Sonntag an	She rings on Sundays.
What does mother buy on Fridays?	Sie kauft Lebensmittel ein.	She buys provisions.
What does the boss lock up?	Er schließt den Laden ab.	He locks the shop up.
What does Peter give up when he is discouraged?	Er gibt seine Arbeit auf.	He gives his work up.
When does Mary go out?	Sie geht am Samstag aus.	She goes out on Saturdays.

PERSONAL PRONOUN + MAIN VERB + another word/expression + AFFIX

Note how these verbs are formed:

1	2	2a	3
	geh		aus
ich		e	
er	räum-	t	auf
Sie	ruf-	t	an
wir	kauf-	en	ein
Sie	geh-	en	aus

← Column 3 contains the verb affixes

↑ These are regular endings to add to the stem of verbs

The most common affixes are: an, auf, aus, bei, ein, her, hin, mit, nach, vor and zu. The affix is put last in the sentence.

Note the formation of the verbs, used in the sentences below:

ich trockne ab	wasche ab	schließe ab	gebe auf
er trocknet ab	wäscht ab	schließt ab	gibt auf
sie trocknet ab	wäscht ab	schließt ab	gibt auf
wir trocknen ab	waschen ab	schließen ab	geben auf
Sie trocknen ab	waschen ab	schließen ab	geben auf

Looking up verbs with separable affixes in the dictionary

If you want to look up one of these verbs in the dictionary, or a vocabulary list, you must look up the right form of the verb. For example, you will not find wäscht ... ab, or trocknet ... ab; you must look up abwaschen or abtrocknen; these forms are called the *infinitive*. Here are some more examples:

steht auf	aufstehen	infinitive
macht ... zu	zumachen	(When the infinitive form
fährt ... ab	abfahren	of the verb is used, the
kommt ... an	ankommen	affix is stressed)

4.4 EXERCISES

Section A

Exercise 1
Ask the times of trains to the following places:

Nürnberg	Erlangen
Würzburg	Ansbach
Innsbruck	Großhabersdorf
Frankfurt	Forchheim
Treuchtlingen	Schwabach

Exercise 2
Look at the symbol. You'll see that it is intended to indicate that one person wishes to travel to Berlin, 2nd class; the double-headed arrow indicates that the person wishes to make a return journey, there and back.

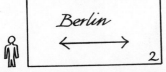

Reisender: Einmal zweiter Klasse nach Berlin, bitte.
Angestellte: Einfach oder hin und zurück?
Reisender: Hin und zurück, bitte.

Make up similar dialogues to match the following symbols. If you can work with a partner, take it in turns to play the part of the Reisender and the Angestellte.

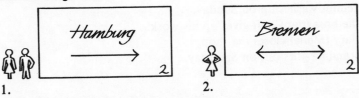

1. 2.

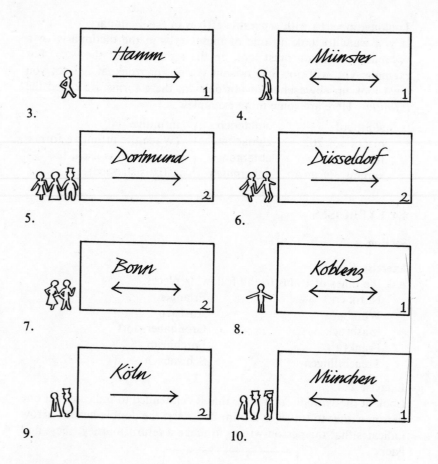

3.

4.

5.

6.

7.

8.

9.

10.

Section B

Exercise 3

Put into German:
1. Grandma (Oma) rings up on Saturday.
2. Ingrid goes out on Tuesday.
3. The children (die Kinder) tidy up the shop.
4. Mother (Mutter) clears up the toys.
5. Peter washes up the plates.
6. Inge buys provisions.
7. Helmut washes up on Sunday.
8. The boss (der Chef) gives up his work.
9. Mary (Maria) closes the shop.
10. Grandma goes out on Saturday.

Exercise 4

The words in these sentences are jumbled up. Sort them out so that they are in the correct order.

1. Wann ab fährt der Zug nach Bonn?
2. Wir ab Laden den schließen.
3. Geht Dienstag aus am Oma.
4. Am an Mittwoch Peter ruft.
5. Lebensmittel ein Chef kauft der.
6. Wäscht Teller Mutter ab die.
7. Kinder Teller ab trocknen die die.
8. Er ein Lebensmittel kauft.
9. Gibt Arbeit der seine auf Chef.
10. Ich auf Spielsachen räume die.

CHAPTER 5

TRAVELLING BY TAXI, BUS OR TRAM

5.1 DIALOGUES

Dialogue 1

Elke is late for her appointment with Fritz, and in order to avoid having another row with him about punctuality, she decides to take a taxi.

1   *Elke*: (dials taxi number) Ich möchte ein
          Taxi bitte.
    Angestellte: Ihr Name?
    Elke: Kustmann.
5   *Angestellte*: Adresse?
    Elke: Fürstenstraße 15.
    Angestellte: Wohin?
    Elke: Zur Nietzschestraße.
    Angestellte: Das Taxi ist in 10 Minuten da.
10 *Elke*: Danke.

    Taxifahrer: (rings frontdoor bell)
          Frau Kustmann?
    Elke: Ja.
    Taxifahrer: Ihr Taxi ist hier.
15 *Elke*: (gets in) Zur Nietzschestraße, bitte.
          Nummer 30.
    Taxifahrer: Ja, ist in Ordnung.
    Taxifahrer: (arriving in Nietzschestraße)
          So, bitte schön.
20 *Elke*: Was macht das?
    Taxifahrer: Das macht 6 Mark 50.
    Elke: (giving him 7 Marks)
          Danke.
          Das stimmt so.

Ihr Taxi ist hier!

Photograph: Bavaria-Verlag/Ludwig Windstosser

25 *Taxifahrer*: Danke schön.
          Auf Wiedersehen.

Dialogue 2

Frau Meyer wants to go to the centre of Munich for her annual visit to the Christkindl Markt during the week before Christmas.

The Christkindl Markt takes place on the Marienplatz in front of the town hall. There are many stalls selling fried sausages, hot punch, sweets, nuts, and Christmas delicacies of all sorts. There are also many stalls selling Christmas decorations and presents.

1 *Frau Meyer*:   Entschuldigung!
       Fährt die Nummer 23 zum Rathaus?
   Mann: Nein, nicht die Nummer 23.
   Frau Meyer: Ach du lieber Himmel!
5   Welche Straßenbahn fährt denn zum Rathaus?
   Mann: Sie brauchen die Nummer 18.
       Sie fährt zum Rathaus.
   Frau Meyer: Ach, vielen Dank.
       Die Nummer 18.
10 *Mann*:   Ja, sie fährt zum Rathaus.
   Frau Meyer: (to herself)
       Das ist ja unerhört!!
       Das war immer die 23!!

5.2 INFORMATION

(a) Notes on Dialogue 1

6. Fürstenstraße 15

Note that in German you say the name of the street first and the number afterwards.

9. Das Taxi ist in 10 Minuten da

Note that here German uses the present tense to indicate future time.

24. Das stimmt so

The customer indicates that he or she requires no change with the phrase Das stimmt so. It is common practice to round up bills to the next highest mark.

(b) Word list

Here is a list of the most important words in this chapter. They should be learnt by heart. They are given here in the order in which they occur in the chapter.

das **Taxi** (-en)	taxi
der **Name**	name
die **Adresse** (-n)	address
wohin?	where to?

die **Minut**e (-n)	minute
da	there
hier	here
Ent**schul**digung	excuse me
die **Numm**er (-n)	number
welch-?	which?
die **Straß**enbahn (-en)	tram
brauchen	to need
fahren (**fährt**)	to go (of transport)
immer	always
der **Haupt**bahnhof	main station
der **Flug**hafen (:)	airport
das **Zen**trum	centre
das **Rat**haus (:er)	town hall
nicht	not
die Stadt (:e)	town
das Schloß (:er)	castle or palace
die Stadt**mitt**e (-n)	town centre
die **Op**er (-n)	opera or opera house
die **Quitt**ung (-en)	receipt
der Bus (-se)	bus
das **Frei**bad (:er)	open-air swimming pool
die Sekret**är**in (-nen)	secretary
der Freund (-e)	friend
das Geld	money
das **Zimm**er (-)	room
der Zug (:e)	train

Some phrases
Ach, du **lieb**er **Himm**el!   Good Heavens!

5.3 STRUCTURAL EXPLANATIONS

(a) Structures to learn
(i) Ordering a taxi (how to state your address)

Hindenburgstraße 17
Mozartstraße 25
Nietzschestraße 30
Oskar von Müller Ring 129
Neue Straße 6
Kennedy Allee 43

The name of the street is stated
first. The number comes after.

(ii) How to state your destination

zum
{
Hauptbahnhof
Flughafen
Rathaus
Stadtzentrum
Schloß Nymphenburg
}
(all these words are masculine or neuter)

zur
{
Hindenburgstraße
Kennedy Allee
Stadtmitte
Oper
}
(all these words are feminine)

Zum is used with masculine and neuter nouns, zur is used with feminine nouns. These expressions are used in the directions which the customer gives when streets or buildings are named, particularly when they are within the town where one takes the taxi.

nach
Perlach
Wedding
Wellingsbüttel
Zirndorf

Nach is used when the customer names an area or district or when the taxi has to go to another town.

(iii) How to pay the taxi driver

Was macht das?   How much is that?

(iv) How to get a receipt for the taxi fare

Eine Quittung über   A receipt for

elf
neun   } Mark
zwanzig

eleven
nine   } marks
twenty

(v) How to enquire where a bus or tram goes to

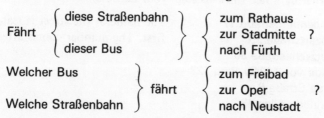

Fährt
{
diese Straßenbahn
dieser Bus
}
{
zum Rathaus
zur Stadtmitte
nach Fürth
}
?

Welcher Bus
Welche Straßenbahn
} fährt
{
zum Freibad
zur Oper
nach Neustadt
}
?

(b) Grammar
(i) The indefinite article

As we saw in Chapter 1, all German nouns can be categorised in one of three genders: masculine, feminine or neuter. When you want to say, for instance, *a* boy, or *an* apple, these words, which are called *indefinite articles*, vary according to the gender of the noun they accompany. Here are some examples:

Masc.	Fem.	Neut.
ein Professor	eine Sekretärin	ein Zimmer
ein Zug	eine Straße	ein Taxi

We can summarise this rule by tabulating the *indefinite articles* alone.

Masc.	Fem.	Neut.
ein	eine	ein

N.B. If you think about it, there can be no plural of 'a', or 'an'.

(ii) The negative

If you want to say 'not a', or 'not an', then the word is kein. It behaves just like the *indefinite article*.

Masc.	Fem.	Neut.
Der ist kein Professor!	Sie ist keine Sekretärin!	Das ist kein Taxi!

We can summarise this rule thus:

Masc.	Fem.	Neut.	Plur.
kein	keine	kein	keine

N.B. The play *St Joan* begins with the memorable phrase 'No eggs! No eggs!', from which you see that there can be a plural form of the German word kein. Keine Eier! 'No eggs!'

The word for 'not' is nicht. Nicht die Nummer 13. 'Not the number 13.'

(iii) Subjects and direct objects

a) The subject of a sentence is the person or thing which *does* the action or event indicated by the verb. All the forms of the indefinite and negative article, described above, are the subjects of sentences. In German, the subjects of sentences are said to be in the 'nominative case'. We can summarise this rule thus:

	Masc.	Fem.	Neut.
	ein	eine	ein
NOMINATIVE	kein	keine	kein

b)   Consider the sentence 'The dog bit the postman'. We know who did the biting. It was the dog; the subject of the sentence. We also know who shouted 'Ouch!' It was the postman! We can say therefore, that whatever is bitten, bought, kicked, liked, etc., is the *direct object* of a verb. In the following sentences, the *direct objects* are printed in italics. Note that verbs describing states, as well as actions, have direct objects.

> Peter kicked *a ball*
> We bought *a house*
> I have *a room*
> He likes *beer*
> She has not got *a cheque book*

Here are some German sentences with the *direct objects* underlined.

> Der Professor hat eine Sekretärin
> Sie hat keinen Freund
> Ich habe kein Geld
> Frau Meyer braucht eine Tasse Kaffee

In German, the direct objects of sentences are said to be in the 'accusative case'. We can summarise this rule thus:

	Masc.	**Fem.**	**Neut.**
	einen	eine	ein
ACCUSATIVE	keinen	keine	kein

N.B. It is the *masculine* form of the *indefinite article* which is different in the *accusative case*. The difference is the letter n.

N.B. There is no direct object after the verb sein: 'to be'.

(iv) The definite article

a)   When you want to say *the* professor, *the* street, or *the* house, these words, which are called *definite articles* vary according to the gender of the noun they accompany. Here are some examples:

Masc.	**Fem.**	**Neut.**
der Professor	die Straße	das Haus
der Zug	die Sekretärin	das Taxi

We can summarise this rule by tabulating the definite article alone:

	Masc.	**Fem.**	**Neut.**
NOMINATIVE	der	die	das

b) If you think back to that postman who got bitten a little while ago, you will remember what *direct objects* are. They are said to be in the 'accusative case'. Now, we can summarise the rule about the *definite article* as we did for the *indefinite article*:

	Masc.	**Fem.**	**Neut.**	**Plur.**
NOMINATIVE	der	die	das	die
ACCUSATIVE	den	die	das	die

Notice the definite article has a *plural form*, because we can talk about 'the dogs', or even 'the postmen'. Notice, too, that the difference between the nominative and the accusative case is again the letter n.

You will find a full list of definite and indefinite articles in the appendix.

(v) 'Some' or 'any'

These words which are so important in English are generally not required in German:

Haben Sie Geld?	Have you any money?
Nein, ich habe kein Geld	No, I haven't got any money
(at a party):	
Herr Müller, Sie haben kein Bier	Herr Müller, you haven't got any beer

(vi) Prepositions

Consider the following sentences, taken from the dialogues:

Zur Nietzschestraße	To Nietzsche Street
Die Nummer 18 fährt zum Rathaus	The number 18 goes to the town hall

As we saw earlier, zum is used with *masculine* and *neuter* nouns, zur is used with *feminine* nouns.

Now, we must understand that each of these two words is a contraction of two other words:

zum = zu dem
zur = zu der

The two words dem and der are examples of our old friends, the definite articles. Here, where they accompany the *preposition* zu, they are said to be in the *dative case*. Another case!! There will be more about this in Chapter 9.

(vii) Some prepositions accompany the *accusative case*, and others accompany the *dative case*. (Some prepositions may be used with both cases!) You will find a complete list in the appendix.

5.4 EXERCISES

Section A

Exercise 1
See how many sentences you can make.

| Fährt | dieser Bus
diese Straßenbahn
dieser Zug
die Nummer 15 | nach

zum

zur | Egersdorf
Steinach
Stadttheater
Rathaus
Flughafen
Stadtmitte
Goethestraße | ? |

Exercise 2
1. You're at the Number 17 tram stop and you want to go to the town hall. What do you say to the lady who is already waiting there?
2. Perhaps you're an opera singer visiting the town for the first time.
3. Perhaps you want to go to the district of Munich called Perlach.
4. You think you want the Number 23, but does it go to the town centre?
5. Was it the 31 that goes to the airport?
6. You're pretty certain that it's the Number 1, but does it go to the open-air swimming pool?
7. Which tram is it that goes to the station?
8. And which bus goes to the Heidenstraße?
9. You know there's a bus to Egersdorf, but which one?
10. Which bus goes to Göttingen?

Section B

Exercise 3
Convert the following sentences into the negative. The first one is done for you:

e.g. Ich habe ein Buch.
　　 Ich habe kein Buch.

1. Er hat ein Auto.
2. Sie möchte einen Kaffee.
3. Er ist Professor.
4. Sie hat eine Einladung.
5. Wir haben einen Hund.

6. Das ist der Bahnhof.
7. Der Garten ist groß.
8. Der Vater ist alt.
9. Frau Meier ist jung.
10. Santos ist in Hamburg.

CHAPTER 6

ILLNESS

6.1 DIALOGUES 📼

Dialogue 1

Frau Meyer has had another very bad night, so she decides to go and see her doctor. She rings for an appointment.

1   *Assistentin*: Praxis Doktor Storm.
        Guten Morgen.
  Frau Meyer: Guten Morgen.
        Ich möchte den Arzt sehen.
5   *Assistentin*: Haben Sie einen Termin?
  Frau Meyer: Nein.
        Geht es heute vormittag?
  Assistentin: Nein.
        Es tut mir leid.
10   Heute vormittag ist nichts mehr frei.
  Frau Meyer: Donnerwetter!
        Ist nichts mehr frei?
  Assistentin: Nein.
        Es tut mir leid.
15   *Frau Meyer*: Geht es heute nachmittag?
  Assistentin: Ja. Kommen Sie um 16 Uhr.
  Frau Meyer: Gott sei Dank!
        Um 16 Uhr.
        Ja, das geht.
20   Danke schön.
  Assistentin: Auf Wiederhören!
  Frau Meyer: Auf Wiederhören!

Dialogue 2

Fritz Löb went out to his Stammtisch at the Gasthaus Adler last night. It was his regular Wednesday night out and as sometimes

Patienten – Wartezimmer

Photograph: Bavaria-Verlag/Laurinpress

happens he had too much to drink. The following morning he finds himself in Dr Storm's surgery explaining his symptoms.

1 *Doktor Storm*: Nun, was fehlt Ihnen denn?
  Fritz: Ich habe Kopfschmerzen.
  Doktor Storm: Ist das alles?
  Fritz: Nein, Herr Doktor.
5   Mein Bauch tut weh, und ich habe Durchfall.
  Doktor Storm: Seit wann haben Sie Durchfall?
  Fritz: Seit gestern.
  Doktor Storm: Ich verschreibe Ihnen etwas für den Durchfall.
  Fritz: Vielen Dank, Herr Doktor.

Dialogue 3

Antonio once entertained ambitions of playing for Inter Milan. He has had to settle for something less exalted, however, and he plays for a Munich club called TSV 1886. On Sunday afternoon he had a difference of opinion with an opposing goalkeeper and on this Monday morning he finds himself in Dr Storm's surgery.

1 *Doktor Storm*: Nun, wo tut es weh?
  Antonio: Hier.
  Es ist mein Rücken.

Doktor Storm: Hier?
(He pokes Antonio's back)
5 *Antonio*: Au!! Ja!
Doktor Storm: Ist das ein stechender Schmerz?
Antonio: Ja! Stichartig.
Doktor Storm: Ist der Schmerz immer stichartig?
Antonio: Nein.
10   In der Nacht war es ein dumpfer Schmerz.
Doktor Storm: So, so.
Kein Fußball für Sie.
Antonio: O weh.

6.2 INFORMATION

(a) Notes on Dialogue 1

5. Termin	der Termin means a date or a fixed time for an appointment.
7. Geht es	The expressions Geht es? or Es geht are very useful expressions which can be used in many situations. It is the equivalent, in English, of expressions such as 'It's all right' or 'It's OK' or 'It's working'.
11. Donnerwetter	This is a fairly acute expression of impatience or irritation but one which can be used in society without giving offence.
16. 16 Uhr	Note that the 24-hour clock is used in any sort of formal situation.

(b) Notes on Dialogue 2

Stammtisch	A Stammtisch is a table in a Gasthaus which is reserved for certain regular customers on a particular day each week. Nearly every Gasthaus has its Stammtisch and there is often a notice on it indicating that it is reserved on a particular day.

The Stammtisch customers sometimes meet in order to talk about matters of mutual interest but they may also often play cards and in particular the very popular German card game Skat.

6. Seit wann?

Note that the English expression 'How long?' is rendered in German by the expression 'Since when?' It is, therefore, quite logical, as in the next line, to have the expression Seit gestern.

(c) Notes on Dialogue 3
TSV 1886

The letters TSV stand for Turn- und Sportverein and the date indicates the year in which the club was founded.

(d) Word list
Here is a list of the most important words in this chapter. They should be learnt by heart. They are given here in the order in which they occur in the chapter.
N.B. Parts of the body are given in the appendix.

die **Prax**is	practice (of a doctor)
der Arzt (⁻e)	doctor
sehen	to see
heute	today
der **Vor**mittag (-e)	morning
nichts	nothing
der **Nach**mittag (-e)	afternoon
nun	now
die **Kopf**schmerzen (plural)	headache
alles	everything
der Bauch	stomach
der **Durch**fall	diarrhoea
seit	since
gestern	yesterday
ver**schrei**ben	to prescribe
etwas	something

der **Rü**cken (-)	back
der Schmerz (-en)	pain
stechend	sharp (of a pain)
stichartig	shooting (of a pain)
immer	always
die Nacht (¨e)	night
dumpf	dull
der **Fuß**ball (-)	football
der **Zahn**arzt (¨e)	dentist
das **Fie**ber	fever or high temperature
die **Stun**de (-n)	hour
der Tag (-e)	day
leicht	slight
stark	strong or severe
trocken	dry
ge**broch**en	broken
die **Reise** (-n)	journey
nett	nice

(e) Some phrases

Heute **Vor**mittag	this morning
Heute **Nach**mittag	this afternoon
Es tut mir leid	I'm sorry
Gott sei Dank!	Thank Goodness!
Das geht	That's all right
Auf **Wie**dersehen	Goodbye
Was fehlt **Ih**nen?	What's the matter?
. . . tut weh	. . . hurts
O weh!	Oh dear!

6.3 STRUCTURAL EXPLANATIONS

(a) Structures to learn

(i) How to make an appointment to see the doctor

Ich möchte		I'd like to see the
den Arzt	} sehen	{ doctor
den Zahnarzt		{ dentist

Geht es		Is	
heute vormittag		this morning	}
heute nachmittag	?	this afternoon	} possible?
morgen		tomorrow	

Kommen Sie um	Come at
10 Uhr	ten o'clock
14 Uhr	two o'clock
16 Uhr 30	four thirty

(ii) How to describe symptoms of illness

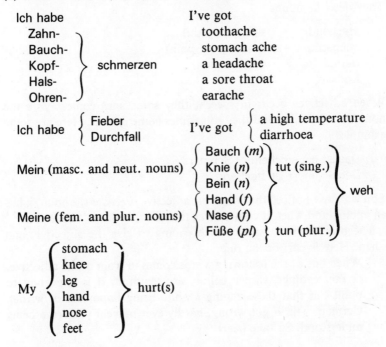

Ich habe		I've got
Zahn-		toothache
Bauch-		stomach ache
Kopf-	schmerzen	a headache
Hals-		a sore throat
Ohren-		earache

Ich habe { Fieber / Durchfall }   I've got { a high temperature / diarrhoea }

Mein (masc. and neut. nouns) { Bauch (*m*) / Knie (*n*) / Bein (*n*) } tut (sing.)

Meine (fem. and plur. nouns) { Hand (*f*) / Nase (*f*) / Füße (*pl*) tun (plur.) } weh

My { stomach / knee / leg / hand / nose / feet } hurt(s)

(iii) How to express how long symptoms have lasted

Seit	gestern	Since yesterday
	mehreren Stunden	For several hours
	drei Tagen	For three days

(iv) How to describe the type of pain

Es tut weh	It hurts or aches
Wo tut es weh?	Where does it hurt?

Ist es	Is it
Es ist	It's

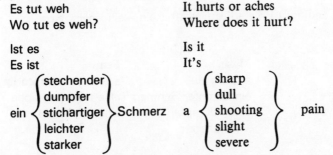

ein { stechender / dumpfer / stichartiger / leichter / starker } Schmerz   a { sharp / dull / shooting / slight / severe } pain

(b) Grammar

(i) Parts of the body

You will find a list of parts of the body in the appendix.

(ii) Adjectives

The following words appeared in the dialogues. They are *adjectives*. They *describe* nouns.

stechend	–	sharp (of pain)
stichartig	–	shooting (of pain)
dumpf	–	dull (of pain)
trocken	–	dry

When adjectives occur in speech, they sometimes come *before* the noun they describe, and they sometimes come *after* it. Here are some examples.

Das ist ein stechend*er* Schmerz
Der Schmerz ist stechend

You will have noticed that when the adjective *precedes* the noun, it has an ending and when it comes *after* the noun, it doesn't have one.

The problem is to know which ending to give the adjective, and when. Here is part of the rule:

When one of the following words comes in front of the adjective, certain endings, shown below, are required. It is important to point out that these endings, while being important in *written* German, will, if got wrong, hardly ever prevent you from being understood. So take heart!

ein	–	a; an	unser	–	our
kein	–	not a	euer	–	your (familiar plural)
mein	–	my			
dein	–	your (familiar)	Ihr	–	your (polite)
sein	–	his	ihr	–	their
ihr	–	her			
sein	–	its			

Note the endings of the adjectives after ein, kein, mein, etc.

	Sing.	
	Masc.	**Fem.**
	a dull pain	a sore or chapped lip
NOMINATIVE	ein dumpf*er* Schmerz	eine trocken*e* Lippe
ACCUSATIVE	einen dumpf*en* Schmerz	eine trocken*e* Lippe

Neut.

a broken leg

NOMINATIVE ein gebrochen*es* Bein
ACCUSATIVE ein gebrochen*es* Bein

Plur. (all genders)

	Masc.	Fem.	Neut.
NOMINATIVE	keine gebrochen*en* Arme	Rippen	Beine
ACCUSATIVE	keine gebrochen*en* Arme	Rippen	Beine

(iii) The 24-hour clock

In German-speaking countries the 24-hour clock is used for all formal expressions of time and in particular for travelling in order to express times of arrival and departure, etc. As long as you know the cardinal numbers up to 60, it is very easy (see Chapter 2).

1. 13:00   dreizehn Uhr
2. 12:00   zwölf Uhr
3. 09:05   neun Uhr fünf
4. 18:15   achtzehn Uhr fünfzehn
5. 16:25   sechzehn Uhr fünfundzwanzig
6. 21:30   einundzwanzig Uhr dreißig
7. 11:10   elf Uhr zehn
8. 06:20   sechs Uhr zwanzig
9. 21:30   einundzwanzig Uhr dreißig
10. 14:45   vierzehn Uhr fünfundvierzig

6.4 EXERCISES

Section A

Exercise 1

What would you say if:

1. The filling in your wisdom tooth has come out.
2. You have eaten too many cherries.
3. You drank too much wine last night.
4. You have been coughing all night.
5. Your neuralgia has returned.
6. You have a fever.
7. Your shoes are too tight.
8. That meat you had yesterday wasn't fresh.
9. You have tripped up and fallen on your knee.
10. Your temperature is 103°.

N.B. *Normal* body temperature is 98.4° Fahrenheit, but 36.6° Celsius, the system used in Germany.

Exercise 2

Play the role of the patient in the following dialogue. Make up the part of the patient and read aloud the part of the doctor. If you are working with a partner, take it in turns to play the role of the doctor and the patient.

Patient	*Arzt*
1. Greet the doctor	
	2. Guten Tag. Was fehlt Ihnen?
3. Say you have a sore throat.	
	4. Seit wann haben Sie Halsschmerzen?
5. Say you've had it for three days.	
	6. Ich verschreibe Ihnen etwas für die Halsschmerzen.

Exercise 3

Say the following parts of your body hurt:

Your	head	Your	arm
	leg		stomach
	foot		ear
	hand		knee
	back		tooth

Section B

Exercise 4

You are feeling very negative about life. Answer all the following questions in the negative.
1. Ist das ein gutes Buch?
2. Ist das eine schöne Frau?
3. Ist das eine ruhige Straße?
4. Ist das ein ruhiges Zimmer?
5. War das ein schöner Abend?
6. War das eine gute Reise?
7. War das eine ruhige Nacht?
8. War das ein schöner Ausblick?

Exercise 5

You are still feeling very negative.
1. Haben Sie eine ruhige Frau?
2. Haben Sie ein gutes Zimmer?

3. Haben Sie einen schönen Ausblick?
4. Haben Sie ein neues Buch?
5. Haben Sie einen neuen Fußball?
6. Haben Sie einen guten Doktor?
7. Haben Sie eine nette Schwester?
8. Haben Sie eine ruhige Straße?

CHAPTER 7

SHOPPING

7.1 DIALOGUES 🖭

Dialogue 1

It will soon be Elke's birthday, and Fritz Löb wants to buy her a pullover. However, he is rather unused to buying ladies' clothes.

1 *Verkäuferin*: Was darf es sein?
Fritz: (speaking by instinct)
Ich schaue mich nur um.
Verkäuferin: Ja, bitte schön.
Fritz: (clears his throat)
Fräulein!
5 *Verkäuferin*: Ja? Was darf es sein, bitte?

Ich möchte einen Damenpullover

Photograph: Bavaria-Verlag / Rudolf Holtappel

Fritz: Ich möchte einen Pullover.
Verkäuferin: Ja. Herren- oder Damenpullover?
Fritz: Einen Damenpullover suche ich.
Verkäuferin: Ja. Welche Größe trägt die Dame?
10 *Fritz*: O, ich weiß es nicht genau.
   Mittelgröße, glaube ich.
Verkäuferin: So wie ich?
Fritz: (embarrassed and trying not to look too closely)
   Ja, so ungefähr.
Verkäuferin: Ja, Größe vierzig.
15   An welches Material hatten Sie gedacht?
Fritz: Ach ja. Das Material. Natürlich.
Verkäuferin: Wolle? Baumwolle? Oder eine Kunstfaser?
Fritz: Wolle! Ja, aus Wolle.
Verkäuferin: Ich habe hier einen schönen roten Pullover.
20   Der ist aus Wolle.
Fritz: Nein. Sie hat schon einen roten Pullover.
   Haben Sie diese Art in blau?
Verkäuferin: Hat die Dame blaue Augen?
Fritz: Eigentlich ja.
25 *Verkäuferin*: Ich habe hier einen blauen Pullover.
Fritz: Ja. Der blaue Pullover ist bestimmt schön.
   Was kostet er?
Verkäuferin: 65 Mark.
Fritz: Ich nehme ihn.

Dialogue 2
Frau Meyer has been needing a pair of new shoes for ages.
1 *Verkäufer*: Kann ich Ihnen helfen?
Frau Meyer: Ich brauche neue Schuhe.
Verkäufer: Ja, bitte schön.
   (looking at Frau Meyer's shoes)
   Sie tragen Größe 37, glaube ich.
5 *Frau Meyer*: Nein. Ich trage immer Größe 36.
Verkäufer: (sceptically)
   Ach so.
Frau Meyer: Was kosten die braunen Schuhe im
   Schaufenster?
Verkäufer: Die sind Größe 37.
10 *Frau Meyer*: Haben Sie die braunen Schuhe eine Nummer
   kleiner?
Verkäufer: Ja, die gleichen Schuhe habe ich hier.
   Sie sind aber schwarz.

Kann ich sie anprobieren?

Photograph: Bavaria-Verlag/Rudolph Holtappel

Frau Meyer: Kann ich sie anprobieren?
15 *Verkäufer*: Selbstverständlich können Sie sie anprobieren.
Frau Meyer: (taking a few steps)
Au!!! Das tut weh!
Sie sind zu klein.
Verkäufer: Möchten Sie die braunen Schuhe anprobieren?
Frau Meyer: Sind die Sohlen aus Leder?
20 *Verkäufer*: Nein. Die braunen Schuhe haben
Kunststoffsohlen.
Frau Meyer: Kunststoffsohlen! Furchtbar!
Das gefällt mir überhaupt nicht.
Haben Sie keine Schuhe mit Ledersohlen.
25 *Verkäufer*: Na, freilich.
Schauen Sie.
Diese blauen Schuhe sind sehr elegant.
Sie sind hundertprozentig aus Leder.
Frau Meyer: Welche Größe?
30 *Verkäufer*: Größe 37.
Frau Meyer: Was kosten sie?
Verkäufer: Sie kosten 145 Mark.
Frau Meyer: Was? Das ist mir zu teuer!
Auf Wiedersehen!
35 *Verkäufer*: Auf Wiedersehen!
Frau Meyer: (grumbling to herself) Allerhand! Allerhand ist
das! 145 Mark!!

7.2 INFORMATION

(a) Notes on Dialogue 1

4. Fräulein!

This word is used, regardless of age, to summon the attention of a salesgirl or saleslady.

8. Einen Damenpullover

Note how the positions of the subject and the object in this sentence have been reversed. In German the object quite often comes at the beginning of a sentence, so that it can be emphasised. German is able to do this quite easily because the masculine object of a sentence is 'marked', in this case by the letters -en, which are added to the word ein.

10. Ich weiß es

Note how German has to say Ich weiß es – 'I know it', where English would normally just say 'I know'.

15. An welches Material . . . ?

Note that where English says 'I think of', German says denken an.

18. aus Wolle

English says 'made of wool'. German says aus Wolle.

20. Der ist . . .

The subject pronoun is normally er, or sie. However, to give the pronoun emphasis the words der or die are frequently used.

(b) Notes on Dialogue 2

6. Ach so

This is one of the most useful expressions you can learn in German because it allows you to express polite interest in what other people are saying, even if you don't feel up to uttering a word yourself. By using it judiciously, and with a good pronunciation, you can probably establish a reputation for vast intelligence and language mastery. It means 'really', 'is that what you mean?', 'how interesting!', 'indeed'. Whichever of these meanings you intend the phrase to have, the one constant underlying significance of the phrase is that you are being told something which you did not know before. If you say nothing else, you will probably get full marks for diplomacy.

8.	im Schaufenster	The word im is a contraction of in dem.
9.	Die sind . . .	See note to line 20 on Dialogue 1.
12.	Die gleichen Schuhe	See note to line 8 on Dialogue 1.
26.	Überhaupt nicht	This phrase or gar nicht are very useful idioms meaning 'not at all'.
29.	Schauen Sie	In the north of Germany you may hear an alternative version of this expression: Sehen Sie.
31.	Hundertprozentig	This useful word can be used for expressions such as 'absolutely' or 'completely'.

(c) Word list

Here is a list of the most important words in this chapter. They should be learnt by heart. They are given here in the order in which they occur in the chapter.

der **Pullover** (-)   pullover

der **Herr**enpullover (-)	gentlemen's pullover
suchen	to look for
die **Größe** (-n)	size
tragen	to wear
die **Da**me (-n)	lady
wissen	to know
ge**nau**	exactly
die **Mittelgröße**	medium size
unge**fähr**	approximately
das Mater**ial**	material
na**tür**lich	of course
die **Wol**le	wool
die **Baum**wolle	cotton
rot	red
schon	already
die Art	sort or kind
blau	blue
das **Au**ge (-n)	eye
eigentlich	actually
be**stimmt**	really or certainly
kosten	to cost
nehmen	to take
helfen (hilft)	to help
brauchen	to need
neu	new
der Schuh (-e)	shoe
glauben	to believe
braun	brown
das **Schau**fenster (-)	window (of a shop)
klein	small
groß	large
gleich	the same
aber	but
schwarz	black
anpro**bie**ren	to try on
selbstver**ständ**lich	of course
können	to be able to or to be allowed to
die **Soh**le (-n)	sole
das **Le**der	leather
der **Kunst**stoff	artificial material
furchtbar	terrible
freilich	certainly
schauen	to look

hundertprozentig	entirely
teuer	dear or expensive
der Rock (¨e)	skirt
die Hose	trousers
das Nachthemd (-en)	nightshirt
die Bluse (-n)	blouse
die Weste (-n)	sleeveless jacket
das Kleid (-er)	dress
der Mantel (¨)	coat
die Jacke (-n)	jacket
der Anzug (¨e)	suit
das Bluson (-s)	light jacket
der Sakko (-s)	sports jacket
der Regenmantel (¨)	raincoat
die Farbe (-n)	colour
der Wein (-e)	wine
die Milch	milk
das Bier	beer

Some phrases

Ich schaue mich nur um	I'm just looking round
Was darf es sein?	Can I help you?

7.3 STRUCTURAL EXPLANATIONS

(a) Structures to learn
(i) Here are some phrases to use when you go shopping:

Ich schaue mich nur um	I'm just looking
Ich weiß es nicht genau	I don't know exactly
Das ist mir zu teuer	That's too expensive

(ii) Here are some phrases which you may hear when you go shopping, and which it will help you to understand:

Kann ich Ihnen helfen?	Can I help you?
Was darf es sein?	What would you like?
Welche Größe?	Which size?
Welche Farbe?	Which colour?
Welches Material?	Which material?
Sonst noch etwas?	Anything else?
Darf es noch etwas sein?	Anything else?

| Haben Sie sonst noch einen Wunsch? | Anything else? |
| Zahlen Sie an der Kasse, bitte | Please pay at the counter. |

(iii) How to ask if you can try on an article of clothing (ladies'):

Kann ich	den Rock		skirt
	die Hose		trousers
	das Nachthemd		nightshirt
	die Bluse		blouse
	die Weste	anprobieren?	sleeveless jacket
	das Kleid		dress
	den Mantel		coat
	die Jacke		jacket
	den Sonnenanzug		sunsuit

(iv) Gentlemen, of course, may wish to have the same privileges:

Kann ich	das Hemd		shirt
	das Bluson		light jacket with zip-front
	die Jacke	anprobieren?	jacket
	die Hose		trousers
	den Anzug		suit
	den Sakko		sports jacket
	den Regenmantel		raincoat

(v) This is how you ask for something a little bit different from what you have been shown. The diagrams below allow you to make up lots of different sentences, so that you can ask for something different.

Haben Sie	diese Art diese Farbe diese Größe dieses Material	eine Number	größer kleiner
		in	blau rot weiß
		aus	Wolle Leder Nylon

	something like this	a size	bigger smaller
Have you got	this colour this size this material	in	blue red white
		in	wool leather nylon

(vi) How to ask the price:

The diagram below will cover most things you are likely to want to buy:

Was {
  kostet {
    der Anzug
    die Bluse
    das Hemd
    er
    sie
    es
  } ?
  kosten {
    sie
    die Schuhe
  }
}

What {
  does {
    the suit
    the blouse
    the shirt
    it
  }
  do {
    they
    the shoes
  }
} cost?

(b) Grammar

(i) Verbs

In Chapter 2, we looked at some common *regular* and *irregular* verbs. Here are some more; the regular ones first. Regular verbs, you will remember, keep their stem unchanged and use the standard set of endings. Once again, you will find the most frequently used parts of the verbs given here. The full table is in the appendix.

The verb SUCHEN — to seek/look for   The verb GLAUBEN — to believe

ich	(I)		e	ich	e
er	(he)		t	er	t
sie	(she)	SUCH-	t	sie GLAUB-	t
wir	(we)		en	wir	en
Sie	(you)		en	Sie	en

The verb BRAUCHEN — to need

ich		e
er		t
sie	BRAUCH-	t
wir		en
Sie		en

Now for the *irregular* verbs!

The verb TRAGEN — to wear

Note how the vowel sounds change with the addition of an Umlaut.

ich	trage
er	trägt
sie	trägt
wir	tragen
Sie	tragen

The verb NEHMEN — to take

Here, not only does the vowel change, the stem changes too!

ich	nehme
er	nimmt
sie	nimmt
wir	nehmen
Sie	nehmen

Here is part of the verb MÖGEN — to like. It enables you to say what you *would like*, as in the sentence: Ich möchte einen Pullover — 'I would like a pullover'.

ich	möchte	—	I would like	
er	möchte	—	he would like	
sie	möchte	—	she would like	einen Pullover
wir	möchten	—	we would like	
Sie	möchten	—	you would like	

This part of the verb is slightly irregular, in that the er form and the sie form end in -e instead of the more usual -t.

(ii) Adjectives

a) In the previous chapter, we looked at the endings of adjectives when they are preceded by words like ein, kein, mein, unser, and so on. In this chapter, we look at the endings of adjectives, when they are preceded by words like der (the), dieser (this), and so on.

Der blaue Pullover ist sehr elegant	The blue pullover is very elegant
Die elegante Dame heißt Frau Müller	The elegant woman is called Mrs Müller
Das alte Taxi fährt schnell	The old taxi goes fast
Diese braunen Schuhe sind aus Leder	These brown shoes are made of leather

The above adjectives all form part of the *subject* of their respective sentences, and so, as we saw in Chapter 5, they are said to be in the 'nominative case'. We can summarise this rule thus:

		Masc.	**Fem.**	**Neut.**	**Plur.** (all genders)
Adjectives after der, dieser	NOMINATIVE	-e	-e	-e	-en

Consider the following sentences.

Fritz kauft den blauen Pullover	Fritz buys the blue pullover
Elke braucht die weiße Bluse	Elke needs the white blouse
Wir sitzen um den runden Tisch	We are sitting around the round table
Konrad hat das rote Hemd	Konrad has the red shirt
Haben Sie die blauen Schuhe?	Have you got the blue shoes?

In each of these sentences, the adjectives are part of the *direct object* of their respective sentences, and they are consequently in the 'accusative case', as we saw in Chapter 5. The third sentence contains a phrase with a preposition governing the 'accusative case'. We can summarise the rule about adjectives when they occur in the 'accusative case' thus:

		Masc.	**Fem.**	**Neut.**	**Plur.** (all genders)
Adjectives after der, dieser	ACCUSATIVE	-en	-e	-e	-en

It is the *masculine* form of the adjective which has a different spelling in the accusative case. The difference is the letter n.

You will find a full account of the endings of adjectives in the appendix. It is worth pointing out, however, that although it is very *easy* to explain how the adjectives make their endings, it is very *hard* to remember the rules well enough to get the endings right when you are speaking. Take heart from the thought that mistakes will seldom prevent you from communicating your meaning to a German speaker. Come back to the adjective endings again and again, and you will gradually begin to get them right as you practise them.

7.4 EXERCISES

Section A

Get ready to go shopping in Germany and be ready to get exactly what you want. Here are some more useful words.

Colours

pastellgrün	pastel green
rosa	pink
mittelbraun	medium brown
gold	gold coloured
beige	beige
hellblau	light blue
dunkelrot	dark red
gelb	yellow
natur	natural colour

Materials

Tweed	tweed
Seide	silk
Krepp	crepe
Leinen	linen
Cord	corduroy
Velours	velvet
Gabardine	gabardine

Trade names for artificial materials

Popeline	poplin
Diolen	(trade name of a lightweight man-made fibre)
Polyester	polyester
Trevira	trevira
Acryl	acrylic

Some of these are easily washed in a washing machine. They are then marked:

> Vollwaschbar

Exercise 1

Study this model conversation carefully.

Verkäuferin: Was darf es sein?
Kunde: (Ich möchte einen Pullover.)
Verkäuferin: Welche Größe brauchen Sie?
Kunde: (Größe 40.)

Verkäuferin: An welches Material hatten Sie gedacht?
Kunde: (Wolle.)
Verkäuferin: Welche Farbe möchten Sie?
Kunde: (Ich möchte hellblau.)
Verkäuferin: Der ist sehr elegant.
Kunde: (Ja, der gefällt mir.)
  (Was kostet er?)

Here are some clothes that you want to buy. Don't forget to look up the equivalent sizes in the appendix, page 309.
1. You fancy a skirt made of poplin. It ought to be dark red. Your size is 14. Don't forget to ask the price.
2. You've been thinking about a crepe blouse for some time. Your size is 16. How about a delicate shade of pink?
3. You've been meaning to treat yourself to a silk shirt for ages. You want a white one, size 12.
4. Those leather jackets in Germany are really good value. A dark brown one would just suit you, size 20.

Exercise 2
You are shopping in Hamburg in Karstadt, a well-known shop in the Mönckebergstraße. The salesgirl offers you a number of things and you like them all. Ask what they cost.
1. Hier habe ich einen Rock.
2. Diese Hose ist schön.
3. Hier ist ein schönes Nachthemd.
4. Die Bluse ist elegant.
5. Und hier habe ich eine schöne Weste.
6. Der Regenmantel ist nicht teuer.
7. Dieser Anzug ist aus Wolle.
8. Hier habe ich eine Hose aus Cord.
9. Eine schöne Lederjacke.
10. Hier habe ich ein schönes Hemd.

Section B

Exercise 3
Check that you know what the following German sentences mean.
1. Ich schaue mich nur um.
2. Ich möchte einen Pullover.
3. Ich weiß es nicht genau.
4. An welches Material hatten Sie gedacht?
5. Der blaue Pullover ist bestimmt schön.

6. Ich brauche neue Schuhe.

7. Ich trage immer Größe 40.

8. Kann ich sie anprobieren?

9. Haben Sie keine Schuhe mit Ledersohlen?

10. Das ist mir zu teuer.

Exercise 4

Translate the following sentences into German.

1. What do they cost?

2. I don't like the shoes at all.

3. Are the soles made of leather?

4. Have you got the same sort of thing a size smaller?

5. How much are the brown shoes in the window?

6. I would like a nightdress.

7. I'm just looking.

8. The shirt is made of silk.

9. How much are the shoes?

10. The pullover is too expensive.

Exercise 5

Put the following expressions into German.

1. The white skirt.
2. The red trousers.
3. The black shoes.
4. The long dress.
5. The brown jacket.

6. The light blue shirt.
7. The brown suit.
8. The short raincoat.
9. The green blouse.
10. The little black dress.

CHAPTER 8

FAMILIES AND NATIONALITIES

8.1 DIALOGUES 📼

Dialogue 1

Antonio Santos is always short of money. He notices this fact particularly when Elke wears her fur coat when coming to work. He has decided to try and get a week-end job in an Italian restaurant. He goes off to see the manager of the Pizzeria Giovanni.

1 *Antonio*: Guten Tag!
    Inhaber: Guten Tag!
    Antonio: Ich komme wegen der Stelle als Kellner.
    Inhaber: Ach ja.
5   Haben Sie Erfahrung als Kellner?
    Antonio: Nein, leider nicht.
    Inhaber: Hmm. Sprechen Sie Italienisch?
    Antonio: Natürlich.
      Ich bin Italiener.
10 *Inhaber*: Ah, Sie sind Italiener.
      Von wo kommen Sie?
    Antonio: Ich komme aus Napoli.
    Inhaber: Napoli! Na ja, Napoli!
      Ich komme aus Benevento.
15 *Antonio*: Na. Wunderbar!
      Meine Tante Concetta kommt aus Benevento.
    Inhaber: Nein.
    Antonio: Doch, doch.
    Inhaber: Fantastico, fantastico!
20   Wann können Sie anfangen?

Dialogue 2

Fritz Löb is visiting a lovely church near Landshut. He has come especially to see it (Elke is just not interested in seeing yet another church). The parson is showing him round.

1 *Pfarrer*: Die Kirche ist sehr alt, Herr Löb.

Fritz: Ja, das sieht man.

Pfarrer: Über drei hundert Jahre alt.

Fritz: Tatsächlich?

5 *Pfarrer*: Ja.

Schauen Sie.

Der Altar ist schön, nicht wahr?

Fritz: Das stimmt, wirklich.

Er ist wunderschön.

10 *Pfarrer*: Riemenschneider.

Fritz: Ach so.

Tilman Riemenschneider.

Pfarrer: Ja.

Sagen Sie, Herr Löb.

15 Was sind Sie von Beruf, wenn ich fragen darf?

Fritz: Ich bin Hauptschullehrer.

In München.

Pfarrer: Ach so.

Sind Sie verheiratet?

20 *Fritz*: Ja. Das heißt, wir leben getrennt.

Pfarrer: Das tut mir leid.

Fritz: Danke.

Pfarrer: Haben Sie Kinder?

Fritz: Nein, ich habe keine Kinder.

25 *Pfarrer*: Es ist vielleicht besser so.

Fritz: Ja, es ist besser so.

Kleine Kinder brauchen einen Vater.

Pfarrer: Das stimmt.

8.2 INFORMATION

(a) Notes on Dialogue 1

6. Leider — This word means 'unfortunately'. Another word with the same meaning is unglücklicherweise.

7. italienisch — This word, being an adjective, is spelt with a small letter.

		Compare with Italiener (l.9), which is a noun and therefore written with a capital letter.
8.	Natürlich	Other words meaning the same could be: selbstverständlich, sicher or freilich.
13.	Napoli	The German form of the name of the town Naples is Neapel. Antonio is here speaking in Italian.
18.	Doch, doch	Note that this word means 'yes' when it is used emphatically, after somebody else has used a negative.

(b) Notes on Dialogue 2

2.	Das sieht man	Each verb can have the subject man. It means 'one'. In English we quite often use the 'you' form of the verb, when we mean 'everybody'. We say, for instance 'you mustn't drive fast in a built-up area', when we really mean 'no-one' must do it. We say, for instance, in English 'You can go into a pub after 6 o'clock in the evening'. What we really mean is everyone can, or 'one' can. German always uses man in order to show that the idea is general to many people. The form of the verb is the same as the er form or sie form.
4.	Tatsächlich	Another word meaning the same thing would be wirklich.
6.	Schauen Sie	The verb schauen meaning 'to look' tends to be used more in the south of Germany. In the north it would be more normal to use the verb sehen.

| 7. Nicht wahr? | In this sentence the expression nicht wahr? means 'isn't it?' The same expression, however, will do for 'don't they? can't I? mustn't we?' etc. It is consequently a very useful phrase which doesn't change, and can be used for turning any statement into a question. |

| 10. Riemenschneider | Tilman Riemenschneider was a famous sculptor, who worked principally in wood. He worked during the fifteenth and sixteenth centuries, and there are many fine altars carved by him to be seen in churches, especially in the south of Germany. |

| 14. Sagen Sie | This is a very useful phrase, which indicates to the person you are talking to that you now wish to say something. |

| 15. Wenn ich fragen darf | Do not attempt to analyse this phrase at this time. Simply use it in order to mean 'if you don't mind my asking'. Students wishing to inform themselves about the structure of 'subordinate' clauses introduced by wenn should consult the grammar books listed in the Bibliography. |

| 16. Hauptschullehrer | In Germany all children go to the Grundschule at the age of 6. When they reach 10+ they transfer to the Hauptschule, where many of them stay until they leave to go into paid employment. Some children leave, however, at the age of 10, as a result of tests and teachers' assessment, in order to go to a |

Gymnasium, which is approximately the equivalent of a grammar school.

20. Wir leben getrennt

This literally means 'we live separated'.

23. Haben Sie Kinder?

Note that where English would need the word 'any', this does not occur in German.

(c) Word list

Here is a list of the most important words in this chapter. They should be learnt by heart. They are given here in the order in which they occur in the chapter.

kommen	to come
wegen	on account of
die **Stelle** (-n)	job or position
der **Kell**ner (-)	waiter
die E**rfah**rung	experience
leider	unfortunately
sprechen	to speak
na**tür**lich	naturally
der Itali**e**ner (-)	Italian
wunderbar	wonderful
die **Tan**te (-n)	aunt
wann?	when?
können	to·be able
anfangen	to begin
die **Kir**che (-n)	church
sehr	very
alt	old
sehen	to see
hundert	a hundred
tat**säch**lich?	really?
das Jahr (-e)	year
der A**ltar** (-e)	altar
wirklich	really
wunderschön	very beautiful
sagen	to say
der Be**ruf**	job/profession
fragen	to ask
der **Leh**rer (-)	teacher
ver**hei**ratet	married
leben	to live

getrennt	separated
das Kind (-er)	child
vielleicht	perhaps
besser	better
brauchen	to need
der Vater (¨)	father
klein	small
ein wenig	a little
verlobt	engaged
ledig	single
geschieden	divorced
verwitwet	widowed
Geschwister	brothers or sisters
der Sohn (¨e)	son
die Tochter (¨)	daughter
der Bruder (¨)	brother
die Schwester (-n)	sister

Some phrases

Das stimmt	That's right
Was sind Sie von Beruf?	What is your job?
Das heißt	That is to say
Das tut mir leid	I'm sorry

8.3 STRUCTURAL EXPLANATIONS

(a) Structures to learn

(i) How to ask somebody their nationality and how to state your own

	Men	Women	
Sind Sie	Deutscher	Deutsche	
Ich bin	Engländer	Engländerin	
	Franzose	Französin	(?)
	Spanier	Spanierin	
	Däne	Dänin	

(ii) How to ask where people come from, and how to say where you come from yourself

Woher sind Sie?		England
Von wo kommen Sie?	Ich komme aus	Schottland
		Frankreich
		Spanien
		Dänemark

N.B. Since Germany is divided into two independent countries, Germans very often give the full name of their state when they say where they come from: Thus, Ich komme aus der Bundesrepublik (Deutschland)'. Or, 'Ich komme aus der DDR' (DDR stands for die Deutsche Demokratische Republik. The first two words are adjectives and agree with the word Republik).

(iii) How to ask whether somebody speaks a particular language

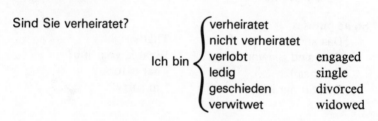

Sprechen Sie
- Deutsch
- Englisch
- Französisch ?
- Spanisch
- Dänisch

- Ja
- Nein
- Ein wenig
- Ein bißchen

} —a little

(iv) How to ask if someone is married, and how to refer to your own status

Sind Sie verheiratet?

Ich bin
- verheiratet
- nicht verheiratet
- verlobt — engaged
- ledig — single
- geschieden — divorced
- verwitwet — widowed

(v) How to ask about a person's family

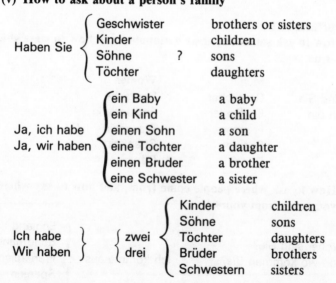

Haben Sie
- Geschwister — brothers or sisters
- Kinder — children
- Söhne ? — sons
- Töchter — daughters

Ja, ich habe
Ja, wir haben
- ein Baby — a baby
- ein Kind — a child
- einen Sohn — a son
- eine Tochter — a daughter
- einen Bruder — a brother
- eine Schwester — a sister

Ich habe }
Wir haben }
{ zwei
{ drei
- Kinder — children
- Söhne — sons
- Töchter — daughters
- Brüder — brothers
- Schwestern — sisters

$$\text{Nein,} \begin{cases} \text{ich habe} \\ \text{wir haben} \end{cases} \begin{cases} \text{kein Baby} \\ \text{kein Kind} \\ \text{keinen Sohn} \\ \text{keine Tochter} \\ \text{keinen Bruder} \\ \text{keine Schwester} \end{cases}$$

$$\begin{rcases} \text{Ich bin} \\ \text{Wir sind} \end{rcases} \text{kinderlos}$$ (We haven't any children/We have no children/We are childless)

(vi) How to ask about someone's job or profession

Was sind Sie von Beruf?

	Men	Women	
	Architekt	Architektin	architect
	Student	Studentin	student
Ich bin	Arzt	Ärztin	doctor
	Lehrer	Lehrerin	teacher
	Polizist	Polizistin	policeman/woman
	Verkäufer	Verkäuferin	salesman/woman

(b) Grammar
(i) You will find a list of nouns of nationality in the appendix.
(ii) There is also a list of European languages there.

(iii) More about adjectives
Sometimes adjectives occur by themselves, as in the sentence:

Kleine Kinder brauchen einen Vater   Young children need a father

When it is said that adjectives 'occur by themselves', this means that they do not follow words such as ein, mein, unser, or der, dieser, etc.

You will find the endings of such 'unaccompanied' adjectives in the appendix.

8.4 EXERCISES

Section A

Exercise 1
Read the following dialogue.
Pfarrer: Sagen Sie, Herr Schmidt.
Sind Sie verheiratet?

Herr Schmidt: Ja.
Pfarrer: Und haben Sie Kinder?
Herr Schmidt: Ja, ich habe zwei Kinder.
Pfarrer: Ach so!

Play out the above scene, imagining that the circumstances are different. If possible, take parts with a partner, each taking a role.
1. Herr Schmidt is divorced and has no children (don't forget what the parson said in the dialogue!).
2. He is widowed and has three children.
3. He is separated and has one child.
4. He is not married (this will be a shorter conversation).

Exercise 2
You are getting to know people and they are all very inquisitive about your family circumstances. What would you say? Here is an example:
Question: Sind Sie verheiratet?
Answer: Ja.
Question: Und haben Sie Kinder?
Answer: Ja, wir haben ein Kind.
1. You are still being woken up at 3 o'clock in the morning.
2. You have one of each.
3. You have two girls.
4. You have three boys.
5. You had to wait to have four boys before you had a girl.

Section B

Exercise 3
State your job as one of the following:
1. Male architect
2. Lady teacher
3. Policewoman
4. Doctor (male)
5. Student (female)
6. Teacher
7. Salesman
8. Saleswoman

CHAPTER 9

PLACES AND WEATHER

9.1 DIALOGUES

Dialogue 1

Elke has taken herself to the Alte Pinakothek, a famous art gallery in Munich. She finds it quite refreshing not to have Fritz trailing about with her for once. Poor Fritz! He'd better watch out!

1 *Mann*: Entschuldigen Sie!
   Elke: Ja?
   Mann: Ich wollte nur sagen ... das ist ein sehr elegantes Kleid.
5 *Elke*: Oh, vielen Dank.
   Das ist sehr nett von Ihnen.
   Mann: Sie haben einen norddeutschen Akzent.
   Elke: Ja. Ich komme aus Mölln.
   Mann: Mölln? Wo ist denn Mölln?
10 *Elke*: In Norddeutschland.
   Nicht weit von Hamburg.
   Mann: Ach so! In der Nähe von Hamburg.
   Elke: Ja. Zwischen Hamburg und Lübeck.
   Mann: Wie ist die Landschaft dort?
15 *Elke*: Es gibt einen großen See dort, und eine sehr schöne Kirche.
   Mann: Haben Sie noch Verwandtschaft dort?
   Elke: Ja. Mein Bruder wohnt in Mölln, bei meinen Eltern.
   Mann: Ach, Sie haben einen Bruder.
20 *Elke*: Ja. Er kommt nächste Woche nach München.
   Er ist begeisterter Skiläufer.
   Mann: Gibt es denn keinen Schnee in Mölln?

In der Alten Pinakothek

Photograph: Bavaria-Verlag/Hans Schmied

> *Elke*:   Nein. Im Winter regnet es sehr viel.
>   Aber es gibt nicht viel Schnee.
> 25 *Mann*:   So, so, so.

Dialogue 2
    Antonio is enjoying the Oktoberfest, a famous beer festival
which is held every year in Munich. He is sitting in a Bierzelt,

where he has been listening to the brass band playing. He has just got talking to a girl sitting opposite him. She is dressed in a very nice Dirndl.

1 *Antonio*: Prost!
  Mädchen: Prost!
  Antonio: Sind Sie Münchnerin?
  Mädchen: Nein. Ich komme aus Bad Reichenhall.
5 *Antonio*: Wo ist denn Bad Reichenhall?
  Mädchen: Nicht weit von Salzburg.
  Und Sie?
  Antonio: Ich komme aus Neapel.
  Aber jetzt bin ich Münchener.

Prost!

Photograph: Bavaria-Verlag / Hans Schmied

10 *Mädchen*:   So.
    Antonio: Was gibt es dort zu sehen, in Bad Reichenhall?
    Mädchen: Es gibt ein schönes Kurhaus und gute Geschäfte.
    Antonio: Und die Landschaft?
    Wie ist dort die Landschaft?
15 *Mädchen*:   Ach, die Landschaft ist wunderbar!
    Es gibt hohe Berge.
    Antonio: Das ist schön.
    Mädchen: Ja. Der Predigtstuhl zum Beispiel.
    Das ist ein sehr hoher Berg.
20 *Antonio*:   Wie ist das Wetter dort?
    Mädchen: Meistens schön.
    Es gibt viel Schnee im Winter.
    Antonio: Und im Sommer?
    Mädchen: Im Sommer regnet es manchmal.
25 Leider.

9.2 INFORMATION

(a) Notes on Dialogue 1

Alte Pinakothek — This is a famous art gallery in Munich containing a very important collection of oil paintings from all over the world.

7. Akzent — Most Germans speak with a regional accent. It is fairly easy to hear whether somebody comes from northern Germany or Bavaria for instance. The practised ear can identify quite easily the different regions of Germany just by listening to a few sentences. This regional accent does not, however, provide any information about social class.

12. in der Nähe von — This expression means 'near'. You can think of it as an abbreviated form of 'in the neighbourhood of'.

13. Hamburg und Lübeck	Hamburg is Germany's most important port. It stands on the river Elbe, with access to the North Sea. Lübeck is about 30 or 40 miles away, standing just back from the Baltic Sea. Hamburg is still an independent city state in the German Federation.
17. Verwandtschaft	This is a very general word which stands for any form of blood relationship.
20. er kommt	Note that German, like English, can use the present tense with an expression of future time, to indicate the future.
23. Im Winter	Notice that the expression im Winter has been brought to the beginning of the sentence in order to emphasise it. The subject consequently follows the verb.

(b) Notes on Dialogue 2

Oktoberfest	This is a festival which attracts many tourists from all over Germany and abroad. It takes place on a large area of ground, specially reserved for this and other festivals. The attractions include a funfair, with lots of roundabouts, shooting booths and stalls selling food and drink. The centre-piece, however, consists of the large tents (Bierzelte) where brass bands play and where large 1 litre tankards of beer (Biersteine) are served by waitresses who manage to carry five in each hand.

	Dirndl	This is a traditional costume still frequently worn in the southern part of Bavaria. It consists of a blouse with a deep décolletage, and short, puffy sleeves. The waist is drawn in tightly to accentuate the hips, and a small apron is worn on top of the skirt. Most women and girls in the south of Bavaria possess a Dirndl and wear it quite frequently.
3.	Münchenerin	This is the feminine form of Münchener and means somebody who lives in Munich.
4.	Bad Reichenhall	This is a well-known spa in the south-eastern tip of Germany, standing on the frontier with Austria.
12.	Kurhaus	This is where guests go to take the waters: the pump room.
18.	Der Predigtstuhl	This is a mountain standing just to the south of Bad Reichenhall which reaches the height of 1617 metres.

(c) Word list

Here is a list of the most important words in this chapter. They should be learnt by heart. They are given here in the order in which they occur in the chapter.

nur	just/only
sagen	to say
sehr	very
elegant	elegant
das Kleid (-er)	dress
nett	nice
der Akzent	accent
wo?	where?
weit	far
von	from
zwischen	between

die **Land**schaft (-en)	countryside
dort	there
schön	beautiful
die **Kir**che (-n)	church
der See (-n)	lake
groß	large
noch	still
die **Verwand**tschaft	relationship
der **Bruder** (⸗)	brother
wohnen	to live
die **El**tern	parents
die **Wo**che (-n)	week
be**gei**stert	enthusiastic
der **Schi**läufer (-)	skier
der Schnee	snow
der **Win**ter	winter
es **reg**net	it is raining
viel	much
Prost!	Cheers!
aber	but
jetzt	now
dort	there
sehen	to see
gut	good
das Ge**schäft** (-e)	shop; business
der Berg (-e)	mountain
das **Wet**ter	weather
meistens	usually
manchmal	sometimes
der **Som**mer	summer
leider	unfortunately
mit	with
von	of; from
zu	to; at
gegen**über**	opposite
die **Fahr**karte (-n)	ticket

(d) Some phrases

Ent**schul**digen Sie	Excuse me; I beg your pardon
Das ist sehr nett von **Ih**nen	That is very nice of you
Nicht weit von	Not far from
In der **Nä**he von	Near
Es gibt	There is; there are

Bei meinen **El**tern	With my parents
Was gibt es dort zu **seh**en?	What is there to see there?
Zum **Bei**spiel	For example

9.3 STRUCTURAL EXPLANATION

(a) Structures to learn

(i)

Wo ist $\begin{cases} \text{Mölln} \\ \text{Bad Reichenhall} \\ \text{Zirndorf} \end{cases}$?   Where is $\begin{cases} \text{Mölln} \\ \text{Bad Reichenhall} \\ \text{Zirndorf} \end{cases}$?

(ii) How to say that one place is near another place

$\begin{rcases} \text{Mölln} \\ \text{Bad Reichenhall} \\ \text{Zirndorf} \end{rcases}$ ist $\begin{cases} \text{nicht weit von} \\ \text{in der Nähe von} \\ \text{bei} \end{cases}$ $\begin{rcases} \text{Hamburg} \\ \text{Salzburg} \\ \text{Nürnberg} \end{rcases}$

$\begin{rcases} \text{Mölln} \\ \text{Bad Reichenhall} \\ \text{Zirndorf} \end{rcases}$ is $\begin{cases} \text{not far from} \\ \text{near} \\ \text{near} \end{cases}$ $\begin{rcases} \text{Hamburg} \\ \text{Salzburg} \\ \text{Nuremburg} \end{rcases}$

(iii) How to ask for information about a place

Wie ist die Landschaft dort?	What is the countryside like there?
Was gibt es dort zu sehen?	What is there to see there?

(iv) How to describe a place

Es gibt $\begin{cases} \text{eine sehr schöne Kirche} \\ \text{einen großen See} \\ \text{ein schönes Kurhaus} \\ \text{gute Geschäfte} \end{cases}$
a very beautiful church
a large lake
a fine kurhaus
good shops

(v) How to ask what the weather is like

Wie ist das Wetter?

(vi) How to describe the weather

(Das Wetter ist) meistens schön	The weather is usually nice

$\begin{rcases} \text{Im Winter} \\ \text{Im Sommer} \end{rcases}$ regnet es $\begin{cases} \text{sehr viel} \\ \text{manchmal} \end{cases}$

N.B. The subject of this sentence is es. However, the sentence begins with the phrases: Im Winter/Im Sommer for emphasis, and the subject comes after the verb.

Es gibt	{ nicht viel / viel }	Schnee	(im Winter)
In winter / In summer	} it rains {	a lot / sometimes	
There is	{ not much / a lot of }	snow	(in winter)

(b) Grammar

(i) You will find a list of expressions about the seasons of the year in the appendix.

(ii) There is a list of the months there too.

(iii) The indirect object

a)   Do you remember how we defined the direct object of a verb in Chapter 5, with the story of the dog biting the postman? Now we have to turn our attention to another concept called the *indirect object*.

Let us imagine that the postman is determined to make friends with the dog. Consider the sentence: *The postman gives the dog a bone.* We know that *the postman* does the giving, and that phrase is consequently the subject of the sentence. The thing that is given is *a bone*, and that is therefore the direct object of the sentence.

The person, or thing, to whom or for whom things are given, bought, sent, taken, etc. – in other words, the recipients – are *indirect objects*. Here are some examples:

I bought (my wife) some flowers
She sent (the man) a letter
We took (him) some chocolate
He threw (her) a kiss
She gave (the car) a good kick

Note that these sentences still make good sense if the *indirect object*, in brackets, is deleted. This would *not* be the case if the *direct objects* were to be deleted.

In German, the *indirect object* is marked or signalled by special forms of the definite and indefinite articles, the personal pronouns and possessive adjectives. They are said to be in the '*dative case*'.

b) **Definite articles**

Er gibt *dem Mann* den Brief	He gives the man the letter
	(He gives the letter to the man)
Er gibt *der Frau* das Geld	He gives the woman the money
	(He gives the money to the
	woman)
Er gibt *dem Mädchen* (das	He gives the girl a kiss
Mädchen) einen Kuß	(He gives a kiss to the girl)

N.B. The gender of the word Mädchen is neuter in German, despite its meaning.

Er gibt *den Kindern*	He gives the children presents
Geschenke	(He gives presents to the
	children)

We can summarise the rule for *definite articles* in the *dative case*, thus:

	Masc.	Fem.	Neut.	Plur. (all genders)
DATIVE CASE	dem	der	dem	den

c) **Indefinite articles and possessive adjectives**

Er gibt *seinem Vater* den	He gives his father the letter
Brief	(He gives the letter to his father
Er gibt *seiner Frau* das Geld	He gives his wife the money
	(He gives the money to his wife)
Er gibt *einem Mädchen*	He gives a girl his coat
seinen Mantel	(He gives his coat to a girl)
Er gibt *ihren Kindern*	He gives her children presents
Geschenke	(He gives presents to her
	children)

We can summarise the rule for *indefinite articles* and *possessive adjectives* in the *dative case*, thus:

		Masc.	Fem.	Neut.	Plur.
DATIVE CASE	(a, an)	einem	einer	einem	–
	(not a)	keinem	keiner	keinem	keinen
	(my)	meinem	meiner	meinem	meinen
	(his)	seinem	seiner	seinem	seinen
	(her)	ihrem	ihrer	ihrem	ihren
	(our)	unserem	unserer	unserem	unseren
	(your)	Ihrem	Ihrer	Ihrem	Ihren

You will find a full list of possessive adjectives in the dative case in the appendix.

d) **Key letters**

For definite and indefinite articles, as well as for possessive adjectives, the key letters, signalling the dative case, are as follows:

	Masc.	Fem.	Neut.	Plur.
DATIVE CASE	m	r	m	n

e) **Personal Pronouns**

Er gibt mir einen Brief	He gives me a letter
Er gibt ihm einen Mantel	He gives him a coat
Er gibt ihr das Geld	He gives her the money
Er gibt uns unsere Fahrkarten	He gives us our tickets
Er gibt Ihnen den Schlüssel	He gives you the key

We can summarise the rule for *personal pronouns* in the *dative case*, thus:

Nominative	Dative
ich	mir
er	ihm
sie	ihr
wir	uns
Sie	Ihnen (polite form)

Note that the polite form has a capital letter. You will find a complete list of personal pronouns in the dative case in the appendix. You will also find there notes on the order of objects in a sentence.

f) **Prepositions**

Certain *prepositions* accompany the *dative case*. Here are some example sentences from the dialogues of this chapter.

Das ist sehr nett von Ihnen
Mein Bruder wohnt bei meinen Eltern
Zum (zu dem) Beispiel

The commonest of the prepositions which always accompany the dative case are: mit (with), von (from, of) and zu (to, at).

Er fährt mit einem Freund nach Deutschland	mit einem Freund – with a friend
Er schreibt mit dem Bleistift	mit dem Bleistift – with the pencil
Sie kommt mit mir	mit mir – with me

Er kommt von meinem Haus	von meinem Haus – from my house
Er wohnt nicht weit von dem Berg	nich weit von dem Berg – not far from the mountain
Ich spreche von ihm	von ihm – of him
Er geht zu meiner Frau	zu meiner Frau – to my wife
Sie geht zur (zu der) Haltestelle	zur Haltestelle – to the bus stop

In the appendix you will find a list of the *prepositions* which always accompany the *dative case*.

N.B. When a noun occurs in the dative case in the plural, it always ends in -n.

9.4 EXERCISES

Section A

Exercise 1
Say where the following towns are.
Example: Wo ist Fürth?
        Nicht weit von Nürnberg.

1. Wo ist Oldenburg?
2. Wo ist Braunschweig?
3. Wo ist Paderborn?
4. Wo ist Limburg?
5. Wo ist Wiesbaden?
6. Wo ist Heidelberg?
7. Wo ist Cadolzburg?
8. Wo ist Augsburg?
9. Wo ist Pforzheim?
10. Wo ist Bad Reichenhall?

1. Oldenburg / Bremen
2. Hannover / Braunschweig
3. Bielefeld / Paderborn
4. Koblenz / Limburg
5. Wiesbaden / Frankfurt
6. Mannheim / Heidelburg
7. Cadolzburg / Nürnberg
8. Augsburg / München
9. Pforzheim / Stuttgart
10. Bad Reichenhall / Salzburg

Exercise 2
Say where the following places are.
Example: Wo ist Lübeck?
        Lübeck ist in Norddeutschland.
1. Wo ist Kiel?
2. Wo ist Passau?

3. Wo ist Lübeck?
4. Wo ist München?
5. Wo ist Hamburg?
6. Wo ist Augsburg?
7. Wo ist Oldenburg?
8. Wo ist Ulm?
9. Wo ist Bremen?
10. Wo ist Freiburg?

Section B

Exercise 3
Translate into German (*c.f.* appendix).
1. At Christmas. (zu)
2. With my parents. (bei)
3. For this reason. (aus)
4. By mistake. (aus)
5. In this weather. (bei)
6. By train. (mit)
7. On foot. (zu)
8. In my opinion (nach)
9. At work. (bei)
10. After half an hour. (nach)

Exercise 4
Complete the following sentences.
1. Sie kommt mit ein ... elegant ... Kleid.
2. Er hat ein ... süddeutsch ... Akzent.
3. Es gibt ein ... schön ... Kirche dort.
4. Mein klein ... Bruder wohnt in Hamburg.
5. Bad Reichenhall ist nicht weit von ein ... hoh ... Berg.
6. Dort gibt ein groß ... Kurhaus.
7. Bei Schaffhausen ist ein groß ... See.
8. Die Zugspitze ist ein hoh ... Berg.
9. Er hat ein weiß ... Hemd.
10. Sie trägt ein ... blau ... Pullover.

CHAPTER 10

REVISION TESTS

In this chapter you will have an opportunity to consolidate the language you have learned in the previous nine chapters. Each test indicates whereabouts in the earlier part of the book you ought to search if you have forgotten a particular point.

Test 1 – How to introduce somebody (Chapter 1)
You live in an old-fashioned family, where all your brothers and your cousins and your aunts live in the same house. You bring a colleague home for a meal and introduce all the members of the family to him one by one. There are some new words in this exercise, and so you ought to consult the pronunciation key before you do it. When you have tried the exercise yourself, check your pronunciation with the tape-recording.
First introduce your wife.
Then your father – Vater (*m*)
Then your mother – Mutter (*f*)
Then your son – Sohn (*m*)
Then your daughter – Tochter (*f*)
Then your uncle – Onkel (*m*)
Then your aunt – Tante (*f*)

Test 2 – Possessive adjectives (Chapter 1)
Like everybody else, you are houseproud about your own house and inquisitive about other people's houses. Together with your husband (or wife), you take your guest round the house and show off its special features.
You show the guests your garden – Garten (*m*)
Your kitchen – Küche (*f*)
Your bedroom – Schlafzimmer (*n*)
Your garage – Garage (*f*)

Your dog – Hund (*m*)
Your cat – Katze (*f*)

Test 3 – Greetings (Chapter 1)

1. What would you say to somebody you met at 8 o'clock in the morning?
2. What would you say to somebody who had just poured you out a drink?
3. What would you say if the telephone rang while you were talking to somebody?
4. What would you say to your son if he was just going off on holiday?
5. What would you say if your boss asked you out to dinner and you spilt your wine all over the best tablecloth?
6. What would you say as you left a friend who was ill in hospital?
7. What would you say to your husband just before you turned the light out at night?
8. What would you say if you stood on somebody's toe?
9. What would you say if you arrived late at the theatre, and had to reach your seat in the middle of the row after the play had started?
10. What would you say to your girlfriend as you prepared to tackle a juicy steak at a restaurant?

Test 4 – Staying in hotels (Chapter 3)

Here is a model letter, written to confirm a hotel booking made by telephone.

An das Hotel Atlantik   Bristol
An der Alster   den 2. April
D – 2000 Hamburg
_____

Sehr geehrte Herren!
Hiermit bestätige ich meine Reservierung für (ein Einzelzimmer mit Dusche) für die Zeit vom (27. Juni) bis zum (30. Juni) einschließlich.

     Hochachtungsvoll

Notes:
1. The address of the hotel you are writing to goes in the top left-hand corner of the writing paper. Note that the name of the town,

together with its postal code, is underlined. The name of the street comes before.

2. When writing your own address on writing paper you only write the name of the town.

3. The date is written as shown. The number is always followed by a full stop.

4. When writing to a hotel, the greeting is as shown. All letter greetings are followed by an exclamation mark.

5. The standard greeting at the end of a letter, written to somebody you do not know is Hochachtungsvoll. A good, standard farewell greeting for somebody you know moderately well would be Mit herzlichen Grüßen.

Translations of key terms in the model letter:

Sehr geehrte Herren!	Dear Sir
Hiermit bestätige ich …	This is to confirm
Einschließlich	Inclusive
Hochachtungsvoll	Yours faithfully

Note that those parts of the letter in brackets can be changed to fit in with your particular requirements. Practise writing the following letters, each of which is intended to confirm a hotel booking made earlier by telephone.

Note the letter D in the address indicates a town in Germany (D is Deutschland). The letter A in the address indicates Austria.

1. Hotel Sonnenhof
   Wagnerstraße 10
   D – 8352 Grafenau

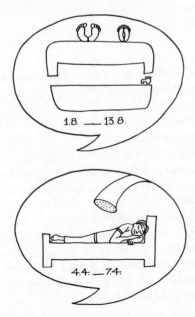

2. Hotel Bergland
   Unterstraße 4
   A – 6416 Obsteig
   Tirol

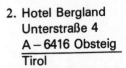

108

3. Hotel Wachtelhof
Mittelstraße 1
A – 5761 Hinterthal

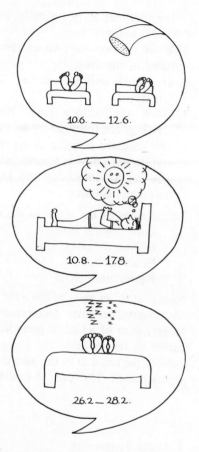

4. Sporthotel Fellhoist
Teichstraße 12
D – 2443 Großenbrode

5. Frühstückspension ,,Olga''
Hauptstraße 91
A – 5600 St. Johann
Salzburger Land

Test 5 – Greetings and making hotel bookings (Chapter 3)

Can you complete your part of the conversation. You will find the complete text on p. 239.

Empfang: Grüß Gott!
You: Greet her.
  Ask if there is a room available.
Empfang: Möchten Sie ein Einzelzimmer oder ein Doppelzimmer?
You: Say you want a double room.
Empfang: Ja, das ist möglich.
  Für wieviele Nächte bitte?
You: Say you want the room for three nights.
Empfang: Möchten Sie das Zimmer mit Bad oder mit Dusche?
You: Say you want it with a shower.
Empfang: Ja, ein Doppelzimmer mit Dusche habe ich.
  Das geht in Ordnung.

You: Ask how much the room is.
Empfang: Das Zimmer kostet 55 Mark pro Nacht.
You: Ask if that includes breakfast.
Empfang: Jawohl.
You: Ask if it includes VAT.
Empfang: Ja, selbstverständlich.
You: Say you'll take the room.
Empfang: Tragen Sie sich bitte ein.

Test 6 – Asking the times of departure and arrival of trains
(Chapter 4)

Look at these dialogues:

a)

HAMBURG – FRANKFURT – BASEL		IC 175
Hamburg – Altona	ab	9.32
Hamburg Dammtor	an	9.38
	ab	9.39
Hamburg Hbf.	an	9.44
	ab	9.45
Hamburg – Harburg	an	9.59
	ab	10.00
Hannover	an	11.10
	ab	11.14
Göttingen	an	12.09
	ab	12.10
Fulda	an	13.36
	ab	13.37
Frankfurt (M)	an	14.36
	ab	14.42
Mannheim	an	15.26
	ab	15.34
Karlsruhe	an	16.02
	ab	16.03
Freiburg	an	17.03
	ab	17.04
Basel	an	17.46

Reisender: Wann fährt der Zug nach Hamburg – Dammtor ab?
Angestellte: Er fährt um 9 Uhr 32 ab.
Reisender: Wann kommt er in Hamburg – Dammtor an?
Angestellte: Er kommt um 9 Uhr 38 an.
Reisender: Muß ich umsteigen?
Angestellte: Nein der Zug fährt direkt.

b)

Reisender: Wann fährt der Zug nach Hamburg Hbf (Hauptbahnhof) ab?
Angestellte: Er fährt um 9 Uhr 39 ab.
Reisender: Wann kommt er in Hamburg Hbf. an?
Angestellte: Er kommt um 9 Uhr 44 an.
Reisender: Muß ich umsteigen?
Angestellte: Nein, der Zug fährt direkt.

Make up dialogues similar to these. If you are studying with a partner, take it in turns to ask the questions.

This is where you are:	This is where you want to go:
1. Hamburg Hbf	Freiburg
2. Hannover	Fulda
3. Göttingen	Basel
4. Mannheim	Freiburg
5. Fulda	Karlsruhe
6. Freiburg	Basel
7. Frankfurt	Freiburg
8. Hamburg – Harburg	Frankfurt
9. Hannover	Frankfurt
10. Karlsruhe	Basel

Test 7 – Verbs with separable affixes (Chapter 4)
Put into German
1. Grandma (Oma) rings up on Saturday.
2. Ingrid goes out on Tuesday.
3. The children (die Kinder) tidy up the shop.
4. Mother (Mutter) clears up the toys.
5. Peter washes up the plates.
6. Inge buys provisions.
7. Helmut washes up on Sunday.
8. The boss (der Chef) gives up his work.
9. Mary (Maria) closes the shop.
10. Grandma goes out on Saturday.

Test 8 – Finding your way by bus and tram (Chapter 5)
Can you complete the following dialogue? If you are working with a partner, take it in turns to play the parts.
Dialogue A
Müller: ......
Meier: Ja, bitte?
Müller: ......
Meier: Nach Opladen?
Nein, dieser Bus fährt nach Ludwigshafen.
Müller: ......
Meier: Sie brauchen die Nummer 14.
Dialogue B
Schmidt: ......
Schüth: Ja. Kann ich Ihnen helfen?
Schmidt: ......
Schüth: Nein, nicht zum Schauspielhaus.
Sie fährt zum Hofgarten.

Schmidt: ......
Schüth: Sie brauchen die Nummer 1.
  Sie fährt zum Schauspielhaus.
Schmidt: ......

Test 9 – The definite article (Chapter 5)
Complete the following sentences:
1. ... Professor heißt Doktor Schmidt.
2. Wo ist ... Tasse?
3. Hier ist ... Buch.
4. ... Kaffee ist heiß.
5. Hier ist ... Frau.
6. ... Auto fährt schnell.
7. ... Mann heißt Herr Müller.
8. ... Einladung kommt heute.
9. ... Schlafzimmer ist groß.
10. ... Küche ist klein.

Test 10 – Describing symptoms of illness (Chapter 6)
Look carefully at the doctor's part of the following dialogue. Then make up the patient's role and speak it aloud. Read aloud the doctor's part (if you are working with a partner, take it in turns to play the role of the doctor and the patient).

Arzt	*Patient*
1. Guten Tag.	
	2. ......
3. Was fehlt Ihnen denn?	
	4. ......
5. Ihr Bein? Ist es ein leichter Schmerz?	
	6. ......
7. Ach so, stichartig. Seit wann tut es weh?	
	8. ......
9. So, so. Drei Tage schon. Kein Fußball für Sie.	

Test 11 – Describing symptoms of illness (Chapter 6)
Poor Sepp Steinbauer has fallen off his bicycle while on his way to a football match. He wanted to see 1.FC Nürnberg versus Bayern München. He's been taken to hospital where the staff nurse is trying to find out how badly he's hurt. From his answers it seems he is only just alive. You play the part of Sepp.

Note: Don't try to make up sentences like the nurse's. Just use her questions as clues to the answers. Example:

Schwester: Tut der Kopf weh?

Sepp: Ja, mein Kopf tut weh.

Schwester: Und das Bein?

Sepp: Ja, mein Bein tut weh.

Now begin:

Schwester: Tut der Kopf weh?
Und das Bein?
Wie geht's Ihrem Knie?
Wie ist mit dem Rücken?
Tut es am Hals weh?
Haben Sie Schmerzen am Ellbogen?
Ist Ihr Ohr wund?
Und die Nase?
Die Schulter ist verletzt, glaube ich.
O, und der Finger auch.

Test 12 – Finding exactly what you want when shopping (Chapter 7)
You are in Munich in the Kaufhaus, Oberpollinger. This time you are a difficult customer to please.

1. *Verkäuferin*:   Hier habe ich ein schönes Hemd.
   (You want something in the same material, but blue.)
2. *Verkäuferin*:   Das ist ein schöner Rock.
   (You want something like this, but a size smaller.)
3. *Verkäuferin*:   Dieser Anzug ist sehr schön.
   (You want the same colour, but in wool.)
4. *Verkäuferin*:   Diese Schuhe sind sehr elegant.
   (You want this colour a size larger.)
5. *Verkäuferin*:   Hier habe ich ein Hemd aus Seide.
   (You want the same material, but in light blue.)
6. *Verkäuferin*:   Das ist ein schöner Regenmantel.
   (You want the same sort of thing in cotton.)
7. *Verkäuferin*:   Der Pullover hier ist nicht teuer.
   (You want the same colour in Polyester.)
8. *Verkäuferin*:   Ein sehr elegantes Nachthemd.
   (You want the same sort of thing in black.)
9. *Verkäuferin*:   Mm, die Jacke ist aber schön.
   (You want the same sort of thing in velvet.)
10. *Verkäuferin*:   Nehmen Sie dieses Hemd?
    (You want the same size in white.)

Test 13 – Describing the weather (Chapter 9)

Expressions

Es ist sehr warm!

Es ist sehr kalt!

Es gibt viel Schnee.

Es regnet.

Example: Using the symbols, describe the climate in Munich

Sommer   Winter

München

Wie ist das Wetter in München?

A: Es ist sehr heiß im Sommer.
       Und es gibt viel Schnee im Winter.

	Sommer	Winter

1. Wie ist das Wetter in Hamburg?

2. Wie ist das Wetter in Bad Reichenhall?

3. Wie ist das Wetter in London?

4. Wie ist das Wetter in Nürnberg?

5. Wie ist das Wetter in Kiel?

CHAPTER 11

EATING OUT

11.1 DIALOGUES

Dialogue 1

Fritz is telephoning the restaurant, in order to reserve a table for himself and Elke.

1 *Besitzer*: Restaurant das Blaue Haus.
Guten Tag.
Fritz: Guten Tag.
Ich möchte einen Tisch für heute abend.
5 *Besitzer*: Für wieviele Personen?
Fritz: Für zwei.
Besitzer: Um wieviel Uhr, bitte?
Fritz: Um acht Uhr.
Besitzer: Ja, um acht Uhr.
10 Ich habe einen Tisch um acht Uhr.
Fritz: Sehr gut.
Besitzer: Auf welchen Namen, bitte?
Fritz: Löb. L – O – umlaut – B.
Besitzer: Herr Löb.
15 Ist in Ordnung, Herr Löb.
Fritz: Auf Wiederhören!
Besitzer: Auf Wiederhören!

(Fritz and Elke have arrived at the restaurant)
Fritz: Guten Abend!
Empfang: Guten Abend!
20 *Fritz*: Ich habe einen Tisch reserviert.
Empfang: Für wieviele Personen?
Fritz: Für zwei Personen.
Empfang: Auf welchen Namen, bitte?

Im Restaurant

Photograph: Bavaria-Verlag/Interfoto

Fritz: Löb.
25 *Empfang*: Ach ja.
 Herr Löb.
 Kommen Sie, bitte.

Dialogue 2

Fritz and Elke are considering the menu.
1 *Fritz*: Möchten Sie eine Vorspeise?
 Elke: Ich möchte eine Suppe – eine Zwiebelsuppe.
 Fritz: Und dann?
 Elke: Ein Texas Steak.
5 Und Sie?
 Was möchten Sie?
 Fritz: Ich glaube, ich möchte auch eine Suppe – eine
 Gulaschsuppe.
 und dann ... auch ein Texas Steak.
10 *Kellner*: Haben Sie gewählt?
 Fritz: Einmal Zwiebelsuppe.
 Einmal Gulaschsuppe.
 Kellner: Einmal Zwiebelsuppe.
 Einmal Gulaschsuppe.

15   *Fritz*:   Und dann – zweimal Texas Steak.
      Elke: Ohne Pommes frites, bitte.
      Kellner: Zweimal Texas Steak.
          Einmal mit Pommes frites.
          Einmal ohne.
20   Jawohl.
      Fritz: Möchten Sie etwas trinken?
      Elke: Ja, ich möchte bitte ein Viertel Rotwein.
      Fritz: Zwei Viertel Rotwein, bitte.
      Kellner: Zwei Viertel Rotwein.
25   Danke schön.

11.2 INFORMATION

(a) Notes on Dialogue 1

7. Um wieviel Uhr

In German you always have to use the word um when you want to ask what time something happens. It is roughly equivalent to our 'at what time?' The same applies when you say at what time something occurs – um acht Uhr.

12. Auf welchen Namen

Note that German uses auf welchen Namen in order to enquire the name of the guest.

16. Auf Wiederhören!

This is a special greeting for terminating a telephone conversation.

(b) Notes on Dialogue 2

1. Vorspeise

This word can mean either 'a starter' or 'hors d'oeuvre'.

2. eine Suppe

Note that German uses *eine* Suppe where in English we say '*some* soup'.

11. Einmal

Literally, this word means 'once'. It is the way you indicate how many portions or dishes you want. Zweimal – two (portions).

22. Viertel

This refers to a quarter of a litre. The wine would be served in a small carafe.

(c) Word list

der Besitzer	owner
das Restaurant (-s)	restaurant
der Tisch (-e)	table
heute	today
heute abend	this evening
wieviel?	how many?
die Person (-en)	person
sehr	very
gut	good
der Name (-n)	name
reservieren	to reserve
kommen	to come
die Vorspeise (-n)	hors d'oeuvre
die Suppe (-n)	soup
die Zwiebelsuppe (-n)	onion soup
das Steak	steak
dann	then
glauben	to believe
auch	also, too
wählen	to choose
die Gulaschsuppe (-n)	goulash soup
ohne	without
mit	with
etwas	something
trinken	to drink
das Viertel (-)	quarter
der Rotwein (-e)	red wine
die Speisekarte (-n)	menu
die Weinkarte (-n)	wine list
sehen	to see
das Wasser (-)	water
essen	to eat
zahlen	to pay
die Rechnung (-en)	bill
wo?	where?
welch-?	which?

wer?	who?
warum?	why?
was?	what?
wohin?	where (to)?
was für?	what sort of?
wie?	how?
heute nachmittag	this afternoon
heute morgen	this morning
morgen	tomorrow
morgen abend	tomorrow evening
morgen nachmittag	tomorrow afternoon
morgen früh	tomorrow morning
gestern	yesterday
gestern abend	yesterday evening
gestern nachmittag	yesterday afternoon
gestern morgen	yesterday morning
die Woche (-n)	week
das Jahr (-e)	year
der Monat (-e)	month
der Tag (-e)	day
die Minute (-n)	minute
die Stunde (-n)	hour
vor	ago

(d) Some phrases

Um wieviel Uhr?	At what time?
Auf welchen Namen?	What name?
Auf Wiederhören	Goodbye (phone)
Was möchten Sie?	What would you like?

(e) Menu vocabulary

garniert	dressed
gebacken	baked
gebraten	fried
gefüllt	stuffed
gegrillt	grilled
gekocht	boiled
geräuchert	smoked
in Essig	in vinegar
mit Sahne	creamed
nach Müllerin Art	meunière
pochiert	poached

*

der **Apfel**kuchen	apple pie
der **Apfel**saft	apple juice
das be**leg**te Brot	sandwich
das **Bier**	beer
die **Bock**wurst	thick, boiled sausage
die **Bowle**	cold punch
das **Brat**hähnchen	roast chicken
Bratkartoffeln	roast potatoes
die **Brat**wurst	fried pork sausages
das **Brötchen**	bread roll
das ge**koch**te Ei	boiled egg
das **Rühr**ei	scrambled egg
Spiegeleier	fried eggs
der **Eis**becher	ice-cream sundae
das **Eis**bein	pork shank in jelly
die **Ente**	duck
der **Fisch**	fish
das **Fleisch**	meat
die **Forelle**	trout
die **Frank**furter	hot-dog sausage
das **Früh**stück	breakfast
das **Geflügel**	poultry
Getränke	beverages
das **Gulasch**	goulash
das **Hack**fleisch	minced meat
das **Hähn**chen	chicken
der **Humm**er	lobster
der **Kaffee**	coffee
das **Kalb**fleisch	veal
die **Kalbs**haxe	leg of veal
das **Kalbs**schnitzel	veal cutlet
der **Kar**toffel	potato
Salzkartoffeln	boiled potatoes
der **Käse**	cheese
der **Kuchen**	cake, tart or flan
der **Lachs**	salmon
die **Leber**	liver
der **Leber**käs	hot sliced meat loaf
der **Leber**knödel	liver dumplings
das **Mat**jesfillet	herring fillet
die **Milch**	milk

das Mineralwasser	mineral water
die Nachspeise	pudding, dessert or sweet
das Obst	fruit
das Omelett	omelette
der Pfannkuchen	pancake
das Pfeffersteak	steak spiced with pepper
Pommes frites	chips
die Portion	portion
das Ragout	ragout
der Rehbraten	venison steak
das Rindfleisch	beef
der Rollmops	rollmop herring
der Saft	juice
die Sahne	cream
der Salat	salad
der grüne Salat	green salad
der Kartoffelsalat	potato salad
das Salz	salt
das Sauerkraut	sauerkraut
der Schinken	ham
die Schlagsahne	whipped cream
der Schnaps	schnapps
das Schnitzel	escalope
das Schweinefleisch	pork
das Schweineschnitzel	pork chop
die Schweinshaxe	leg of pork
der Spargel	asparagus
die Speisekarte	menu
die Suppe	soup
die Tagessuppe	soup of the day
der Tee	tea
eine Tasse Tee	a cup of tea
ein Kännchen Tee	a pot of tea
die Torte	gateau
das Viertel	quarter of a litre
der Wein	wine
der Weinbrand	brandy
das Wienerschnitzel	veal escalope with breadcrumbs
die Wurst	sausage
der Zucker	sugar
die Zwiebel	onion

11.3 STRUCTURAL EXPLANATIONS

(a) Structures to learn

(i) How to ask if there is a table

Haben Sie einen Tisch	Have you got a table
frei	free
für zwei ?	for two ?
für vier	for four

(ii) How to call the waiter or waitress

Herr Ober!	Waiter!
Fräulein!	Miss!
(even if the lady is no longer in the first bloom of youth)	

(iii) How to ask for the menu or the wine list

Die Speisekarte, bitte!	The menu, please
Die Weinkarte, bitte!	The wine list, please
Ich möchte	I'd like to see the
die Weinkarte ⎫ sehen	wine list
die Speisekarte ⎭	menu

(iv) How to ask someone what they would like to eat or drink

(1) Was möchten Sie?   What would you like?

(2)
Ich möchte ⎫ ⎧ einen Cognac
Möchten Sie ⎭ ⎨ eine Vorspeise
                   ⎩ ein Mineralwasser

I'd like ⎫ ⎧ a Cognac
Would you like ⎭ ⎨ a starter
                      ⎩ a mineral water

Note the form of ein

(3) Möchten Sie/Ich möchte   Would you like/I'd like
     etwas essen/etwas trinken   something to eat/something to drink

(v) How to order

Einmal ⎫ ⎧ Texas Steak
Zweimal ⎬ ⎨ Gulaschsuppe
Dreimal ⎭ ⎩

One ⎫ ⎧ Texas steak(s)
Two ⎬ ⎨ goulash soup(s)
Three ⎭ ⎩

N.B. Einmal, zweimal, etc., indicate the number of portions required, corresponding to the number of people who require them. In German, the noun remains in the singular after zweimal, dreimal, etc.

(vi) How to ask for the bill

Zahlen, bitte
Die Rechnung, bitte
Ich möchte zahlen, bitte
Ich möchte die Rechnung, bitte

(vii) How to express the time by clock
(1) *Questions*

Wieviel Uhr ist es? ⎫	What time is it?
Wie spät ist es? ⎭	
Wann . . . ?	When?
Um wieviel Uhr . . . ?	At what time?

(viii) Expressions of time
1. *The hours*

Es ist = It is
Um = At

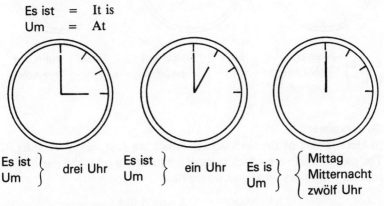

Es ist ⎫	drei Uhr	Es ist ⎫	ein Uhr	Es is ⎫	Mittag
Um ⎭		Um ⎭		Um ⎭	Mitternacht
					zwölf Uhr

2. *Time past the hour*

| Es ist ⎫ | fünf (Minuten) | Es ist ⎰ | fünfundzwanzig (Minuten) |
| Um ⎭ | nach neun | Um ⎱ | nach sechs |

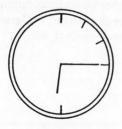 

Es ist	Viertel nach	Es ist	
Um	sechs	Um	halb zehn

N.B.! N.B.! 'Half' TOWARDS the next hour.

3. Time TO the hour

Es ist	zwanzig	Es ist	Viertel vor	Es ist	zehn vor
Um	(Minuten) vor elf	Um	zwölf	Um	zwölf

(b) Grammar

(i) Here is part of the verb MÖGEN, which we first met in Chapter 7. The part of this verb which is most frequently used is the part which enables you to say what you *would like*.

ich	möchte	I would like
er	möchte	he would like
sie	möchte	she would like
wir	möchten	we would like
Sie	möchten	you would like (formal or polite)

You will find the verb in the appendix.

(ii) Note these two question forms

1. Möchten Sie eine Vorspeise?
   Möchten Sie etwas trinken?   The verb comes first

2. Was möchten Sie?
   Was möchten Sie trinken?

The sentence begins with a question word

(iii) Further question words, or interrogatives, are:

Wo?	– Where?	Wo möchten Sie essen? Where would you like to eat?
Welcher? (*m*)	– Which?	Welcher Wein ist billiger? Which wine is cheaper?
Welche? (*f*)	– Which?	Welche Vorspeise ist besser? Which hors d'oeuvre is better?

Welches? (*n*)	– Which?	Welches Mineralwasser
		   schmeckt gut mit Whisky
		   Which mineral water tastes
		   good with whisky?

Wer?	– Who?	Wer ist im Restaurant? Who is in the restaurant?

N.B. 'false friend': don't confuse wer? with wo?

Warum?	– Why?	Warum trinken Sie Pils? Why are you drinking Pils?
Was?	– What?	Was trinken Sie? What are you drinking?
Wohin?	– Where (to)?	Wohin gehen Sie? Where are you going (to)?
Was für?	– What sort of?	Was für Bier trinken Sie? What sort of beer are you drinking?
Wie?	– How?	Wie kochen Sie Jägerschnitzel How do you cook Jägerschnitzel?

(iv) **How to say which day**

a) heute – today
   heute abend – this evening/tonight
   heute nachmittag – this afternoon
   heute morgen – this morning

b) morgen – tomorrow
   morgen abend – tomorrow evening/night
   morgen nachmittag – tomorrow afternoon
   morgen früh – tomorrow morning

c) gestern – yesterday
   gestern abend – yesterday evening/night

gestern nachmittag – yesterday afternoon
gestern morgen – yesterday morning

(v) How to express relative time

a)
diese		this	
nächste	} Woche (*f*)	next	} week
letzte		last	

b)
dieses		this	
nächstes	} Jahr (*n*)	next	} year
letztes		last	

c)
diesen		this	
nächsten	} Monat (*m*)	next	} month
letzten		last	

d)
in drei
Tagen	in three	days
Wochen		weeks
Monaten		months
Jahren		years

e)
vor drei
Tagen	three	days	
Wochen		weeks	} ago
Monaten		months	
Jahren		years	

f)
in fünf
Minuten	in five	minutes
Stunden		hours

11.4 EXERCISES

Section A

Exercise 1
With reference to the menu on page 127, work out how you would order under the following conditions. (If you are working with a partner, take turns to play the part of the waiter.)
1. You are by yourself and want a quick meal; one meat dish will do. You want to spend as little as possible. Nothing to drink.
2. You are dining with an important friend and you can afford the best. Curiously, you both have exactly the same taste in food. You decide to have the lot: hors d'oeuvres, fish, meat, dessert, and, of course, your favourite Rhine wine.

RESTAURANT ZUM RITTER

SPEISEKARTE

VORSPEISEN

Krabbencocktail	6.00
Aal in Aspik	7.00
Austern (12)	12.00

SUPPEN

Hühnerbrühe mit Nudeln	2.00
Gulaschsuppe	2.50
Zwiebelsuppe	3.00

EIERSPEISEN

Rührei	4.50
Spiegeleier mit Schinken	5.00
Omelett – verschiedener Art	5.25

FISCHGERICHTE

Rollmops	7.50
Forelle, blau, mit grünem Salat, Salzkartoffeln	12.00
Seezungenfilet mit grünen Bohnen, Salzkartoffeln	14.50

FLEISCHGERICHTE

Eisbein mit Sauerkraut	7.20
'Texas' Steak mit Pommes frites und gemischtem Salat	13.80
Jägerschnitzel mit Pommes frites	14.00
Wiener Schnitzel mit Spiegelei, Salat, Röstkartoffeln	14.30
Zigeuner Steak mit Zwiebeln, Reis und grünem Salat	15.00

ETWAS FUR DEN KLEINEN APPETIT

Rührei mit Schinken	4.20
Paar Frankfurter mit Pommes frites	4.80

KÄSE

Emmentaler mit Butter, Brot	3.20
Käseplatte, Butter, Brot	3.60

NACHSPEISEN

Gemischtes Kompott	2.50
Pampelmuse	2.50
Pfannkuchen	3.70
Ananas flambiert mit Kirschwasser	6.20

GETRANKE

	Glas	Flasche
Pils	1.50	
Export	1.75	
Viertel Moselwein	4.00	14.00
Viertel Rheinwein	4.00	14.00
Rotwein	4.00	14.00

	Glas	Flasche
Sekt		22.50
Cognac	2.50	
Weinbrand	2.00	
Mineralwasser	1.50	

Tasse Kaffee oder Tee 2.10
Kännchen 3.50

UNSERE PREISE SIND ENDPREISE

3. You are taking the children out for their first meal in a restaurant. Peter can't stand eggs and Paula has an aversion to sausages. You have a weakness for trout yourself. You do like wine, but you want to set the children a good example.
4. You want to have a light lunch with a colleague. Ham and eggs for you and a scrambled egg for him shouldn't have too many calories. Afterwards, you could share a selection of different cheeses, perhaps, and a cup of coffee.

Exercise 2

You go into a Gasthaus for lunch with two friends. What do you say?
1. Ask if there's a table for three.
2. Call the waitress.
3. Say you want to order.
4. Order two prawn cocktails and jellied eels.
5. Say you'd like three Texas steaks.
6. Order two quarters of red wine and a Pils.
7. Ask for the bill.

If you are working with a partner, take it in turns to play the part of the waitress.

Section B

Exercise 3

Ask your guests if they want to have the same dish that you have chosen.

Example: Ich möchte eine Vorspeise.
Möchten Sie auch eine Vorspeise?
Ich möchte ein Mineralwasser.
Möchten Sie auch ein Mineralwasser?

1. Ich möchte eine Vorspeise.
2. Ich möchte ein Mineralwasser.
3. Ich möchte einen Cognac.
4. Ich möchte eine Gulaschsuppe.
5. Ich möchte eine Forelle.
6. Ich möchte Salzkartoffeln.
7. Ich möchte Eisbein.
8. Ich möchte ein Wiener Schnitzel.
9. Ich möchte eine Käseplatte.
10. Ich möchte ein gemischtes Kompott.

Exercise 4

Ask and say what time it is.

Example: 08:00 Wieviel Uhr ist es?
                  Es ist acht Uhr.
          10:30 Wieviel Uhr ist es?
                  Es ist halb elf.

1. 13:00
2. 12:00
3. 09:05
4. 18:15
5. 16:25

6. 21:30
7. 11:10
8. 06:20
9. 21:30
10. 14:45

CHAPTER 12

ASKING PERMISSION

12.1 DIALOGUES 📼

Dialogue 1

Parking is always a problem in every town, and Munich is no exception.

1 *Antonio*:   Entschuldigen Sie!
   (louder) Entschuldigen Sie!
 Polizist: Ja?
 Antonio: Kann ich hier parken?

Fahren Sie zum Parkhaus!

Photograph: J. Allan Cash Ltd

5 *Polizist*: Nein. Es tut mir leid.
Hier dürfen Sie nicht parken.
Antonio: (pointing) Und dort drüben?
Kann ich dort drüben parken?
Polizist: Nein.
10 Dort dürfen Sie auch nicht parken.
Antonio: Herr Gott nochmal!!
Wo kann ich denn hier parken?
Polizist: Im Parkhaus.
Fahren Sie zum Parkhaus.
15 *Antonio*: Zum Parkhaus! Zum Parkhaus!
Also zum Parkhaus.
(sound of squealing tyres)

Dialogue 2

Fritz Löb's car won't start, so he goes to see Frau Meyer, who
lives in the same block, to see if she can help. Perhaps that
dreadful old bicycle of hers is still in working order.
(Fritz rings the frontdoor bell)

1 *Frau Meyer*: Ja, bitte?
Ach, Sie sind es, Herr Löb.
Fritz: Grüß Gott, Frau Meyer!
Entschuldigen Sie die Störung.
5 *Frau Meyer*: Was kann ich für Sie tun?
Fritz: Frau Meyer, mein Auto startet nicht.
Die Batterie ist kaputt, glaube ich.
Frau Meyer: O, das tut mir leid.
Fritz: Darf ich bitte Ihr Fahrrad borgen?
10 *Frau Meyer*: Mein Fahrrad?
Selbstverständlich.
Es ist unten im Keller.
Fritz: Herzlichen Dank.
O, darf ich auch die Pumpe borgen?
15 *Frau Meyer*: Aber natürlich.
Sie dürfen die Pumpe auch borgen.
Fritz: Recht vielen Dank.
Frau Meyer: Gern geschehen.
Fahren Sie vorsichtig.
20 *Fritz*: Ja, ja.

12.2 INFORMATION

(a) Notes on Dialogue 1

5. Es tut mir leid

This expression cannot be translated word for word. It is an expression which should be learned as a whole.

10. auch

The word auch has a number of meanings: 'also', 'too', and in this sentence it means 'either', because it is in a sentence containing a negative. Note in particular the position this word has in the sentence and how it is emphasised by the speaker on the cassette.

11. Herr Gott nochmal

This is an expression of real irritation. It is quite colloquial but can be used in any society where it would be allowed to show one's irritation.

(b) Notes on Dialogue 2

4. die Störung

'The disturbance'. Note that where German uses a noun, English uses the expression 'for disturbing you'.

7. kaputt

This is a very useful phrase which can be used in a large number of situations. Many things, such as a car battery in this instance, can be kaputt where we would normally use an expression in English which was more tailor-made e.g. run down.

12. im Keller

Nearly all German houses have a cellar. In a large house which is divided up into flats or in a block of flats the cellar is divided up into compartments, each one belonging to one of

the families living in the house.
Cellars normally contain central-
heating boilers and are also used
as general storage rooms,
especially for bottles of wine.

18. Gern geschehen

This is a very useful phrase with
which to respond when
somebody thanks you for
something. It can represent
English expressions such as
'that's quite all right', 'you're
welcome' or 'don't mention it'.

(c) Word list

parken	to park
können	to be able; to be allowed
dürfen	to be allowed
auch	also
das **Park**haus (¨er)	multi-storey car park
tun	to do
das **Au**to (-s)	car
starten	to start
die Batte**rie** (-n)	battery
ka**putt**	broken
glauben	to believe
das **Fahr**rad (¨er)	bicycle
borgen	to borrow
selbstver**ständ**lich	of course
unten	downstairs
der **Kel**ler (-)	cellar
die **Pum**pe (-n)	pump
na**tür**lich	of course
vorsichtig	careful; carefully
der **Re**genmantel (¨)	raincoat
die **Zei**tung (-en)	newspaper
nehmen	to take
sehen	to see
die **Zahn**bürste (-n)	toothbrush
die **Zahn**pasta	toothpaste
der **Rasier**apparat (-e)	razor
die **Ho**se (singular only)	trousers
der **Fernseh**apparat	television set
der **Zu**cker	sugar

das Buch ("er)	book
der Kamm ("e)	comb

(d) Some phrases

Ent**schul**digen Sie!	Excuse me!
Es tut mir leid	I'm sorry
Dort **drü**ben	Over there
Herzlichen Dank	Thank you very much
Recht **vie**len Dank	Thank you very much
Das geht nicht	That won't do
Das ist un**mög**lich	That is impossible
Auf **kein**en Fall	Under no circumstances

12.3 STRUCTURAL EXPLANATIONS

(a) Structures to learn

(i) How to ask permission to do something, using the verb KÖNNEN.

a) How to ask permission to *borrow* things

Kann ich { Ihr Fahrrad / Ihren Regenmantel / Ihre Zeitung } borgen?

das Fahrrad – bicycle
der Regenmantel – raincoat
die Zeitung – newspaper

b) How to ask permission to *do other* things

Kann ich { Ihr Fahrrad / Ihren Regenmantel / Ihre Zeitung } { borgen / nehmen / sehen } ?

borgen – to borrow
nehmen – to take
sehen – to see

(ii) If you want to be particularly polite, possibly because you are talking to someone of higher status than yourself, you can ask for permission by using another verb: DÜRFEN.

It may be that you want to refuse permission to somebody to do something, and express the meaning 'you are not allowed to do something'. In both these cases, you use the verb DÜRFEN.

Dort dürfen Sie nicht parken
Darf ich Ihr Fahrrad borgen?
Darf ich die Pumpe borgen?

Here are some sentences which show you how this verb can be used:

Darf ich { Ihr Fahrrad / Ihren Regenmantel / Ihre Zeitung } borgen?

(v) Here are some phrases you can use if you want to give permission to somebody:

Selbstverständlich
Aber natürlich
Sicher   } of course
Bitte

(vi) Here are some expressions you can use if you want to refuse somebody permission. They range from being quite neutral in tone at the top to being very strong at the bottom.

Nein, es tut mir leid
Nein, das geht nicht
Nein, das ist unmöglich
Nein, auf keinen Fall

(b) Grammar

(i) Here are the most frequently used parts of the two verbs we have been looking at in this chapter.

The verb KÖNNEN — to be able to			The verb DÜRFEN — to be allowed to		
ich	kann	I can	ich	darf	I may i.e. am allowed to
er	kann	he can	er	darf	he may
sie	kann	she can	sie	darf	she may
wir	können	we can	wir	dürfen	we may
Sie	können	you can	Sie	dürfen	you may

Both verbs are *irregular* in that their stems change, and their endings do not conform to the standard pattern.

(ii) The verb KÖNNEN has two meanings. One meaning is associated with asking permission, as we have seen earlier. The primary meaning, however, is connected with *ability*. Thus:

Kann er schwimmen?   Can he (is he able to, does he know how to) swim?

Ich kann schwimmen   I can (am able to) swim

(iii) The two verbs KÖNNEN and DÜRFEN can be used in a number of different sentence patterns. Here are some examples:

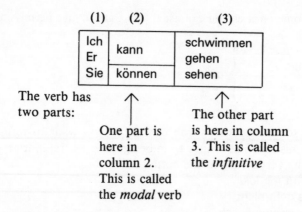

(1)	(2)	(3)
Ich Er	kann	schwimmen gehen
Sie	können	sehen

The verb has two parts:

↑ One part is here in column 2. This is called the *modal* verb

↑ The other part is here in column 3. This is called the *infinitive*

A *modal* verb defines the mode, or manner in which something is done. It refers to the necessity, possibility or impossibility of e.g. swimming, going, seeing, etc.

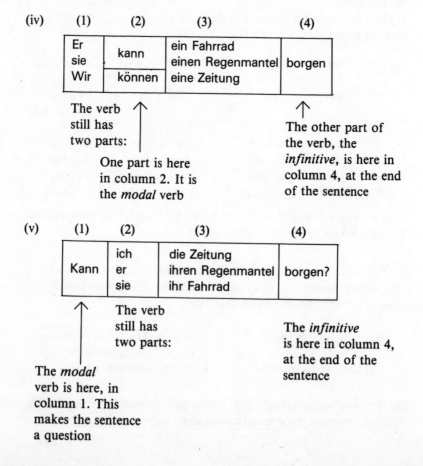

(iv)

(1)	(2)	(3)	(4)
Er sie	kann	ein Fahrrad einen Regenmantel	borgen
Wir	können	eine Zeitung	

The verb still has two parts:

↑ One part is here in column 2. It is the *modal* verb

↑ The other part of the verb, the *infinitive*, is here in column 4, at the end of the sentence

(v)

(1)	(2)	(3)	(4)
Kann	ich er sie	die Zeitung ihren Regenmantel ihr Fahrrad	borgen?

↑ The *modal* verb is here, in column 1. This makes the sentence a question

The verb still has two parts:

The *infinitive* is here in column 4, at the end of the sentence

(vi)

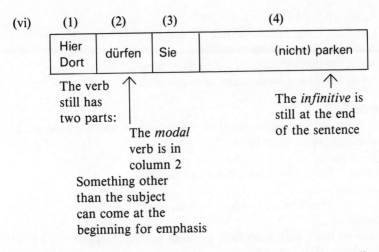

(1)	(2)	(3)	(4)
Hier Dort	dürfen	Sie	(nicht) parken

The verb still has two parts:

The *modal* verb is in column 2

Something other than the subject can come at the beginning for emphasis

The *infinitive* is still at the end of the sentence

(vii) You will find the verbs können and dürfen in the appendix.

12.4 EXERCISES

Exercise 1
Imagine that you are living with a German family and want to borrow some of their things. This is what you would say:
Example: Kann ich Ihr Fahrrad borgen bitte?
Now, how would you ask to borrow the following things? Of course, you might not get them.
1. Das Auto.
2. Die Zahnbürste.
3. Die Zahnpasta.
4. Der Rasierapparat.
5. Die Zeitung.

Exercise 2
Now it's your turn to practise giving or refusing permission. Here are some things which somebody might – with a stretch of the imagination, of course – ask you if they can borrow. When you check the answers, bear in mind that we have printed the answers we think you may have given. We have no means of telling, of course, how generous you are.
1. Kann ich Ihr Fahrrad borgen, bitte?
2. Kann ich Ihre Hose borgen, bitte?
3. Kann ich Ihre Zeitung borgen, bitte?
4. Kann ich Ihren Rasierapparat borgen, bitte?
5. Kann ich Ihre Zahnpasta borgen, bitte?

6. Kann ich Ihr Auto borgen, bitte?
7. Kann ich Ihren Mann borgen, bitte?
8. Kann ich Ihre Frau borgen, bitte?
9. Kann ich Ihren Regenmantel borgen, bitte?
10. Kann ich Ihren Fernsehapparat borgen, bitte?

Exercise 3

Look at the answers which are given below and try and work out what the questions must have been.
1. *Question*: ...... ?
   Answer: Nein, hier dürfen Sie nicht parken.
2. *Question*: ...... ?
   Answer: Aber natürlich. Mein Fahrrad ist dort drüben.
3. *Question*: ...... ?
   Answer: Nein, es tut mir leid. Ich habe keinen Zucker.
4. *Question*: ...... ?
   Answer: Aber sicher. Sie können das Auto nehmen.
5. *Question*: ...... ?
   Answer: Nein, es tut mir leid. Ich habe nur eine Zahnbürste.

Exercise 4

Imagine that you are living with a German family called Fiebiger. You have come rather unprepared and you want to borrow a number of things. What do you say?
Example:
You want to borrow Herr Fiebiger's bicycle.
Kann ich Ihr Fahrrad borgen, Herr Fiebiger?
Now continue:
1. You want to see Herr Fiebiger's newspaper.
2. You'd like to borrow his car.
3. You'd like to have Frau Fiebiger's lamp.
4. It would be nice if you could take their television.
5. You'd like to borrow Herr Fiebiger's radio.
6. It's raining and you want to take Frau Fiebiger's raincoat.
7. You've left your razor at home. Can you have his, I wonder.
8. You're quite out of toothpaste. Can you borrow some?
9. That was an interesting book Frau Fiebiger was reading last night. Perhaps you could see it.
10. Your hair is terribly untidy. Can you have Herr Fiebiger's comb, I wonder.

New words

das Auto – the car
das Buch – the book
der Kamm – the comb

CHAPTER 13

JOBS AND PROFESSIONS

13.1 DIALOGUES 📼

Dialogue 1
Fritz is bringing back Frau Meyer's bicycle which he borrowed
when his car wouldn't start.
(He rings the frontdoor bell)

1 *Frau Meyer*: Ja, bitte?
    Ach, Sie sind es, Herr Löb.
  Fritz: Grüß Gott, Frau Meyer!
    Entschuldigen Sie die Störung.
5   Hier ist Ihr Rad.
  Frau Meyer: Vielen Dank.
    War alles in Ordnung?
  Fritz: Ja, alles war in Ordnung.
    Danke schön.
10 *Frau Meyer*: Sie sind Hauptschullehrer, nicht wahr?
  Fritz: Ja, das stimmt.
  Frau Meyer: Gefällt Ihnen die Arbeit?
  Fritz: O ja, sehr.
  Frau Meyer: Wann beginnen Sie am Morgen?
15 *Fritz*: Wir beginnen um acht Uhr.
  Frau Meyer: Ach so.
    Und wann kommen Sie normalerweise nach Hause?
  Fritz: Ich komme gewöhnlich gegen zwei Uhr nach Hause.
  Frau Meyer: Wieviele Tage arbeiten Sie in der Woche?
20 *Fritz*: Nur fünf.
    Gott sei Dank.
  Frau Meyer: Als ich Schülerin war, hatten wir auch samstags
    Schule.
  Fritz: Ja ja, wir haben es besser.

Er ist Hauptschullehrer

Photograph: Bavaria-Verlag/Jürgen Gaiser

25 Nun. Vielen Dank noch einmal für das Rad.
 Frau Meyer: Gern geschehen, Herr Löb.
 Auf Wiedersehen.

Dialogue 2

You will remember that Elke met a man when she was in the Alte Pinakothek. He has invited her to have a cup of coffee in the museum restaurant.

1   *Mann*: Was sind Sie von Beruf, wenn ich fragen darf?

     Elke: Ich bin Verkäuferin.

     Mann: Hier in München?

     Elke: Ja, bei Mode Zilling.

5   In der Leopoldstraße.

     Mann: Gefällt Ihnen die Arbeit?

     Elke: O, ja und nein.

     Ich verdiene sehr gut.

     Mann: Wann beginnen Sie mit der Arbeit?

10 *Elke*: Um acht Uhr.

     Mann: Und haben Sie eine Mittagspause?

     Elke: Ja. Von zwölf bis eins.

     Mann: Zwischen zwölf und eins habe ich auch Mittagspause.

     Elke: (ironically) Schauen Sie mal!

15 *Mann*: Wann kommen Sie abends nach Hause?

     Elke: Ich habe um fünf Uhr Feierabend.

     Mann: Ich auch.

     Könnte ich Sie an Ihrem Geschäft abholen?

     Ich habe ein Auto.

20   Wir könnten vielleicht aufs Land fahren.

     Elke: Vielen Dank.

     Aber ich habe mein eigenes Auto.

     Mann: Ach so.

     Elke: Und heute kommt mein Freund um fünf Uhr.

25   Wir wollen auf dem Viktualien Markt einkaufen gehen.

     Mann: Schade.

     Ein anderes Mal vielleicht.

     Elke: Vielleicht.

13.2 INFORMATION

(a) Notes on Dialogue 1

7. War — War is the past tense of the verb sein – 'to be'. It is to be translated here as 'was'.

10. Hauptschullehrer — Note that there is no indefinite article in front of the word Hauptschullehrer. In English when we refer to somebody's profession we say, for example, 'He is *a* teacher'. In German the indefinite article is omitted and

Germans say instead Er ist Hauptschullehrer.

10. nicht wahr?

Nicht wahr is a very useful expression for converting a statement into a question. The phrase nicht wahr can be added to any statement in order to turn it into an interrogative.

12. Gefällt Ihnen

No attempt should be made to translate this expression literally. Treat it exactly as if it meant 'Do you like ... ?' Note, however, that in order to say 'I like something', German puts the object of the sentence first, thus: Die Arbeit gefällt mir – 'I like the work'.

17. normalerweise
18. gewöhnlich

These phrases are interchangeable and allow you to refer to what is *usual* or *normal*.

22. Als ich Schülerin war

Students may like to note the position of the verb in this sentence, but they are not required to be able to use it at this stage. Students wishing to inform themselves about the structure of 'subordinate' clauses introduced by als should consult the grammar books listed in the bibliography.

22. hatten

This is the past tense of the verb haben and means 'had'.

22. samstags

Note that by adding an s to the end of the word you make the phrase 'on Saturdays'.

(b) Notes on Dialogue 2

1. wenn ich fragen darf

Students may like to note the position of the verb in this

phrase but at this stage they are only required to use the sentence as if it were an idiom: 'If you don't mind my asking'.

12. eins

In colloquial German you can say either eins or ein Uhr for one o'clock.

16. Feierabend

This is a very frequent and colloquial expression meaning to finish one's work for the day.

25. Viktualien Markt

Name of a famous food market in Munich.

(c) Word list

das Rad (short for Fahrrad)	bicycle
alles	everything
der Lehrer	teacher
die Arbeit (-en)	work
sehr	very much
beginnen	to begin
wann?	when?
der Morgen (-)	morning
wieviel?	how many?
der Tag (-e)	day
arbeiten	to work
die Woche (-n)	week
der Schüler	school pupil (male)
die Schülerin	school pupil (female)
die Schule (-n)	school
noch einmal	once again
besser	better
der Beruf (-e)	job; profession
fragen	to ask
die Verkäuferin (-nen)	sales lady
verdienen	to earn
zwischen	between
abends	in the evening
die Mittagspause (-n)	midday break
das Geschäft (-e)	shop; business
abholen	to call for
das Auto (-s)	car
vielleicht	perhaps

fahren	to drive
eigen	own
heute	today
der Freund (-e)	(boy) friend
wollen	to want to
einkaufen **geh**en	to go shopping
schade	pity
die **Buch**handlung (-en)	bookshop
das Büro (-s)	office
die Fab**rik** (-en)	factory
die Kondito**rei** (-en)	café or cake shop
das **Kauf**haus (⸚er)	store
der Pull**o**ver	pullover
das **Wet**ter	weather
der Schnee	snow
der Schuh (-e)	shoe
der Berg (-e)	mountain

(d) Some phrases

In **Ord**nung	All right
Das stimmt	That's right
Gegen	About
Gott sei Dank!	Thank God!
Gern ge**scheh**en	You're welcome
Aufs Land	Into the country
Ein **an**deres Mal	Another time

12.3 STRUCTURAL EXPLANATIONS

(a) Structures to learn

(i) How to ask somebody what he or she does for a living

Was sind Sie von Beruf?	What do you do?
Sie sind (Lehrer), nicht wahr?	You are (a teacher), aren't you?
Herr Löb ist Lehrer	Mr Löb is a teacher

(ii) How to say what you do (for a living)

Ich bin
{
Angestellter	Polizist
Bäcker	Schüler
Beamter	Student
Busfahrer	Taxifahrer
Friseur	Techniker
Kellner	Verkäufer
Lehrer	Verwaltungsangestellter
}

I am
- an employee
- a baker
- a civil servant
- a bus driver
- a hairdresser
- a waiter
- a teacher
- a policeman
- a school-student
- a student
- a taxi-driver
- a technician
- a sales person
- a government employee

An Angestellter is a salaried employee, or white-collar worker.
A Beamter is a civil servant, holding a tenured position.

(iii) The names of jobs held by women frequently end with the letters -in.

Ich bin

Ärztin	Studentin	lady doctor	girl student
Kellnerin	Sekretärin	waitress	secretary
Lehrerin	Taxifahrerin	lady teacher	lady taxi-driver
Polizistin	Telephonistin	policewoman	lady telephonist
Schülerin	Verkäuferin	girl school-student	sales lady

(iv) There are some exceptions to the above, normally ending in -e.

Ich bin
- Angestellte — woman employee
- Empfangsdame — lady receptionist
- Friseuse — lady hairdresser
- Hausfrau — housewife

(v) How to ask somebody where they work and how to state where you work

Wo arbeiten Sie?   Ich bin bei (name of firm or company)

Ich bin bei
- Siemens
- Grundig
- Ford
- Mode Zilling
- Mercedes

Ich arbeite in
- einer Buchhandlung — die Buchhandlung – bookshop
- einem Büro — das Büro – office
- einer Schule — die Schule – school
- einer Fabrik — die Fabrik – factory
- einem Hotel — das Hotel – hotel
- einer Konditorei — die Konditorei – café or cakeshop

| einem Kaufhaus | das Kaufhaus – store |
| einem Geschäft | das Geschäft – shop |

(vi) How to ask about somebody's conditions of work

1. Wann beginnen Sie
   { am Morgen?
   { mit der Arbeit?

   When do you begin
   { in the morning?
   { work?

   Ich beginne
   Wir beginnen } um acht Uhr

   I begin
   We begin } at eight o'clock

2. Wann kommen Sie (abends) nach Hause?
   When do you come home (in the evening)?

   Um sechs Uhr — At six o'clock
   Ich habe um fünf Uhr Feierabend — I finish at five o'clock

3. Wieviele { Tage
   { Stunden } arbeiten Sie in der Woche?

   How many { days
   { hours } do you work a week?

   Nur fünf Tage — Only five days
   Ich arbeite fünfunddreißig Stunden — I work 35 hours (a week)

4. Haben Sie eine Mittagspause? — Do you have a midday break?

   Wann
   Wie lange } haben Sie Mittagspause?

   When
   How long } is your midday break?

   Von zwölf bis eins — From twelve to one

(b) Grammar

(i) Expressions of time (frequency)

meistens
in der Regel
normalerweise
gewöhnlich
} = usually, as a rule

(ii) Approximate and exact time

gegen drei Uhr — about or towards three o'clock
gerade drei Uhr — exactly (or just) three o'clock

(iii) **Today, tomorrow, etc.**

heute	today
morgen	tomorrow
übermorgen	the day after tomorrow
gestern	yesterday
vorgestern	the day before yesterday

(iv) **Time of day**

morgens	in the morning
vormittags	in the morning
nachmittags	in the afternoon
abends	in the evening
nachts	in the night

(v) **Time of day**

heute früh	early this morning
heute morgen	this morning
heute nachmittag	this afternoon
heute abend	this evening
morgen früh	early tomorrow morning
gestern abend	yesterday evening

(vi) **The use of the accusative**

jeden Abend	every evening
jeden Freitag	every Friday
diesen Abend	this evening
heute abend	this evening
nächsten Freitag	next Friday

(vii) **Use of prepositions**

heute in acht Tagen	a week today
heute in vierzehn Tagen	a fortnight today
heute vor acht Tagen	a week ago

(viii) **Regularity**

montags	on Mondays
dienstags	on Tuesdays
mittwochs	on Wednesdays
donnerstags	on Thursdays
freitags	on Fridays
samstags	on Saturdays
sonntags	on Sundays

N.B. A small letter is used because it is the notion of regularity which is meant, rather than the name of the day.

(ix) The use of the dative to express liking

Gefällt Ihnen (singular)
{ der Pullover
  das Wetter   ?
  der Schnee

Do you like
{ the pullover
  the weather   ?
  the snow

Gefallen Ihnen (plural)
{ die Schuhe
  die Geschäfte   ?
  die Berge

Do you like
{ the shoes
  the shops   ?
  the mountains

Der Pullover
Das Wetter   } gefällt mir
Der Schnee   (singular)

I like { the pullover
  the weather
  the snow

Die Schuhe
Die Geschäfte   } gefallen mir
Die Berge   (plural)

I like { the shoes
  the shops
  the mountains

13.4 EXERCISES

Section A

Exercise 1
1. Was ist Herr Moezer von Beruf?
2. Was ist Frau Hacker von Beruf?
3. Was ist Fräulein Siegling von Beruf?
4. Was ist Herr Mader von Beruf?
5. Was ist Frau Meyer von Beruf?
6. Was ist Fräulein Bauer von Beruf?
7. Was ist Frau Augustin von Beruf?
8. Was ist Herr Flohr von Beruf?
9. Was ist Herr Kahle von Beruf?
10. Was ist Herr Löb von Beruf?

Herr Kahle is a technician.
Fräulein Augustin is a waitress.
Herr Mader is a taxi-driver.
Herr Löb is a teacher.
Herr Moezer is a baker.

Fräulein Siegling is a student.
Frau Hacker is a hairdresser.
Fräulein Bauer is a secretary.
Frau Meyer is a housewife.
Herr Flohr is a policeman.

Exercise 2

Practise this conversation, speaking both the answers and the
questions. The first one is done for you.

A: Was sind Sie von Beruf, Herr Flohr?   Herr Flohr (Polizist)
B: Ich bin Polizist.   0830 – 1600
A: Wann beginnen Sie mit der Arbeit?
B: Um 8.30 Uhr.
A: Wann haben Sie Feierabend?
B: Ich habe um 16 Uhr Feierabend.

Now do these conversations, with a partner, if possible.

1. Herr Löb (Lehrer)
   0800 – 1400
2. Frau Hacker (Friseuse)
   0900 – 1800
3. Frau Augustin (Kellnerin)
   1400 – 2230
4. Herr Mader (Taxifahrer)
   0500 – 1300
5. Herr Moezer (Bäcker)
   0400 – 1100

Section B

Exercise 3

Give questions which will produce the following answers.

1. Die Farbe gefällt mir.
2. Die Landschaft gefällt mir.
3. Das Auto gefällt mir.
4. Die Schuhe gefallen mir.
5. Der Wind gefällt mir nicht.
6. Das Material gefällt mir.
7. Das Wetter gefällt mir.
8. Der Schnee gefällt mir.
9. Die Geschäfte gefallen mir.
10. Der Regen gefällt mir nicht.

CHAPTER 14

ACCOMMODATION

14.1 DIALOGUES 📼

Dialogue 1

Antonio Santos has come to love the folklore which is so much part of the life in Munich. On this particular day, just before Christmas, he has travelled into the centre of the city on the underground in order to visit the Christkindl Markt. This is held every year in the days leading up to Christmas and is situated on the Marienplatz just in front of the town hall. One important aspect of the Christkindl Markt is the many stalls where you can drink Glühwein. Antonio has met Fritz Löb there and has got into conversation with him.

1 *Antonio*: Prost!
  Fritz: Prost!
  Antonio: Der Glühwein ist schön warm, nicht wahr?
  Fritz: Ja, schön warm.
5 *Antonio*: Wohnen Sie hier in München?
  Fritz: Ja, ich wohne in der Nietzschestraße.
  Antonio: Wohnen Sie in einem Mietshaus?
  Fritz: Ja, ich habe eine Einzimmerwohnung, in einem großen Mietshaus.
10 *Antonio*: Haben Sie nur ein Zimmer?
  Fritz: Na, ich habe ein Badezimmer und eine Küche.
  Antonio: Und sonst?
  Fritz: Sonst habe ich ein Wohn- und Schlafzimmer.
  Antonio: Ist die Wohnung schön?
15 *Fritz*: Ja, sie ist klein, aber ganz schön.
  Ich habe viele Bilder dort.
  Antonio: Bilder?

Christkindlmarkt, München

Photograph: *Bavaria-Verlag/GEWE-Foto*

> *Fritz*: Ja.
>   Ich sammle Bilder.
> 20 *Antonio*: Hmm. Interessant.

Dialogue 2
   Antonio and Fritz continue talking together.
 1 *Antonio*: Mein Onkel hat auch viele Bilder.

Fritz: Wo wohnt er?

Antonio: In Napoli.

Fritz: Ach, in Neapel.

5 *Antonio*: Er hat ein Einzelhaus.

Fritz: Das ist schön.

Antonio: Er hat sechs Schlafzimmer und zwei Gästezimmer.

Fritz: Du liebe Zeit!

Antonio: Stellen Sie sich mal vor!

10 Sechs Schlafzimmer!

Fritz: Hat er auch einen Garten?

Antonio: Und ob!

Er hat Bäume und Sträucher überall.

Fritz: Sehr schön.

15 *Antonio*: Aber ich ...

Ich habe eine Sozialwohnung in der Kaufmannsstraße.

Fritz: Wieviele Zimmer haben Sie?

Antonio: Ich habe ein Eßzimmer und ein Schlafzimmer.

Fritz: Haben Sie ein Badezimmer und eine Küche?

20 *Antonio*: Selbstverständlich!

Und ich habe einen Balkon.

Das ist schön.

14.2 INFORMATION

(a) Notes on Dialogue 1

Christkindl Markt

The Christkindl Markt in Munich consists of rows of brightly lit stalls where you can buy sweets, Christmas tree decorations and small items to give as presents. The air is full of the smell of frying sausages and sweetmeats which are being prepared on the spot. Many people take refuge from the very cold air by drinking Glühwein, a sort of punch made of hot red wine containing spices.

5. Wohnen Sie?

Notice that in English we form many questions by using the words 'do' or 'does'. For example:

Do you live in Munich?
Does he live in Stuttgart?
Do they live in London?

In German the question form is made by inverting the order of the subject and the verb. For example:

> Er wohnt in München
> Wohnt er in München?
> Wohnen Sie in Stuttgart?
> Wohnt sie in Hamburg?

8. Ich habe ...

Notice that in English we often use the verb 'have got'. For example, we say 'I've got a flat in King Street' or 'How many rooms have you got?' German does not have the word 'got'. Consequently, there is no equivalent for this word in a sentence such as Ich habe eine Einzimmerwohnung.

12. sonst

The expression Und sonst? is a very useful one because it has the function of inviting somebody to enlarge on what he or she has been saying.

13. Sonst habe ich ...

Note that when sonst is brought to the beginning of the sentence in order to give it emphasis, then the subject comes after the verb.

(b) Notes on Dialogue 2

1. auch

Note the position of the word auch which means 'too' or 'also'.

4. Neapel

The names of certain towns have a special German equivalent. The German equivalent of the Italian word 'Napoli' is Neapel.

8. Du liebe Zeit

This is a very useful expression which can be used in many situations in order to express mild astonishment. It can be used equally by men and women in any sort of society, without giving offence.

9. Stellen Sie sich mal vor

This expression is a bit of a tongue-twister and may need some practice before you can get your tongue round it adequately. It is, however, a very useful expression which can be used on many occasions in order to express surprise tinged with mild disbelief.

12. Und ob!

Like the above two expressions, this has a very wide currency and can be used very frequently in order to give emphasis to something which has been said just previously.

(c) Word list

Prost!	Cheers!
der **Glüh**wein	hot punch
die **Einzimmerwohnung** (-en)	one-room flat
warm	warm
wohnen	to live
das **Miets**haus (¨-er)	house divided up into flats
groß	big
nur	only
das **Zimm**er (-)	room
schön	beautiful
klein	small
aber	but
ganz	quite
viel-	many
das Bild (-er)	picture

sammeln	to collect
interes**sant**	interesting
der **Onk**el (-)	uncle
über**all**	everywhere
selbstver**ständ**lich	of course
das **Haus** (-̈er)	house
das **Einz**elhaus (-̈er)	detached house
das **Ein**familienhaus (-̈er)	one-family house
die **Wohn**ung (-en)	flat
die **Sozial**wohnung (-en)	council flat
die **Eigentums**wohnung (-en)	owner-occupied flat
die **Küch**e (-n)	kitchen
das **Bad**ezimmer (-)	bathroom
das **Wohn**zimmer (-)	living room
das **Eß**zimmer (-)	dining room
das **Schlaf**zimmer (-)	bedroom
das **WC**	toilet
das **Gäs**tezimmer (-)	guest room
der **Balk**on (-e)	balcony
der **Gart**en (-̈)	garden
die **Garage** (-n)	garage
das **Schwimm**bad (-̈er)	swimming pool
der **Tenn**isplatz (-̈e)	tennis court
die **Terrass**e (-n)	terrace
der **Baum** (-̈e)	tree
die **Blum**e (-n)	flower
der **Strauch** (-̈er)	bush
der **Enk**el (-)	grandson
der **Flüg**el (-)	wing
der **Schlüss**el (-)	key
der **Kuch**en (-)	cake
der **Reif**en (-)	tyre
der **Kof**fer (-)	suitcase
der **Kell**ner (-)	waiter
die **Hand** (-̈e)	hand
die **Wand** (-̈e)	wall
die **Stadt** (-̈e)	town
das **Boot** (-e)	boat
das **Ding** (-e)	thing
der **Arm** (-e)	arm
der **Ort** (-e)	place
der **Schuh** (-e)	shoe

der **Ap**fel (⁻)	apple
der **Ha**fen (⁻)	harbour
der **Vo**gel (⁻)	bird
die Saat (-en)	seed
die Uhr (-en)	clock
die Tür (-en)	door
die Zahl (-en)	number
der Mann (⁻er)	man
der Wald (⁻er)	wood
das Dorf (⁻er)	village

der Flur (-e)	entrance hall, vestibule
die **Die**le (-n)	entrance hall, vestibule

14.3 STRUCTURAL EXPLANATIONS

(a) Structures to learn

(i) How to ask where someone lives

Wo wohnen Sie?	Where do you live?
Wo wohnt er?	Where does he live?
Wohnen Sie hier in München?	Do you live here in Munich?

(ii) How to ask in what sort of a house somebody lives

Wohnen Sie in einem
{ Haus
Einfamilienhaus
Mietshaus } ?

Do you live in a
{ house
one-family house
house divided up into flats } ?

Other types of accommodation

ein Zweifamilienhaus	a two-family house
eine Wohnung	a flat
eine Sozialwohnung	a council flat
ein Einzelhaus	a detached house
ein Reihenhaus	a terraced house
eine Mietwohnung	a rented flat
eine Eigentumswohnung	an owner-occupied flat

N.B. Approximately half the population in Germany lives in rented accommodation. In the cities there are large numbers of blocks of flats while in the country districts it's more likely that rented flats are in large houses where the owner also lives.

(iii) How to describe where one lives

Wieviele Zimmer haben Sie?	How many rooms have you got?
Ich habe	I've got a
eine Küche	kitchen
ein Badezimmer	bathroom
ein Wohnzimmer	living room
ein Eßzimmer	dining room
ein Schlafzimmer	bedroom
ein WC	toilet
ein Gästezimmer	guest room
eine Einzimmerwohnung	one-room flat
eine Zweizimmerwohnung	two-room flat

(iv) How to ask about other amenities

Haben Sie	Have you got a
einen Balkon	balcony
einen Garten ?	garden ?
eine Garage	garage
ein Schwimmbad	a swimming pool

Ich habe	I've got
einen Garten	a garden
einen Balkon	a balcony
einen Tennisplatz	a tennis court
eine Garage	a garage
eine Terrasse	a terrace
viele Bäume	many trees
viele Blumen	many flowers
viele Sträucher	many bushes

(b) Grammar

(i) The verb HABEN takes a *direct object* (see Chapter 5). The direct object of a sentence is said in German to be in the *accusative case*. The accusative case is 'marked' or 'signalled' by the indefinite article ein, thus:

Ich habe ein*en* Garten (der Garten)

Ich habe eine Garage (die Garage)
Ich habe ein Einzelhaus (das Einzelhaus)

N.B. Only the masculine singular article carries this marker.

(ii) Plurals of nouns
In English, we usually indicate that there are *more than one* of a thing
by adding the letters 's' or 'es' to a word.

boy	–	boys	window	–	windows
girl	–	girls	door	–	doors

The plural of German nouns may be formed in any one of a number
of different ways. There is no foolproof way of predicting how a
German noun will make its plural and therefore the best thing to do is
to learn the plural form of each noun as it occurs. Below are given
some of the most frequently occurring plural formations with a
number of nouns in common use in each category.

No change in the plural
indicated thus (-)

der Onkel (-)	uncle
der Enkel (-)	grandson
der Flügel (-)	wing
der Schlüssel (-)	key
der Kuchen (-)	cake
der Reifen (-)	tyre
der Koffer (-)	case
der Kellner (-)	waiter

Some nouns make their plurals
by adding an e. This is shown
like this (e)

das Boot (-e)	boat
das Ding (-e)	thing
der Arm (-e)	arm
der Ort (-e)	place
der Schuh (-e)	shoe

Other plurals are made by
adding an Umlaut over the
vowel and an e. This is
shown thus (¨e)

die Hand (¨e)	hand
die Wand (¨e)	wall
die Stadt (¨e)	town

Some nouns make their plural
by just adding an Umlaut. This
is shown thus (¨)

der Apfel (¨)	apple
der Garten (¨)	garden
der Hafen (¨)	harbour
der Vogel (¨)	bird

Many nouns make their
plural by adding en. This is
indicated thus (-en)

die Saat (-en)	seed
die Uhr (-en)	clock
die Tür (-en)	door
die Zahl (-en)	number

Some nouns make their plural
by adding an Umlaut and er. It
is indicated like this (¨er)

der Mann (¨er)	man
der Wald (¨er)	wood
das Dorf (¨er)	village
das Buch (¨er)	book
das Haus (¨er)	house

If you don't know a plural, here is a rule-of-thumb which will be correct some of the time.

1. Masculine nouns ending in -el, -en and -er don't change in the plural.
2. Many feminine nouns make their plural by adding -(e)n.
3. Many neuter nouns make their plural by adding -er, and an Umlaut if feasible, i.e. on a, o, u.
4. Many masculine nouns make their plural by adding -e. Many of these add an Umlaut if possible.

14.4 EXERCISES

Section A

Exercise 1

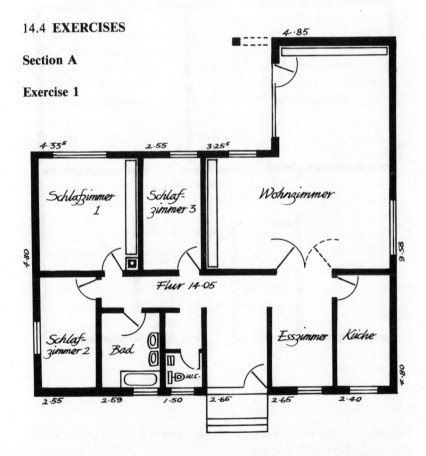

Imagine that this house belongs to you. Here is a conversation you might have with an acquaintance:

Acquaintance: Haben Sie ein Wohnzimmer?
You: Ja, ich habe ein Wohnzimmer.

Answer the following questions in the same way:
1. Haben Sie ein Wohnzimmer?
2. Haben Sie ein Eßzimmer?
3. Haben Sie eine Küche?
4. Haben Sie ein Badezimmer?
5. Haben Sie ein Schlafzimmer?
6. Haben Sie eine Toilette?

Exercise 2

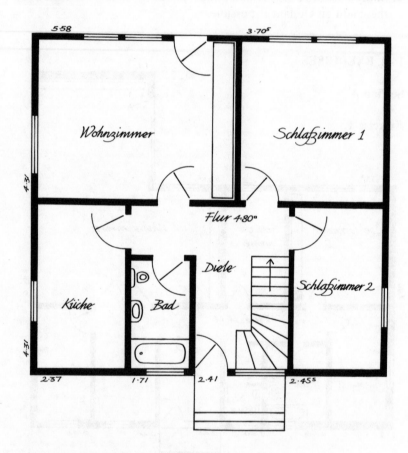

Imagine that this house belongs to you. Here is a conversation which you might have with a friend:

Friend: Haben Sie ein Wohnzimmer?
You: Ja, ich habe ein Wohnzimmer.
Friend: Haben Sie eine Garage?
You: Nein, eine Garage habe ich nicht.

Answer the following questions in the same way:
1. Haben Sie ein Wohnzimmer?
2. Haben Sie eine Garage?
3. Haben Sie ein Eßzimmer?
4. Haben Sie eine Terrasse?
5. Haben Sie eine Küche?
6. Haben Sie einen Balkon?
7. Haben Sie ein Badezimmer?
8. Haben Sie einen Garten?

Exercise 3
The temptation to keep up with the Joneses sometimes simply cannot be resisted. The case of Helmut Schwarz is a case in point. He thought that he had built the most splendid house in the village but when a retired dentist from the city came and built an even larger house just beside his, he found that he had to keep up with the Winklers. Here is the beginning of a conversation between the two of them. You continue by playing the part of Helmut.
Example:
Winkler: Ich habe einen Garten.
Helmut: Ich habe auch einen Garten.

Winkler: Ich habe ein Schwimmbad
Ich habe einen Balkon
Ich habe einen Tennisplatz
Ich habe eine Terrasse
Ich habe viele Bäume
Ich habe viele Sträucher

Section B

Exercise 4
Listen to the recorded dialogues again or read the script in the book. Then answer the following questions.
1. Wohnt Fritz in München?
2. Hat er eine Zweizimmerwohnung?
3. Hat er ein Badezimmer?
4. Hat er eine Küche?
5. Hat er viele Bilder?
6. Wo wohnt Antonios Onkel?
7. Hat er eine Sozialwohnung?
8. Wieviele Schlafzimmer hat er?
9. Wieviele Gästezimmer hat er?

10. Hat Antonio ein Einzelhaus?
11. Hat er ein Eßzimmer?
12. Hat er ein Badezimmer?
13. Hat er eine Küche?
14. Hat er einen Garten?

CHAPTER 15

HOBBIES AND INTERESTS

15.1 DIALOGUES 📼

Dialogue 1

Fritz has taken the plunge and invited Elke to come home to his flat after work to have some coffee and cakes.

1 *Fritz*: Kommen Sie bitte herein.
    Elke: Danke.
    Fritz: Das ist meine Einzimmerwohnung.
    Elke: Sie ist sehr schön.
5 *Fritz*: Sie ist leider etwas zu klein.
    Elke: Sie haben viele Bilder.
        Aber sie sind alle von Kirchen.
    Fritz: Ja, ich interessiere mich für Kirchen.
    Elke: Ja, das sehe ich.
10 *Fritz*: Wissen Sie . . .
        Ich fotografiere sehr gern.
        Ich fotografiere gern Kirchen.
    Elke: (meaningfully)
        Ja, das sehe ich.
    Fritz: Möchten Sie eine Tasse Kaffee?
15 *Elke*: O ja, bitte schön.
    Fritz: Schauen Sie . . .
        die Kirche hier ist schön, nicht wahr?
    Elke: (without enthusiasm)
        Hmm.
    Fritz: Sie ist romanisch.
20 *Elke*: Tatsächlich?
    Fritz: Ja. Ich interessiere mich sehr für romanische Kirchen.
        Ich fotografiere sie sehr gern.

Ich interessiere mich für Kirchen

Photograph: Bavaria-Verlag/Dr Wilfred Bahnmüller

Elke: (yawning)
Ja, das sehe ich.
Fritz: O, entschuldigen Sie.
25   Ihr Kaffee.
Nehmen Sie Zucker?
Elke: Nein, danke.

Dialogue 2

Antonio is talking to a fellow student at the Meisterschule für Mode.

1 *Student*: Du! Antonio!
  Antonio: Was ist los?
  Student: Gar nichts.
     Ich wollte dir nur etwas sagen.
5 *Antonio*: Na und ... ?
  Student: Du weißt ... .
     Ich interessiere mich für italienisch.
  Antonio: Ja, das weiß ich.
  Student: Und ich esse sehr gern italienisches Essen.
10 *Antonio*: Ja, das weiß ich auch.
  Student: Also ... .
     Gestern war ich in einem italienischen Restaurant.
  Antonio: Wo denn?
  Student: In der St Markus Straße.
15   Restaurant Giovanni heißt es.
  Antonio: Das kenne ich nicht.
     Ist es gut?
  Student: Na, ich esse sehr gern Pizza.
     Und die Pizza war wirklich gut.
20 *Antonio*: Warst du allein?
  Student: Nein, die Birgit war dabei.
     Sie ißt lieber Canneloni.
  Antonio: Hm. Waren die Cannelloni auch gut?
  Student: Nicht schlecht.
25 *Antonio*: Da muß ich auch hin.
     Ich esse furchtbar gern Pizza.

15.2 INFORMATION

(a) Notes on Dialogue 1

1. Kommen Sie — Note that the English translation gives the typically English rather tentative form where the German tends to be more direct.

8. für — Notice that where in English we say 'I'm interested *in* something', German uses the word für.

10. Wissen Sie	This is a very useful expression for indicating that you want to say something. It has the effect of telling other people 'Stop talking for a minute and listen to what I'm going to say'.

(b) Notes on Dialogue 2

5. Na und ... ?	This is another very useful phrase but you should take care to use it only with people you are on fairly good terms with. It can be slightly challenging and provocative. It has a touch of 'So what?' about it.
11. Also	One of the most useful words in German because it has the function of allowing you to say something, while you are still making up your mind what you want to say.
21. die Birgit	The word die is not necessary but it is very colloquial to say die Birgit or der Peter. It tends to be rather more frequently used in the south of Germany than in the north. It will make you sound very competent to use it occasionally but don't feel obliged to use it every time you say somebody's name.

(c) Word list

kommen	to come
etwas	somewhat
die **Einzimmerwoh**nung (-en)	one-roomed flat
sehr	very
schön	beautiful
leider	unfortunately
klein	small
das Bild (-er)	picture

alle	all
die **Kir**che (-en)	church
sich interes**sier**en für	to be interested in
sehen	to see
wissen	to know
fotogra**fier**en	to photograph
die **Tas**se (-n)	cup
der **Kaff**ee (-)	coffee
tat**säch**lich	indeed
nehmen	to take
der **Zuck**er (-)	sugar
nur	only
sagen	to say
essen	to eat
das **Ess**en (-)	food
gestern	yesterday
heißen	to be called
kennen	to know (a person or a place)
wirklich	really
all**ein**	alone
dab**ei**	there
schlecht	bad
furchtbar	terribly
der **Fuß**ball (¨e)	football
die **Leich**tath**let**ik (-)	athletics
das Land (¨er)	country
die **Brief**marke (-n)	stamp
die **Münz**e (-n)	coin
tanzen	to dance
wandern	to go walking
malen	to paint
lesen	to read
basteln	to make things as a hobby
singen	to sing
kochen	to cook
spielen	to play
fahren	to go

(d) Some phrases

Kommen Sie **bit**te her**ein**	Please come in
Das **sehe** ich	I can see that
Was ist los?	What's the matter?
Gar nichts	Nothing at all
Das weiß ich	I know

15.3 STRUCTURAL EXPLANATIONS

(a) Structures to learn

(i) How to ask about somebody's interests

Interessieren Sie sich für { Musik / Bilder ? / Bücher

Musik – music
Bilder – pictures
Bücher – books

(ii) How to say what you are interested in

Ich interessiere mich für

Fotografie
Fußball
Leichtathletik
andere Länder

Fotografie – photography
Fußball – football
Leichtathletik – athletics
andere Länder – other countries

(iii) How to say that you collect things

Ich sammle { Briefmarken / Münzen / Kupferstiche / alte Bücher

Briefmarken – stamps
Münzen – coins
Kupferstiche – etchings
alte Bücher – old books

(iv) How to say what you enjoy doing

Ich { tanze / wandere / male / lese / bastele / singe / koche } gern

tanzen – to dance
wandern – to go hiking or walking
malen – to paint
lesen – to read
basteln – to make things as a hobby
singen – to sing
kochen – to cook

(v)

Ich {
spiele gern { Karten / Bridge / Klarinette / Klavier
fahre gern { Ski / mit dem Rad
koche gern { Spaghetti / Pizza
}

Karten spielen – to play cards
Klavier spielen – to play the piano
Ski fahren – to go skiing
mit dem Rad fahren – to go cycling

(vi) Intensifiers

gern	nicht gern
sehr gern	gar nicht gern
wirklich sehr gern	überhaupt nicht gern
außerordentlich gern	
furchtbar gern	

These expressions allow you to convey your liking with increasing enthusiasm.	These expressions allow you to express your dislike with increasing strength.

Ich koche
gern	I like cooking
sehr gern	I like cooking very much
wirklich sehr gern	I really like cooking a lot
außerordentlich gern	I like cooking tremendously
furchtbar gern	I adore cooking

Ich koche
nicht gern	I don't like cooking
gar nicht gern	I don't like cooking at all
überhaupt nicht gern	I can't stand cooking

(b) Grammar

(i) In German, you use the word gern in order to express the idea of *liking to do something*. Observe the position of the word gern in the sentence, when there is a simple verb.

(1)	(2)	(3)	
Ich	lese reite male	gern	I like reading I like riding I like painting

↑
Gern comes
after the verb

(ii) Observe the following sentences, and see where the word gern occurs.

(1)	(2)	(3)	(4)	
Ich	höre gehe fahre	gern	Musik schwimmen Auto	I like listening to music I like going swimming I like driving a car

↑
Here you see
that the word
gern 'belongs
to' the verb

(iii) If you compare two activities, both of which you enjoy doing, it is possible that you prefer one to the other. The idea of preference is expressed in German as follows:

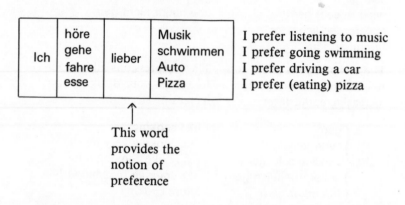

Ich	höre gehe fahre esse	lieber	Musik schwimmen Auto Pizza

I prefer listening to music
I prefer going swimming
I prefer driving a car
I prefer (eating) pizza

↑
This word
provides the
notion of
preference

(iv) If it is things, rather than activities, that you wish to compare, then you will need to know the *comparative form of adjectives*. Then you will be able to say that things are *bigger* and *better*.

Let us look first at some simple adjectives, and see how they make their comparative form.

schön — schöner (more beautiful)
tief — tiefer (deeper)
leicht — leichter (easier)
angenehm — angenehmer (more pleasant)

Note how there is only one way of expressing this comparison in German although we have two ways in English.

Let us put these comparative adjectives into sentences:

Elke ist schöner als Petra — Elke is more beautiful than Petra
Der Atlantik ist tiefer als die Nordsee — The Atlantic is deeper than the North Sea
Deutsch ist leichter als französisch — German is easier than French
Schlafen ist angenehmer als Arbeit — Sleeping is more pleasant than work

We can summarise the rule about making the comparative form of the adjective thus:

Add -er

(v) Perhaps you will want to say that something is *biggest* or *best*. Then you will need to know the *superlative form of adjectives*. Here is how the same adjectives make their superlative form

schön	–	der, die, das schönste
tief	–	der, die, das tiefste
leicht	–	der, die, das leichteste
angenehm	–	der, die, das angenehmste

Let us put these superlative adjectives into sentences.

Elke ist die schönste Frau	Elke is the most beautiful woman
Der Stille Ozean ist das tiefste Meer	The Pacific is the deepest sea
Deutsch ist die leichteste Sprache	German is the easiest language
Schlafen ist die angenehmste Tätigkeit	Sleeping is the most pleasant activity

We can summarise the rule about making the superlative form of the adjective thus:

Add -(e)st

(vi) Unfortunately, there are a number of irregular ways of forming comparative and superlative adjectives. You will find the rules set out in the appendix.

15.4 EXERCISES

Section A

Exercise 1
Here are five questions about what you like. Express your liking for each one of them with an increasing degree of enthusiasm.

1. Tanzen Sie gern?
2. Wandern Sie gern?
3. Malen Sie gern?
4. Lesen Sie gern?
5. Singen Sie gern?

Exercise 2

Here are three questions about your likes and dislikes. Answer each of them with an increasing degree of distaste.

1. Kochen Sie gern?
2. Basteln Sie gern?
3. Tanzen Sie gern?

Exercise 3

Imagine that you are one of those people who only likes doing those things which can be done comfortably at home, sitting down in the warmth. Answer the following questions appropriately.

1. Tanzen Sie gern?
2. Wandern Sie gern?
3. Malen Sie gern?
4. Spielen Sie gern Karten?
5. Fahren Sie gern Ski?
6. Lesen Sie gern?
7. Singen Sie gern?
8. Reiten Sie gern?

Section B

Exercise 4

There are two footballers playing in Germany at the moment. One is the veteran Beckenbauer and the other is the younger man Rumenigge. Here are some statements about Beckenbauer. See if you can trump them by making comparative statements about Rumenigge.

1. Beckenbauer ist groß.
2. Er ist schnell.
3. Er ist gesund.
4. Er ist stark.
5. Er ist jung.
6. Er ist klug.
7. Er spielt hart.
8. Er spielt gut.

(*See Grammatical Summary, Section D.*)

CHAPTER 16

'WANT' AND 'MUST'

16.1 DIALOGUES 📼

Dialogue 1

Elke is passionately fond of opera. She has succeeded in obtaining tickets to go to the Richard Wagner festival in Bayreuth.

1 *Elke*: Fritz! Wissen Sie was?

    Fritz: Nein.

    Elke: Herr Zilling hat Karten für Parsifal, und er kann nicht gehen.

5 *Fritz*: Das ist Pech.

    Elke: Für ihn, aber nicht für uns.

    Fritz: Wieso?

    Elke: Wollen wir die Karten nehmen?

    Fritz: Was kosten sie?

10 *Elke*: Die Karte sechzig Mark.

    Fritz: Das ist aber teuer.

    Elke: Es ist doch Bayreuth, wissen Sie?

    Fritz: Ja.

        Muß ich meinen Smoking anziehen?

15 *Elke*: Das ist ja normal.

        Ich will mein neues Kleid anziehen.

    Fritz: Schön!

    Elke: Ich will auch meinen Nerzmantel tragen.

    Fritz: Ha!

20 *Elke*: Und natürlich meine Perlenkette.

    Fritz: Wann müssen wir uns entscheiden?

    Elke: O, sofort.

        Wir wollen doch gehen, oder?

    Fritz: (hastily) O ja, selbstverständlich.

25   Wann müssen wir die Karten abholen?

Bayreuth

Photograph: Bavaria-Verlag/Siegfried Lauterwasser-Bavaria

Dialogue 2

Frau Meyer has gone to see her doctor because she has been feeling a bit giddy recently.

1 *Doktor Storm*:   Nun, Frau Meyer, was fehlt Ihnen denn?
Frau Meyer: Es ist mein Kopf, Herr Doktor.
   Mir ist immer wieder schwindlig.

Doktor Storm:　Wie alt sind Sie, Frau Meyer?

5　*Frau Meyer*:　Ich bin fünfundsiebzig Jahre alt.

Doktor Storm:　Und wo wohnen Sie?

Frau Meyer:　In der Nietzschestraße.

Doktor Storm:　Wo ist Ihre Wohnung?
Im Parterre?

10　*Frau Meyer*:　Nein, Herr Doktor.
Im dritten Stock.

Doktor Storm:　Und Sie gehen jeden Tag einkaufen?

Frau Meyer:　Ja, und ich hole die kleine Sandra von der
Schule.

15　*Doktor Storm*:　Ja, ja. nun, Frau Meyer, Sie müssen etwas
weniger herumlaufen.
Wann stehen Sie morgens auf?

Frau Meyer:　Um sechs Uhr.

Doktor Storm:　Sie müssen etwas länger im Bett bleiben, und

20　Sie müssen sich jeden Nachmittag eine Stunde hinlegen.

Frau Meyer:　Muß ich daheim bleiben, Herr Doktor?

Doktor Storm:　Nein, Sie brauchen nicht daheim bleiben, aber
Sie müssen diese Tabletten nehmen.

Frau Meyer:　Muß ich sie abends nehmen?

25　Ich werde nicht einschlafen.

Doktor Storm:　Nein, Sie brauchen sie nicht abends nehmen.

Frau Meyer:　Gott sei Dank!

16.2 INFORMATION

(a) Notes on Dialogue 1

Bayreuth	Bayreuth is a town in the north of Bavaria where Richard Wagner established a theatre for the performance of his operas. Each summer there is a festival of his operas there.
3.　Parsifal	Parsifal is the name of one of Richard Wagner's operas.
8.　Wollen wir	Although the verb wollen means literally 'to want to', when it is used in this way wollen wir . . . ? it has the function of making a suggestion. It is

		consequently best translated in this case as 'Shall we ... ?'
10.	Die Karte	In order to show the cost of each individual item, German places the name of the item first thus: Die Karte sechzig Mark – Each ticket sixty marks; das Glas eine Mark zwanzig – DM 1.20 per glass.
14.	Smoking	Smoking is the term for a dinner jacket and matching trousers. It is here translated as evening dress.
23.	doch	The word doch in this sentence is rendered in the English by 'do', which changes the straightforward statement into a request for confirmation: 'We *do* want to go, (don't we?)'.
23.	oder?	The word oder? has the same function as nicht wahr?. It can be rendered in English as: 'don't we?' 'haven't I?' 'shan't we?' etc.

(b) Notes on Dialogue 2

2.	Herr Doktor	When people speak to a doctor and refer to him by his title, the word Herr is used as well as the title.
3.	immer wieder	This phrase indicates that something happens over and over again and can therefore be translated as 'always' or 'again and again'.
11.	im	Note that German uses the word in where English uses the word 'on'. Im dritten Stock – 'on the third floor'.

| 17. | morgens | This is a general term and has the force of 'every morning', or 'regularly every morning'. |

(c) Word list

wissen	to know
die **Kar**te (-n)	ticket
ge**h**en	to go
wie**so**?	how? or why?
nehmen	to take
kosten	to cost
teuer	expensive
anziehen	to put on
das Kleid (-er)	dress
nor**mal**	usual
der **Nerz**mantel (¨)	mink coat
neu	new
tragen	to wear
na**tür**lich	naturally
die **Perlenket**te (-n)	pearl necklace
wann?	when?
sich ent**schei**den	to decide
so**fort**	at once
selbstver**ständ**lich	of course
abholen	to fetch; pick up
der Kopf (¨e)	head
schwindlig	giddy
alt	old
das Jahr (-e)	year
die **Woh**nung (-en)	flat
der Stock (Stockwerke)	floor (of a building)
jed-	every
der Tag (-e)	day
einkaufen	to go shopping
holen	to fetch
die **Schu**le (-n)	school
he**rum**laufen	to run about
aufstehen	to get up
lang	long, a long time
das Bett (-en)	bed
bleiben	to remain, stay
der **Nach**mittag (-e)	afternoon
die **Stun**de (-n)	hour

sich **hin**legen	to lie down
da**heim**	at home
die **Tablet**te (-n)	tablet; pill
abends	in the evening
einschlafen	to go to sleep
kochen	to cook
rauchen	to smoke
lesen	to read
die **Zahn**bürste (-n)	toothbrush
die **Bade**hose	swimming trunks
der **Reise**paß (ˉe)	passport
die **Ein**trittskarte (-n)	(entry) ticket
das **Geld**	money
die **Land**karte (-n)	map
der **Tennisschläger** (-)	tennis racket
der **Stie**fel (-)	boot
der **Regenschirm** (-e)	umbrella

(d)) Some phrases

Das ist Pech	That's bad luck
Was fehlt **Ihnen**?	What's the matter (with you)?
Im Par**terre**	On the groundfloor
Gott sei Dank!	Thank heavens!

16.3 STRUCTURAL EXPLANATIONS

(a) Structures to learn

  (i) How to say what you want to do

Ich will $\left.\begin{array}{l}\text{kochen}\\\text{rauchen}\\\text{gehen}\\\text{lesen}\end{array}\right\}$
Wir wollen

I want to $\left.\begin{array}{l}\text{cook}\\\text{smoke}\\\text{go}\\\text{read}\end{array}\right\}$
We want to

In order to express what you want to do, you use part of the verb WOLLEN, and the infinitive of some other verb.

(ii) Look at some of the sentences from the dialogues:

Ich will $\left.\begin{array}{l}\text{mein neues Kleid}\\\text{meinen Nerzmantel}\end{array}\right\}$ anziehen
Wir wollen   die Karten   nehmen

I want to $\left\{\begin{array}{l}\text{put on my new dress}\\\text{put on my mink coat}\end{array}\right.$
We want to   take the tickets

If you look at these sentences carefully, you will see that the infinitive is placed at the end of the sentence.

(iii) How to express what you have to do

Ich muß / Wir müssen	kochen / rauchen / gehen / lesen	I must / We must	cook / smoke / go / read

(iv) When there are other elements in the sentence besides the modal verb, müssen or wollen, and an infinitive, then the infinitive is placed at the end of the sentence. Here are some sentences from the dialogue:

Sie müssen	etwas weniger / etwas länger im Bett / sich / diese Tabletten	herumlaufen / bleiben / hinlegen / nehmen

(v) Exactly the same applies if you want to ask a question using a modal verb and an infinitive. Have a look at these sentences taken from the dialogue:

Wann müssen wir	uns / die Karten	entscheiden? / abholen?

Or have a look at these sentences:

Muß ich	sie abends / daheim / meinen Smoking	nehmen? / bleiben? / anziehen?

(vi) How to say that you don't have to do something
In these sentences, taken from the dialogue, the verb which expresses absence of obligation is the verb BRAUCHEN used in the negative.

Sie brauchen	nicht daheim / sie nicht abends	bleiben / nehmen

You don't need to stay at home
You don't need to take them in the evening

(b) Grammar
(i) The three verbs you have been using in this chapter are:

WOLLEN — to want to
MÜSSEN — to 'must'/to have to
BRAUCHEN NICHT — to 'not have to'/not need to

In order to see how these verbs can be used in sentences, see Chapter 12.

(ii) Further notes on the modal verbs WOLLEN, MÜSSEN, BRAUCHEN
1. The verb wollen indicates a wish, willingness or intention.

Wollen Sie Brot?	Do you want some bread?
Wollen Sie mit (kommen)?	Do you want to come (with me)?
Ich will ihn nicht stören	I don't want to disturb him
Ich will das nicht tun	I don't want to do it

2. The verb müssen denotes some kind of compulsion.

Ich muß nach Hause (gehen)	I must go home
Ich muß lachen	I must laugh, I can't help laughing
Ich muß einen Brief schreiben	I must/have to write a letter

3. The verb brauchen is not normally considered to be amongst the set of modal verbs. Absence of obligation can be expressed by using the verb müssen in the negative form. However, it is probably easier to learn how to express this function of language by using a separate verb. That is why the verb brauchen has been introduced here. Here are some further examples of sentences showing its use.

Sie brauchen keinen Brief schreiben	You don't have to write a letter
Sie brauchen jetzt nicht gehen	You don't have to go now
Sie brauchen nicht zu mir kommen	You don't have to come to me

16.4 EXERCISES

Section A

Exercise 1
Which of the things in the list would you have to take with you (mitnehmen) under the following circumstances? For instance, if it was raining, you would need to take your raincoat and you would say Ich muß meinen Regenmantel mitnehmen.

1. What would you need to take if you were going shopping?

die Zahnbürste

2. Suppose you wanted to play football.   die Badehose
3. You want to play tennis.   der Reisepaß
4. How about a drive in the country?   die Eintrittskarten
5. You're just off to the theatre.   das Geld
6. You want to go swimming.   die Landkarte
7. You're going abroad for your holiday.   der Tennisschläger
8. A weekend away?   der Stiefel
9. It's raining   der Regenschirm

Exercise 2

Below you will find a page from Fritz's diary. What does he have to do on each day? The first one is done for you.

Question: Was muß Fritz am Sonntag machen?

Answer: Er muß Elke besuchen.

So	Elke besuchen	Was muß Fritz am Sonntag machen?
Mo	die Karten abholen	Was muß Fritz am Montag machen?
Di	nach Nürnberg fahren	Was muß Fritz am Dienstag machen?
Mi	eine Kette für Elke kaufen	Was muß Fritz am Mittwoch machen?
Do	einen Tennisschläger kaufen	Was muß Fritz am Donnerstag machen?
Fr	nach Stuttgart fahren	Was muß Fritz am Freitag machen?
Sa	im Bett bleiben (müde!)	Was muß Fritz am Samstag machen?

Exercise 3

You have arranged to go on holiday with a friend. This friend is notoriously careless at getting things ready and so you have collected everything that he might need and put it in your car. When he rings up, therefore, to find out if he should bring certain things with him, you are able to say that you have already got everything organised. The first answer is done for you to show you how to do it.

Question: Muß ich meinen Tennisschläger mitnehmen?

Answer: Nein, Sie brauchen Ihren Tennisschläger nicht mitnehmen.

Here are the questions.
1. Muß ich meine Stiefel mitnehmen?
2. Muß ich meine Landkarte mitnehmen?
3. Muß ich meine Badehose mitnehmen?
4. Muß ich meine Zahnbürste mitnehmen?
5. Muß ich meine Schuhe mitnehmen?
6. Muß ich meinen Smoking mitnehmen?
7. Muß ich meinen Mantel mitnehmen?
8. Muß ich meine Tabletten mitnehmen?
9. Muß ich mein Buch mitnehmen?
10. Muß ich meinen Tennisschläger mitnehmen?

CHAPTER 17

SUGGESTIONS AND PROPOSALS

17.1 DIALOGUES 📼

Dialogue 1

The irrepressible Antonio Santos has spotted a rather nice-looking girl sitting outside a Gasthaus on the Leopoldstraße. Sensing the possibility of an upturn in his love-life, he sits down at the same table.

1 *Antonio*: Ist dieser Platz frei?
   Mädchen: Ja.
   Antonio: Schönes Wetter, nicht wahr?
   Mädchen: Ja. Sehr schön.
5 *Antonio*: Ich heiße Antonio.
   Mädchen: Hmm.
   Antonio: Antonio Santos.

. . .

   Antonio: Wie heißen Sie?
     Wenn ich fragen darf?
10 *Mädchen*: Claudia.
   Antonio: Claudia. Ein schöner Name.
   Mädchen: Danke.

. . .

   Antonio: Sagen Sie, Claudia?
     Können Sie Tennis spielen?
15 *Mädchen*: Ja.
   Antonio: Schön! Wollen wir Tennis spielen?
   Mädchen: Wann?
   Antonio: Morgen, vielleicht?
   Mädchen: Ja, gern.
20 *Antonio*: Spielen Sie oft?
   Mädchen: Ziemlich oft.

Schönes Wetter, nicht wahr?

Photograph: Bavaria-Verlag/Klaus Meier-Ude

Vier oder fünf mal in der Woche.
Antonio: Wo spielen Sie?
Mädchen: Im Carlton Club.
25   *Antonio*:   Ach?
Spielen Sie gut?
Mädchen: Ach, ganz gut.
Und Sie?
Antonio: Nicht sehr gut.
(To himself) Das gibt's doch nicht!!

Dialogue 2

Fritz has decided that his relationship with Elke ought to take a more positive turn, so he goes to visit her at her flat. He is encouraged when she uses the familiar du form.

1 *Fritz*: Hallo, Elke!
  Elke: Du, Fritz!
    Komm doch herein!
  Fritz: Danke.
5   Wie geht's dir?
  Elke: Prima!
  Fritz: Du, Elke . . . .
    Wollen wir am Wochenende wegfahren?
  Elke: O, ja! Wohin?
10 *Fritz*: Ich kenne eine sehr hübsche Kirche.
    In der Nähe von Rosenheim.
  Elke: O nein, Fritz!
    Schon wieder eine Kirche!!!
  Fritz: Was ist denn los?
15 *Elke*: Jedes Mal eine Kirche!
  Fritz: Kirchen interessieren mich.
    Das weißt du.
  Elke: Aber du hast jede Woche eine andere Kirche.
    Das ist mir zu viel.

Auf dem Idiotenhügel

Photograph: J. Allan Cash Ltd

20 *Fritz*: Es tut mir leid.
  Elke: Wollen wir nach Kufstein fahren?
    Dort können wir Ski fahren.
  Fritz: Aber ich kann nicht Ski fahren.
  Elke: Aber ich kann sehr gut Ski fahren.
25 *Fritz*: Na gut.
    Fahren wir nach Kufstein.
  Elke: Ja, du kannst es lernen.
    (to herself) (Auf dem Idiotenhügel!)

17.2 INFORMATION

(a) Notes on Dialogue 1

9. Wenn

Despite appearances to the contrary, this word very often means 'if'. Here it means 'if I may ask', or as we would say 'if you don't mind my asking'. Students wishing to inform themselves about the structure of 'subordinate' clauses introduced by wenn should consult the grammar books listed in the bibliography.

13. Sagen Sie

This phrase is excellent for indicating that you want to say something, or for breaking into a conversation, or simply for establishing that it is now your turn to speak. In English we would say, 'Tell me ... ' or 'I say ... '.

14. spielen

Note that this word comes at the end of the sentence. See Section 16.2.

17. Wann

Note this word carefully because it is very similar to the word in line 9. This word, however, is always used in a question: 'When?'

19.	gern	This short word is a very economic way of expressing the idea 'I'd like to'.
26.	gut	This word can serve both as an adjective or an adverb. We would here have to translate it as 'well'.

(b) Notes on Dialogue 2

7.	Du	This is a fairly emphatic, but very typical way of addressing somebody, in the familiar form.
8.	wegfahren	Note the position of this word in the sentence. See Section 16.2.
9.	Wohin	Germans are very punctilious about indicating the distinction between locality and direction. In English we would simply say 'Where?' In German, however, it is essential to indicate the meaning which we still have in our archaic form 'Whither?' It is probably best to think of the meaning of the word wohin? as 'where to?'
11.	In der Nähe von	This rather long phrase is the German for 'near'.
16.	interessieren mich	Note how German says: (things, e.g. churches) interest me.
22.	Dort	This word is placed at the beginning of the sentence for emphasis.
28.	Idiotenhügel	Although we would say 'nursery slope' in English, the term in German for the slopes where many people can learn to ski is very condescending. It is best translated as 'idiots' slope'.

(c) Word list

dies-	this
der Platz (¨e)	place; seat
frei	free; vacant
schön	nice, beautiful
das **Wet**ter	weather
heißen	to be called
der Name (-n)	name
sagen	to say
können	to be able
spielen	to play
wollen	to wish; want to
wann?	when?
morgen	tomorrow
viel**leicht**	perhaps
oft	often
ziemlich	fairly
die **Wo**che (-n)	week
gut	well (as an adverb)
ganz	quite
Prima!	splendid!
das **Woch**enende (-n)	weekend
wegfahren	to go away
wo**hin?**	where to?
kennen	to know (a person or a place)
hübsch	pretty
die **Kir**che (-n)	church
interes**sie**ren	to interest
wissen	to know (a fact)
ander-	other
Ski fahren	to go ski-ing
lernen	to learn
der **Fuß**ball (¨e)	football
die **Kar**te (-n)	card(s)
schwimmen	to swim
tanzen	to dance
essen	to eat
der **Spazier**gang (¨e)	walk
machen	to make, to do
reiten	to ride
malen	to paint
singen	to sing
ausgezeichnet	very well indeed

(d) Some phrases

Nicht wahr?	Isn't it, etc.
Wie **heiß**en Sie?	What is your name?
Komm doch her**ein**	Come in, won't you? (familiar form)
Wie geht's dir?	How are you? (familiar form)
Was ist denn los?	What's the matter?
Schon **wie**der!	Again!
Jedes Mal	Every time
Das ist mir zu viel	That's too much (for me)
Es tut mir leid	I'm sorry
Sehr gut	Very well
Ziemlich gut	Fairly well
Nicht sehr gut	Not very well
Nur **etw**as	Only a little bit
Im **groß**en und **gan**zen	On the whole

17.3 STRUCTURAL EXPLANATIONS

(a) Structures to learn

(i) How to make a suggestion or proposal

190

(ii) How to ask what you can do

Können Sie / Kannst du

schwimmen
Ski fahren
reiten
malen
singen
tanzen
Tennis } spielen
Fußball }

?

Can you

swim
ski
ride
paint
sing
dance
play { tennis, football

?

(iii) How to say what you can do

Ich kann

schwimmen
Ski fahren
reiten
malen
singen
tanzen
Tennis } spielen
Fußball }

I can

swim
ski
ride
paint
sing
dance
play { tennis, football

(iv) How to ask how well someone can do something

Schwimmen Sie gut?
Reiten Sie gut?

Singen Sie gut?
Tanzen Sie gut?

BUT:

Fahren Sie gut Ski?
Spielen Sie gut Tennis?
Spielen Sie gut Fußball?

(v) **Here are some replies you can give**

ausgezeichnet	–	very well indeed
sehr gut	–	very well
ziemlich gut	–	fairly well
nicht sehr gut	–	not very well
nur etwas	–	only a little bit

(b) Grammar

(i) Here are the most frequently used parts of the two verbs we have been looking at in this chapter.

The verb WOLLEN – to want to

ich will	I want to
er will	he wants to
sie will	she wants to
wir wollen	we want to
Sie wollen	you want to

The verb KÖNNEN – to be able to

ich kann	I can
er kann	he can
sie kann	she can
wir können	we can
Sie können	you can

Both these verbs are *irregular* in that their stems change, and their endings do not conform to the standard pattern. However, they are amongst the most important verbs in the whole language and there is no alternative to learning them.

(ii) The most frequent sentence patterns in which these verbs operate is as follows:

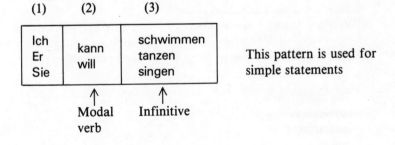

(1)	(2)	(3)
Ich Er Sie	kann will	schwimmen tanzen singen

↑ Modal verb   ↑ Infinitive

This pattern is used for simple statements

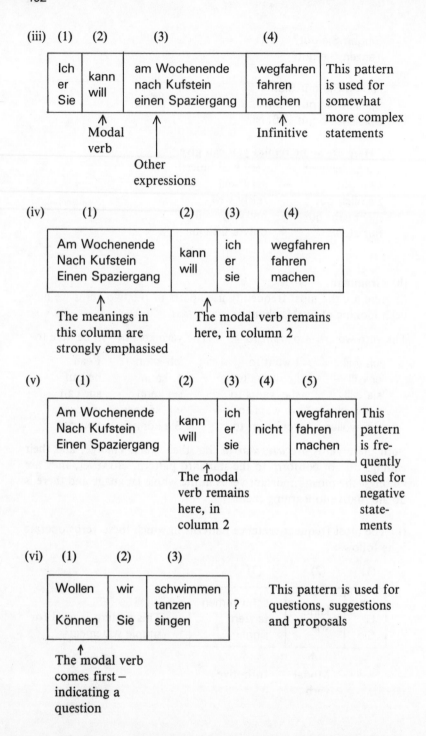

(iii)

(1)	(2)	(3)	(4)	
Ich er Sie	kann will	am Wochenende nach Kufstein einen Spaziergang	wegfahren fahren machen	This pattern is used for somewhat more complex statements

↑ Modal verb   ↑ Other expressions   ↑ Infinitive

(iv)

(1)	(2)	(3)	(4)
Am Wochenende Nach Kufstein Einen Spaziergang	kann will	ich er sie	wegfahren fahren machen

↑ The meanings in this column are strongly emphasised

↑ The modal verb remains here, in column 2

(v)

(1)	(2)	(3)	(4)	(5)	
Am Wochenende Nach Kufstein Einen Spaziergang	kann will	ich er sie	nicht	wegfahren fahren machen	This pattern is frequently used for negative statements

↑ The modal verb remains here, in column 2

(vi)

(1)	(2)	(3)	
Wollen Können	wir Sie	schwimmen tanzen singen	? This pattern is used for questions, suggestions and proposals

↑ The modal verb comes first – indicating a question

(vii) You will find the verbs wollen and können in the appendix.

(viii) We now come to one of the trickiest problems in German; it concerns the two concepts of *position* and *direction*.

POSITION: this concept enables you to *express where you are*, or *where something is*.

MOVEMENT TOWARDS: this concept enables you to express movement towards a thing, a person, or a place.

Consider the following sentences:

1. a) Ich bin in dem (im) Garten   I am *in* the garden
   b) Ich gehe in den Garten   I go *into* the garden
2. a) Ich bin in dem (im) Haus   I am *in* the house
   b) Ich gehe in das (ins) Haus   I go *into* the house
3. a) Ich bin in dem (im) Park   I am *in* the park
   b) Ich gehe in den Park   I go *into* the park
4. a) Ich bin in der Kirche   I am *in* the church
   b) Ich gehe in die Kirche   I go *into* the church

Notice that in all the above pairs of sentences, the a) sentence expresses POSITION and has its definite article in the *dative case*. All the b) sentences express MOVEMENT TOWARDS something, and have their definite article in the *accusative case*.

This concept can be illustrated visually:

Jochen läuft in den Wald   Jochen runs into (i.e. towards) the wood

Jochen läuft in dem (im) Wald   Jochen is running in (i.e. within/inside) the wood

The above pictures show how important this concept is in German. The only difference between the two sentences is the definite article, once in the *accusative* indicating MOVEMENT TOWARDS the wood, and once in the *dative* indicating Jochen's POSITION inside the wood. Consequently, the only way German speakers have of understanding correctly what is meant is by correct use of the two cases.

Certain verbs, such as wohnen (to live), sein (to be) and sitzen (to be sitting) always indicate POSITION.

Other verbs, such as fahren (to go, to drive), and gehen (to go, to walk) always indicate MOVEMENT.

When you use one of these verbs, therefore, it is especially important to use the correct case.

The following three prepositions are the most frequently used for indicating either MOVEMENT TOWARDS or POSITION:

an	—	to, by
auf	—	on, onto
in	—	in, into

The rule can be summarised thus:

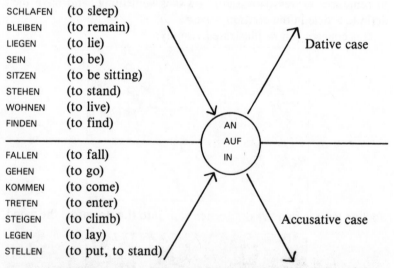

SCHLAFEN	(to sleep)
BLEIBEN	(to remain)
LIEGEN	(to lie)
SEIN	(to be)
SITZEN	(to be sitting)
STEHEN	(to stand)
WOHNEN	(to live)
FINDEN	(to find)

Dative case

AN
AUF
IN

FALLEN	(to fall)
GEHEN	(to go)
KOMMEN	(to come)
TRETEN	(to enter)
STEIGEN	(to climb)
LEGEN	(to lay)
STELLEN	(to put, to stand)

Accusative case

You will find a list of those prepositions which can be used with either the *accusative* or the *dative* case in the appendix.

Do not forget, however, that there are also prepositions which can *only* be used with the *accusative*, just as there are those which can *only* be used with the *dative*. You will find these in the appendix. They were dealt with in Chapters 5 and 9.

17.4 EXERCISES

Section A

Exercise 1

This is Karlheinz. He enjoys playing football and cards. He likes ski-ing and going for walks.

This is Gertraute. She likes dancing, swimming and riding and playing tennis.

Make some proposals to Karlheinz and Gertraute. Here are some sample conversations:

You: Karlheinz! Wollen wir Fußball spielen?
Karlheinz: Ja, gern.

You: Gertraute! Wollen wir Karten spielen?
Gertraute: Nein, ich kann nicht Karten spielen.

Suggest to Karlheinz that you
 1. play football,
 2. go riding,
 3. play cards,
 4. play tennis,
 5. go swimming.

Then propose to Gertraute that you
 6. go dancing,
 7. go ski-ing,
 8. go for a walk,
 9. play football,
10. play cards.

Exercise 2

You are one of those people who are either extremely good at a thing, or absolutely awful. As it happens your strengths lie in swimming, riding, tennis and cards, and your weaknesses in ski-ing, dancing, football, singing and painting. Answer the following questions:

1. Können Sie gut Tennis spielen?
2. Können Sie gut malen?
3. Können Sie gut reiten?
4. Können Sie gut Ski fahren?
5. Können Sie gut tanzen?
6. Können Sie gut schwimmen?
7. Können Sie gut singen?
8. Können Sie gut Fußball spielen?
9. Können Sie gut Karten spielen?

Section B

Exercise 3

Complete the following sentences:

1. Der Junge geht in d— Schule.
2. Der Lehrer arbeitet in d— Schule.
3. Die Klasse kommt in d— Klassenzimmer.
4. Die Mädchen warten in d— Klassenzimmer.
5. Das Radio steht auf d— Tisch.
6. Ich stelle die Milch in d— Kühlschrank.
7. Das Bild hängt an d— Wand.
8. Ich halte meine Zeitung unter d— Arm.
9. Ich gehe an d— Tür.
10. Ich stelle die Tasse auf d— Tisch.

CHAPTER 18

DREAMS AND WISHES

18.1 DIALOGUES 📼

Dialogue 1

Elke and Fritz have been enjoying the ski-ing at Kufstein (she possibly somewhat more than he). Now they are lying side by side on camp beds in the sun at the top of the ski slope. Elke is looking through some travel brochures.

1 *Elke*: Fritz?
    Fritz: Ja?
    Elke: Es ist schön hier, nicht?
    Fritz: Ja. Sehr schön.
5 *Elke*: Du bist wirklich lieb, weißt du?
    Fritz: Ja?
    . . .
    Elke: Fritz?
    Fritz: Ja?
    Elke: Weißt du was?
10 *Fritz*: Nein?
    Elke: Ich möchte nach Amerika fahren.
    Fritz: Tatsächlich?
    Elke: Ja. Ich möchte Hollywood sehen.
    Fritz: Hollywood?
15 *Elke*: Ja. Und ich möchte New York besuchen.
    Fritz: Ach, New York ist doch nicht schön.
    Elke: Doch, doch!
    Und ich möchte mit einer Straßenbahn in San Francisco fahren.
20 *Fritz*: Warum möchtest du mit einer Straßenbahn fahren?
    Das kannst du in München tun.

. . . ist das so romantisch

Photograph: Bavaria-Verlag / Werner Stuhler

> *Elke*:   Ach, du verstehst nicht.
> In San Francisco ist das so romantisch.
> *Fritz*:   Aber teuer.
> 25 *Elke*:   Das ist typisch ‚Mann'!!
> Du denkst nur ans Geld.
> Ich möchte reisen.
> Ich möchte die Welt sehen.

Dialogue 2

Frau Meyer is telephoning her best friend in order to impart the great news.

> 1 *Frau Meyer*:   Leni? Weißt du was?
> Die Inge kriegt ein Kind!
> *Leni*:   Nein. Das ist ja wunderbar!
> Wo ist sie denn?
> 5 *Frau Meyer*:   In Liverpool.
> *Leni*:   Ach ja, richtig.
> In England.
> *Frau Meyer*:   Ich fahre natürlich nach Liverpool.
> *Leni*:   Ja, natürlich.

10   *Frau Meyer*: Ich muß meinen Pelzmantel reinigen lassen.
     Leni: Ja, selbstverständlich.
     Frau Meyer: Und ich muß mir ein neues Kleid machen lassen.
     Leni: Ja, freilich.
     Frau Meyer: Dann brauche ich einen Fotoapparat.
15   Ich muß meinen alten Fotoapparat reparieren lassen.
     Leni: Sicher.
     Frau Meyer: Dann muß ich auch etwas Geld wechseln.
     Leni: Ja, klar.
     Frau Meyer: Was für Geld haben sie dort in England?
20   Dollar, nicht?
     Leni: Nein. Sie haben Pfund und 'Pence'.
     Frau Meyer: Ach so. Ja.
     Dann muß ich mir die Haare waschen lassen.
     Leni: Moment, Irmgard.
25   Wann erwartet Inge ihr Kind?
     Frau Meyer: Nächstes Jahr.
     Im März.
     Leni: Hör' mal, Irmgard!
     Du hast doch noch viel Zeit.

18.2 INFORMATION

(a) Notes on Dialogue 1

11. fahren

Note the difference in the word order between German and English. In German the infinitive comes at the end of the sentence. See also lines 13, 15, 19, 20 and 28.

17. Doch, doch!

The word doch means 'yes' after someone has made a negative statement in the previous sentence. See line 16.

26. ans Geld

The meaning of an in this sentence is 'of'. Denken an – 'to think of'.

(b) Notes on Dialogue 2

2. kriegt

There are two verbs in German which mean 'to get' or 'to

receive'. They are kriegen and bekommen. Of the two, kriegen is slightly more colloquial. In this particular sentence the word kriegen is probably best rendered by 'to have', since in English we say 'to have a child'.

The present tense of the verb can be used to indicate something that is going to happen in the future. As the story makes clear, Inge's confinement lies in the future and the verb kriegt is consequently translated as 'is going to have'.

6. richtig

In German there are several expressions with which you can agree with what somebody else has just said. Leni uses a number of them.

richtig (line 6)
natürlich (line 9)
selbstverständlich (line 11)
freilich (line 13)
sicher (line 16)
klar (line 18)

14. brauche

As with the comment on line 2, this verb is formally in the present tense, though its meaning is to convey the future. Therefore it is translated as 'am going to need'.

17. etwas

This word when used together with a noun means 'some'. Etwas Geld – 'some money', etwas Milch – 'some milk', etwas Butter – 'some butter'.

19. Was für ... ?

This useful phrase means 'What sort of ... ?'

(c) Word list

wirklich	really
lieb	sweet, nice
tatsächlich	really; indeed
sehen	to see
besuchen	to visit
schön	beautiful
die Straßenbahn (-en)	tram
warum?	why?
verstehen	to understand
romantisch	romantic
teuer	dear; expensive
typisch	typical
denken	to think
nur	only
das Geld	money
reisen	to travel
die Welt	world
wissen	to know
kriegen	to get
das Kind (-er)	child
wunderbar	wonderful
richtig	right; correct
natürlich	naturally
der Pelzmantel (¨)	fur coat
reinigen	to clean
selbstverständlich	of course
neu	new
das Kleid (-er)	dress
freilich	of course
brauchen	to need
der Fotoapparat (-e)	camera
alt	old
reparieren	to repair
sicher	certainly
wechseln	to change
klar	obviously
die Haare (used in plural)	hair
waschen	to wash
erwarten	to expect
das Jahr (-e)	year
die Zeit	time

sprechen	to speak
zahlen	to pay
telefo**nier**en	to make a telephone call
schlafen	to sleep
schmutzig	dirty
die **Arm**banduhr (-en)	wristwatch
ka**putt**	broken
dreckig	dirty
das Hemd (-en)	shirt
die **Bri**lle	glasses, spectacles

18.3 STRUCTURAL EXPLANATIONS

(a) Structures to learn

(i) How to say you would like to do something and how to ask somebody what they would like to do

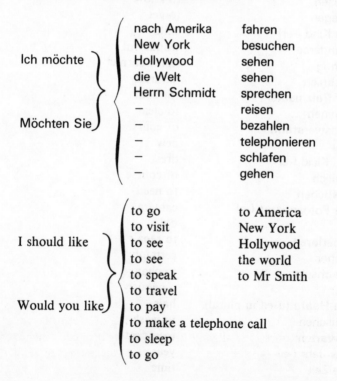

Ich möchte	nach Amerika	fahren
	New York	besuchen
	Hollywood	sehen
	die Welt	sehen
	Herrn Schmidt	sprechen
Möchten Sie	–	reisen
	–	bezahlen
	–	telephonieren
	–	schlafen
	–	gehen

I should like	to go	to America
	to visit	New York
	to see	Hollywood
	to see	the world
	to speak	to Mr Smith
Would you like	to travel	
	to pay	
	to make a telephone call	
	to sleep	
	to go	

(ii) **How to say that you would like to have something done**

Ich muß Ich möchte	{	meinen Pelzmantel meinen Fotoapparat ein neues Kleid mir die Haare	{	reinigen reparieren machen waschen } lassen

I must I should like to	have	{	my fur coat my camera a new dress my hair	{	cleaned repaired made washed

(iii) When you have things done for you, you often want to ask when the services requested will be complete. Here are some ways of asking when things will be done:

Wann ist { der Pelzmantel
der Fotoapparat
das Kleid } fertig?

When will { the fur coat
the camera
the dress } be ready?

(iv) **How to ask when you can collect things**

Wann kann ich { den Pelzmantel
den Fotoapparat
das Kleid } abholen?

When can I collect { the fur coat
the camera
the dress } ?

18.4 EXERCISES

Section A

Exercise 1

You had an accident on the way home and fell off your bicycle. All your clothes are dirty and all your breakables are broken. You have to set about restoring the damage. You go to the various shops. What do you say?

1. Dieser Mantel ist schmutzig.   Ich möchte ......
2. Diese Armbanduhr ist kaputt.   Ich möchte ......
3. Mein Hut ist dreckig.   Ich möchte ......
4. Mein Fotoapparat ist kaputt.   Ich möchte ......
5. Dieses Hemd ist schmutzig.   Ich möchte ......
6. Diese Hose ist dreckig.   Ich möchte ......
7. Meine Brille ist kaputt.   Ich möchte ......

Exercise 2

What would you say?

1. You're dreaming of far-off shores.
2. You want to leave the restaurant.
3. You want to speak to a friend on the phone.
4. You want to go to bed at last.
5. You want to leave.
6. You want to visit Peter.
7. You want to have a word with Miss Braun.
8. You want to see Munich.
9. You want to travel to Bonn.
10. You want to change your money.

Section B

Exercise 3

Unscramble the following sentences:

1. Ich möchte mir die Haare   a) Hamburg fahren.
2. Er will seinen   b) wechseln.
3. Elke will New York   c) Kleid machen lassen.
4. Ich möchte die   d) Herrn Schmidt sprechen.
5. Er möchte nach   e) reinigen lassen.
6. Wir müssen das Geld   f) waschen lassen.
7. Wir möchten   g) bezahlen.
8. Sie muß sich ein neues   h) Apparat reparieren lassen.
9. Kann ich bitte   i) Welt sehen.
10. Sie will ihren Pelzmantel   j) besuchen.

CHAPTER 19

TALKING ABOUT THE PAST

19.1 DIALOGUES 🔲

Dialogue 1

Fritz is furious that Elke has kept him waiting – yet again.

1   *Fritz*:   Mensch!
          Wo warst du denn?
      Elke: Was ist denn los?
          Mein Bus hatte Verspätung.
5   *Fritz*:   Er hatte gestern Verspätung.
          Und heute hat er schon wieder Verspätung.
      Elke: Gestern hatte mein Bus nicht Verspätung.
      Fritz: Doch, doch!
          Er hatte dreißig Minuten Verspätung.
10   *Elke*:   Das stimmt nicht.
      Fritz: Doch! Das stimmt.
          Ich war um sieben Uhr vor dem Kino.
          Und du warst erst um sieben Uhr dreißig da.
      Elke: Ich war pünktlich da.
15   Du warst einfach zu früh am Kino.
      Fritz: Und warum warst du vorgestern nicht pünktlich?
      Elke: Ich war im Geschäft.
      Fritz: Was? Bis acht Uhr?
          Das glaube ich nicht!
20   *Elke*:   Ich hatte sehr viel zu tun.
      Fritz: Und der Chef war auch da, nicht wahr?
      Elke: Natürlich.
          Er hatte auch viel zu tun.
      Fritz: Ah hah. Jetzt verstehe ich ...

Dialogue 2

Antonio is walking along the street when he sees Frau Meyer apparently searching for something.

1   *Antonio*:   Kann ich Ihnen helfen?
  Frau Meyer: Ach, ich habe meine Armbanduhr verloren.
  Antonio: Hier, auf der Straße?
  Frau Meyer: Ja, das glaube ich.
5   Ich bin in die Stadt gefahren.
  Und ich habe dort Kaffee getrunken.
  Antonio: Haben Sie die Uhr vielleicht in der Stadt verloren?
  Frau Meyer: Nein.
  Ich habe sie in der Straßenbahn noch gesehen.
10   *Antonio*:   Haben Sie an der Haltestelle gesucht?
  Frau Meyer: Ja, natürlich.
  Dort habe ich Frau Moezer getroffen.
  Ich bin mit ihr zur Post gegangen.
  Antonio: Haben Sie die Uhr vielleicht in der Post verloren?
15   *Frau Meyer*:   Nein, das glaube ich nicht.
  Antonio: Sind Sie direkt von der Post hierher gekommen?
  Frau Meyer: Nein. Ich habe zuerst Äpfel gekauft.
  Bei Schötz.
  Antonio: Ach so. Bei Schötz.
20   Wie lange sind Sie bei Schötz geblieben?
  Frau Meyer: Ach, nicht lange.
  Fünf Minuten vielleicht.
  Antonio: Haben Sie in Ihrer Tasche gesucht?
  Frau Meyer: Was?
25   *Antonio*:   Haben Sie in Ihrer Tasche gesucht?
  Frau Meyer: Um Gottes Willen!
  Da ist sie!

19.2 INFORMATION

(a) Notes on Dialogue 1

1. Mensch!   This is a much-used expression in German, which you will hear very frequently if you go there. It conveys a certain feeling of indignation on the part of the speaker, and you should be wary of using it unless you feel you know the person you are speaking to well enough.

4.	Verspätung	Note that where in English we say something or someone *is* late, in German one says something has *lateness*.
7.	Gestern	The word gestern is put at the beginning of the sentence for emphasis, and this means that the subject comes after the verb.
10.	Das stimmt nicht	This phrase should be treated as an idiom, and not translated.
12.	um sieben Uhr	In German, expressions of time always come before expressions of place.
13.	erst	In expressions of time, this word means 'not until'.

(b) Notes on Dialogue 2

2.	verloren	Note that the past participle comes at the end of the sentence.
4.	das glaube ich	Get used to the order of the words in this expression, and use it as an idiom when you want to say 'I think so'.
6.	getrunken	English very often uses the verb 'to have' with food or drink. German, however, always specifies whether one is eating or drinking.
7.	vielleicht	This word means 'perhaps'.
10.	Haben Sie ... ?	Remember that English very often forms its questions with the word 'Do' or 'Did'. In German the subject and the verb are inverted in order to make the question form.

(c) Word list

der Bus (-se)	bus
gestern	yesterday

heute	today
schon **wie**der	again
die Minute (-n)	minute
vor	in front of
das **Ki**no (-s)	cinema
pünktlich	on time
einfach	simply
früh	early
vor**gest**ern	the day before yesterday
das Ge**schäft** (-e)	shop; business
bis	until
glauben	to believe
sehr viel	very much
tun	to do
der Chef	boss
ver**steh**en	to understand
helfen	to help
die **Arm**banduhr (-en)	wristwatch
ver**lier**en	to lose
die **Straß**e (-n)	street
die Stadt (¨e)	town
die **Straß**enbahn	tram
der **Kaff**ee	coffee
trinken	to drink
die **Halt**estelle	bus or tram stop
sehen	to see
suchen	to seek, look for
na**tür**lich	of course, naturally
treffen	to meet
die Post	post office
di**rekt**	straight directly
zu**erst**	first of all
der **Ap**fel (¨)	apple
kaufen	to buy
wie **lange**?	how long?
bleiben	to stay; remain
nicht **lange**	not long
viel**leicht**	perhaps
die **Ta**sche (-n)	pocket; bag

(d) Some phrases

Was ist denn los?	What's the matter?
Das stimmt nicht	That's not true, correct

Das **glaub**e ich nicht   I don't believe it
Um **Gottes Will**en!   Good Lord!

19.3 STRUCTURAL EXPLANATIONS

Grammar

(i) When referring to the past, two tenses are used in German. The first past tense is known as the *Imperfect* or *Simple Past*, and the other is known as the *Perfect* tense or *Compound Past*.

(ii) **The Simple Past (also known as the Imperfect tense)**

When talking German and wishing to refer to the past, this tense is used mainly with the verbs haben and sein, and with a number of other verbs of speaking, i.e. sagen – 'to say'.

Here are some examples, taken from Dialogue 1:

Wo warst du denn?
Ich war um sieben Uhr vor dem Kino
Du warst erst um sieben Uhr dreißig da
Ich war pünktlich da
Ich war im Geschäft

Mein Bus hatte Verspätung
Er hatte gestern Verspätung
Ich hatte sehr viel zu tun
Er hatte auch viel zu tun

(iii) Here are the forms of the Simple Past tense of SEIN – to be.

ich war	I was
du warst	you were (familiar)
er war	he was
sie war	she was
es war	it was
wir waren	we were
ihr ward	you were (familiar)
Sie waren	you were (formal or polite)
sie waren	they were

(iv) Here are the forms of the Simple Past tense of HABEN – to have.

ich hatte	I had
du hattest	you had (familiar)
er hatte	he had

sie hatte	she had
es hatte	it had
wir hatten	we had
ihr hattet	you had (familiar)
Sie hatten	you had (formal or polite)
sie hatten	they had

(v) Remember when you want to say: 'I was', or 'we were', or 'I had', or 'they had', these are the forms to use.

You should use the same tense if you want to say 'I said'. The Simple Past tense of the verb 'to say' is given in the appendix.

(vi) The Compound Past (also known as the Perfect tense)

In this course, you are going to learn the Compound Past of verbs *other than* haben, sein and sagen. As the word *compound* indicates, this tense is made by using parts of two verbs.

Consider the following sentences, taken from Dialogue 2 and try to discover how this tense is constructed.

Ich *habe* meine Armbanduhr *verloren*	(verlieren – to lose)
Ich *habe* dort Kaffee *getrunken*	(trinken – to drink)
Ich *habe* sie in der Straßenbahn *gesehen*	(sehen – to see)
Ich *habe* zuerst Äpfel *gekauft*	(kaufen – to buy)

Here is an analysis of these sentences.

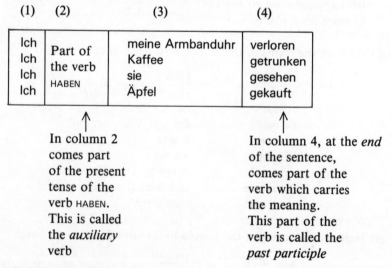

(vii) Here are some more sentences from Dialogue 2. Look and see how they are constructed.

Haben Sie die Uhr in der Stadt *verloren?*
Haben Sie an der Haltestelle *gesucht?*
Haben Sie die Uhr in der Post *verloren?*
Haben Sie in Ihrer Tasche *gesucht?*

Here is an analysis of these sentences.

(1)　　　(2)　　　(3)　　　　　　　(4)

Part of the verb HABEN	Sie	die Uhr in der Stadt	verloren
	Sie	an der Haltestelle	gesucht
	Sie	die Uhr in der Post	verloren
	Sie	in Ihrer Tasche	gesucht

↑

The *auxiliary* verb is at the beginning of the sentence in column 1. This indicates that the sentences are questions

↑

The *past participle* comes in column 4, at the end of the sentence

(viii) All the verbs we have looked at so far make their *Compound Past* tense by using the verb HABEN. Unfortunately, this is not always the case. A small group of very important verbs make the *Compound Past* by using the verb SEIN.

(ix) Consider the following sentences taken from Dialogue 2.

Ich bin in die Stadt gefahren.　　　(fahren – to go/drive)
Ich bin mit ihr zur Post gegangen.　　(gehen – to go)

Here is an analysis of the sentences.

(1)　(2)　　　　　(3)　　　　　(4)

| Ich | Part of the verb SEIN | in die Stadt | gefahren |
| Ich | | zur Post | gegangen |

↑

Part of the present tense of the verb SEIN

↑

At the *end* of the sentence comes the *past participle*

(x) Here are some more sentences from Dialogue 2. Look and see how they are constructed.

> Sind Sie direkt von der Post hierher gekommen?
>   (kommen – to come)
> Wie lange sind Sie bei Schötz geblieben?
>   (bleiben – to stay/remain)

Here is an analysis of these sentences.

(1)	(2)	(3)	(4)	(5)
– Wie lange	Part of the verb SEIN	Sie Sie	von der Post bei Schötz	gekommen? geblieben?

The *auxiliary*
verb: SEIN
is here

The *past participle*
is at the *end* of
the sentence

(xi) We can summarise the rule about making the Compound Past tense thus:

1. The *Compound Past* is made with part of the present tense of the verb HABEN or SEIN. This is called the *auxiliary verb*.
2. The other part of this tense is called the *past participle*.
3. The *past participle* comes at the end of the sentence, whether it is a question or a statement.

(xii) Two vital questions remain:
1. How does each individual verb make its past participle?
2. Which verbs make their Compound Past tense with HABEN, and which with SEIN?

These questions may be answered by consulting the list of verbs in the appendix.

19.4 EXERCISES

Section A

Exercise 1
Imagine that this is your diary. Say what you did on each day of the week. Here is an example:

Montag – Ich bin nach Solingen gefahren.

Mo	*nach Solingen fahren.*
Di	*Armbanduhr kaufen.*
Mi	*Kette für Inge suchen.*
Do	*mit Elke ins Kino gehen.*
Fr	*Wein mit Peter trinken.*
Sa	*Bayern-München gegen Hamburg sehen.*
So	*in die Kirche gehen.*

Exercise 2
Here is a page from your diary, which shows your movements throughout the day. Imagine that you are being questioned by a policeman, who says: 'Wo waren Sie um 9 Uhr?' You can answer: 'Ich war im Büro'. Now answer the following questions.

1. Wo waren Sie um 9 Uhr?
2. Wo waren Sie um 10 Uhr?
3. Wo waren Sie um 11 Uhr?
4. Wo waren Sie um 12 Uhr?
5. Wo waren Sie um 13 Uhr?
6. Wo waren Sie um 14 Uhr?
7. Wo waren Sie um 15 Uhr?

Dienstag 2 Mai

09·00	im Büro
10·00	in der Post
11·00	am Marktplatz
12·00	im Gasthaus Bauer
13·00	bei Müller
14·00	im Café
15·00	im Zug
16·00	
17·00	
18·00	

Section B

Exercise 3

Put the following sentences into the Perfect tense.

1. Ich trinke Bier.
2. Ich gehe in die Stadt.
3. Er fährt nach Bremen.
4. Wir kommen um 8 Uhr.
5. Sie bleiben zu lange.
6. Sie kauft ein Hemd.
7. Wir suchen eine Wohnung.
8. Sie verliert ihre Armbanduhr.
9. Ich sehe einen guten Film.
10. Sie treffen Herrn Schüth.

CHAPTER 20

REVISION TESTS

In this chapter you will have an opportunity to consolidate the language you have learned in the previous nine chapters. Each test indicates whereabouts in the later part of the book you ought to search if you have forgotten a particular point.

Test 1 – Ordering a Meal (Ch. 11)
You're taking a friend out to dinner to celebrate his/her birthday.
Waiter: Guten Abend!
You: Greet him.
  Ask for a table for two.
Waiter: Kommen Sie, bitte.
You: Call for the waiter.
Waiter: Bitte schön?
You: Ask for the menu.
Waiter: Die Speisekarte, bitte schön.
You: Ask your friend if he/she would like an hors d'oeuvre.
Friend: Ja, bitte.
You: Ask your friend if he/she would like oysters.
Friend: Austern, O ja!
You: Order the oysters for both of you.
Waiter: Zweimal Austern.
You: Ask your friend if he/she would like a Zigeuner Steak.
Friend: Nein, danke, ich möchte ein Jägerschnitzel.
You: Order one Jägerschnitzel and a Wienerschnitzel.
Waiter: Jawohl.
You: Ask your friend if he/she would like something to drink.
Friend: O ja. Ich möchte einen Rotwein. Und Sie?
You: Say you'd like red wine too.
  Order two red wines.
Waiter: Jawohl, mein Herr.
If you are learning with a friend, take it in turns to play the parts.

Test 2 – Finding a table in a restaurant (Ch. 11)

Sort out these phrases spoken by a head waiter and a customer at his restaurant in order to make an intelligible conversation. If you are working with a partner, take a part each. The customer begins.

Customer	*Head waiter*
Für zwei	Für wieviele Personen?
Ich möchte einen Tisch	Guten Abend
Guten Abend	Kommen Sie, bitte

Test 3 – Reserving a table by phone (Ch. 11)

Now try to sort this one out. The customer begins.

Customer	*Head waiter*
Um acht Uhr	Auf welchen Namen
Für zwei	Für wann?
Guten Tag!	Ist in Ordnung
Ich möchte einen Tisch	Für wieviele Personen?
Auf Wiederhören!	Um wieviel Uhr?
Schmidt	Guten Tag!
Für heute Abend	

Test 4 – Ordering food in a restaurant (Ch. 11)

Order the following dishes:

One apple pie	Three herring fillets
Two roast chickens	Two fruit cocktails
One boiled egg	One pepper steak
Two portions of duck	Two grape juices
Three portions of liver	One portion of pickled cabbage
One meat loaf	Three portions of pork

Test 5 – Asking to borrow things (Ch. 12)

What would you say if you had very accommodating neighbours?

1. You want to borrow a table for a party.
2. Could you have a friend's dress, just for the evening?
3. There's one extra for dinner; you need another chair.
4. Your pullover has a stain.
5. You didn't have time to wash your shirt.
6. You ought really to have a blouse to go with that skirt.
7. There's a button off your jacket.
8. You have just torn your trousers.
9. It's raining and you have left your raincoat at the office.
10. The children need another nightdress for dressing up in.

Test 6 – A Riddle (Ch. 13)
How can you mention all the days of the working week, without saying Monday, Tuesday, Wednesday, etc.?

Test 7 – Using the dative to express liking (Ch. 13)
Answer the following questions. The ticks and crosses will give you a clue as to the answer you should give.
1. Gefällt Ihnen das Wetter? ✓
2. Gefällt Ihnen der Sonnenschein? ✓
3. Gefällt Ihnen der Regen? ✗
4. Gefällt Ihnen der Schnee? ✓
5. Gefällt Ihnen der Wind? ✗
6. Gefällt Ihnen die Landschaft? ✓
7. Gefällt Ihnen das Meer? ✓
8. Gefällt Ihnen der Nebel? (fog) ✗
9. Gefällt Ihnen der Strand? ✗
10. Gefallen Ihnen die Berge? ✓

Test 8 – Types of accommodation (ch. 14)
      (cf. also indefinite article, Ch. 5)
Translate into German
1. I live in a house.
2. I live in an owner-occupied flat.
3. I live in a one-family house.
4. I live in a terraced house.
5. I live in a house divided up into flats.
6. I live in a detached house.
7. I live in a two-family house.
8. I live in a flat.
9. I live in a council flat.
10. I live in a rented flat.

Test 9 – Saying what you like doing (Ch. 15)
How would it be if you were the sort of person who only likes doing things which can be done in the open air and which involve being very energetic?
1. Reiten Sie gern?
2. Fahren Sie gern Ski?
3. Fahren Sie gern mit dem Rad?
4. Reisen Sie gern?
5. Spielen Sie gern Klavier?
6. Spielen Sie gern Karten?

Test 10 – Describing hobbies and interests (Ch. 15)

What would you say to somebody who said to you Haben Sie ein Hobby?

1. Assuming that you were interested in music.
2. If you were interested in pictures.
3. If your passion was collecting books.
4. Assuming you were a keen photographer.
5. If you were a football fan.
6. If you liked watching athletics.

Test 11 – Saying what you must/have to do (Ch. 16)

Here is a page from Fritz's diary. Can you answer the questions below?

So	Elke besuchen
Mo	die Karten abholen
Di	nach Nürnberg fahren
Mi	eine Kette für Elke kaufen
Do	einen Tennisschläger kaufen
Fr	nach Stuttgart fahren
Sa	im Bett bleiben

1. Was muß Fritz am Donnerstag machen?
2. Was muß er am Dienstag machen?
3. Was muß er am Sonntag machen?
4. Was muß er am Mittwoch machen?
5. Was muß er am Montag machen?
6. Was muß er am Freitag machen?
7. Was muß er am Samstag machen?

Test 12 – Können and wollen (Ch. 17)

Translate into German

1. Can you play tennis?
2. Shall we go for a walk?
3. Can you dance?
4. He can swim.

5. They want to play football.
6. We can play cards.
7. Shall we go to London?
8. Can she sing?
9. He doesn't want to drink.
10. You can't swim.

II REFERENCE MATERIAL

PRONUNCIATION KEY

The best way to get a good pronunciation is to practise with the sound recording. You should listen to each word as it is spoken on the tape, concentrating on the particular sound to be practised. This is indicated by underlining. You should pay particular attention to the vowel sounds because, in comparison with English pronunciation, a greater proportion of them in German are pure, that is to say they consist of one vowel sound only. There are, however, some diphthongs in German, and these are indicated separately. When a word, or part of a word, begins with a vowel, it is uttered with a slight explosion of breath at the back of the throat, similar to a very slight cough. This is called a 'glottal stop'. On the whole the consonants of German are the same as in English, and the learning problem here is to become used to the fact that certain letters of the alphabet indicate different sounds in German from English.

VOWELS

/a/ is pronounced like /bunker/
Example: Danke – thank you
/a/	– long is pronounced like /father/	Example: Tag – day
/e/	is pronounced like /pet/	Example: welcher – which
/e/	– long is pronounced like /fey/	Example: Tee – tea
/i/	is pronounced like /bit/	Example: bitte – please
/ie/	– long is pronounced like /here/	Example: hier – here
/o/	is pronounced like /coffer/	Example: Koffer – suitcase
/o/	– long is pronounced like /grown/	Example: wohnen – to live
/u/	is pronounced like /pull/	Example: und – and
/u/	– long is pronounced like /moot/	Example: Guten Tag – Good Day

MODIFIED VOWELS

The vowel sounds shown above are changed slightly by the addition of an *Umlaut* (¨).
/ä/	is pronounced like /peck/	Example: Äpfel – apples
/ä/	– long is pronounced like /late/	Example: spät – late
/ö/	– is pronounced like /cur/	Example: Streichhölzer – matches

/ö/   – long is pronounced like /t<u>ur</u>n/   Example: schön – beautiful

/ü/   This sound does not exist in English, and the way to make it is to purse your lips as if to whistle, and then without moving them say a short /i/   Example: hübsch – pretty

/ü/   – long   Purse the lips the same way, as if to whistle, and without moving them say /ee/   Example: Bücher – books

/ei/   is pronounced like /m<u>i</u>ne/   Example: nein – no

/au/   is pronounced like /h<u>ow</u>l/   Example: Frau – Mrs

/eu/   is pronounced like /c<u>oy</u>/   Example: heute – today

/äu/   is pronounced like /c<u>oy</u>/   Example: Fräulein – Miss

When a vowel comes before two consonants, it is usually 'short', e.g. Äpfel, bitte. When a vowel comes before a single consonant, or the letter 'h', it is usually 'long', e.g. wohnen, hier.

CONSONANTS

These are the main differences from English:

/j/   is pronounced like /<u>y</u>acht/   Example: ja – yes

/r/   This sound is made at the back of the mouth when it comes at the beginning or the middle of a word. Example: Frau – Mrs

/v/   is pronounced like /<u>f</u>an/   Example: von – from

/w/   is pronounced like /<u>v</u>ase/   Example: wieder – again

/z/   is pronounced like /cat<u>s</u>/   Example: Zimmer – room

     Note that English has this sound, but does not put it at the beginning of a word as German does.

/ch/   when it follows the vowels a, o, u, or au is pronounced like /lo<u>ch</u>/   Example: Bach – stream

/ch/   when it comes anywhere else is pronounced like /h<u>u</u>ge/   Example: ich – I

/sch/   is pronounced like /<u>sh</u>ip/   Example: schön – beautiful

/sp/   is pronounced like /<u>sh</u>p/   Example: spät – late

/st/   is pronounced like /<u>sh</u>t/   Example: Stein – stone

/s/   when it comes before vowels has a buzzing sound like /<u>zoo</u>/   Example: Sie – you

/s/   in other positions is pronounced like /hou<u>s</u>e/   Example: ist – is

               Rathaus – town hall

/b/   when it occurs at the end of a word or a syllable is pronounced like /p/   Example: grob – vulgar

/d/   when it comes at the end of a word or a syllable is pronounced like /t/   Example: Hand – hand

/g/   when it comes after /i/ (-ig) is pronounced like /ch/ as in the Scottish 'lo<u>ch</u>'   Example: hungrig – hungry

Students are warned that the pronunciation key given here is only an approximation. Treat the key as a rough guide. If you are able to implement it, it will make you understandable amongst speakers of German, but to obtain a really good accent you should practise with the sound recording.

STRESS

The best way to learn how the syllables of German words are stressed is to listen carefully to the recorded dialogues.

As an additional help, the *word lists* show the stressed syllables in bold type. The letters of the German alphabet are virtually the same as in English. There are four exceptions. These are asterisked.

Aa	The two dots over the vowels /a/o/u/
Ää *	are called an UMLAUT.
Bb	
Cc	The symbol between /s/ and /t/ is called sz
Dd	
Ee	
Ff	
Gg	
Hh	
Ii	
Jj	
Kk	
Ll	
Mm	
Nn	
Oo	
Öö *	
Pp	
Qq	
Rr	
Ss	
ß *	
Tt	
Uu	
Üü *	
Vv	
Ww	
Xx	
Yy	
Zz	

ANSWERS TO EXERCISES

Chapter 1 Greetings and Introductions

Answers to Exercise 1
1. Gute Nacht!
2. Viel Glück!
3. Prost/Zum Wohl!
4. Guten Morgen!
5. Gute Reise!
6. Gute Besserung!
7. Guten Abend!
8. Viel Spaß/Viel Vergnügen!
9. Guten Tag/Grüß Gott!

Answers to Exercise 2
1. Guten Abend, Herr Doktor!
2. Darf ich meine Frau vorstellen?
3. Angenehm.
4. Kommen Sie herein.
5. Bitte, nehmen Sie Platz.
6. Danke schön für die Einladung.
7. Eine Tasse Kaffee?
8. Bitte sehr!
9. Nein, danke.
10. Entschuldigen Sie!

Answers to Exercise 3
1. Guten Abend!
2. Danke/Danke schön.
3. Sehr gut, danke.
4. Angenehm.
5. Danke.
6. It depends, doesn't it? Either Bitte sehr or Nein, danke.

Chapter 2 Getting about

Answers to Exercise 1
1. Wie komme ich zum Krankenhaus?
2. Wie komme ich zur Sparkasse?
3. Wie komme ich zum Bahnhof?
4. Wie komme ich zum Sportplatz?
5. Wie komme ich zum Hallenbad?
6. Wie komme ich zum Freibad?
7. Wie komme ich zur Grundschule?
8. Wie komme ich zum Altenheim?
9. Wie komme ich zur Kapuzinerkirche?
10. Wie komme ich zum Campingplatz?
11. Wie komme ich zum Kindergarten?
12. Wie komme ich zur Reithalle?
13. Wie komme ich zum Minigolfplatz?
14. Wie komme ich zum Waldrestaurant?
15. Wie komme ich zum Marktplatz?
16. Wie komme ich zur Post?
17. Wie komme ich zum Rathaus?
18. Wie komme ich zum Dom?
19. Wie komme ich zum Parkplatz?

Answers to Exercise 2
1. Wie komme ich zur Audi-Werkstatt?
2. Wie komme ich zur Volkswagen-Werkstatt?
3. Wie komme ich zur Opel-Werkstatt?
4. Wie komme ich zur Ford-Werkstatt?
5. Hard luck, you'd better go on to Munich.

Answers to Exercise 3
1. Wie komme ich nach Warburg?
2. Wie komme ich nach Brakel?
3. Wie komme ich nach Eissen?
4. Wie komme ich nach Manrode?
5. Wie komme ich nach Offendorf?
6. Wie kommen wir nach Paderborn?
7. Wie kommen wir nach Detmold?
8. Wie kommen wir nach Peckelsheim?
9. Wie kommen wir nach Steinheim?
10. Wie kommen wir nach Holzminden?

Answers to Exercise 4
1. *A*: Wie weit ist es nach Dessau?
   B: Einundzwanzig Kilometer ungefähr.
2. *A*: Wie weit ist es nach Halle?
   B: Zweiundfünfzig Kilometer ungefähr.
3. *A*: Wie weit ist es nach Jena?
   B: Hundertein Kilometer ungefähr.

4. *A*: Wie weit ist es nach Linz?
   B: Dreiundzwanzig Kilometer ungefähr.
5. *A*: Wie weit ist es nach Kitzbühel?
   B: Neununddreißig Kilometer ungefähr.
6. *A*: Wie weit ist es nach Kufstein?
   B: Neun Kilometer ungefähr.
7. *A*: Wie weit ist es nach Zürich?
   B: Sechsundfünfzig Kilometer ungefähr.
8. *A*: Wie weit ist es nach Tübingen?
   B: Einundsiebzig Kilometer ungefähr.
9. *A*: Wie weit ist es nach Ansbach?
   B: Sechsundfünfzig Kilometer ungefähr.
10. *A*: Wie weit ist es nach Fulda?
    B: Fünfundvierzig Kilometer ungefähr.

Chapter 3 Staying in hotels

Section A

Answers to Exercise 1

1. *Guest*: Haben Sie ein Zimmer frei?
   Hotel: Jawohl. Was für ein Zimmer?
   Guest: Ein Einzelzimmer.
   Hotel: Für wie lange?
   Guest: Für eine Nacht.

2. *Guest*: Haben Sie ein Zimmer frei?
   Hotel: Jawohl. Was für ein Zimmer?
   Guest: Ein Einzelzimmer mit Dusche.
   Hotel: Für wie lange?
   Guest: Für eine Nacht.

3. *Guest*: Haben Sie ein Zimmer frei?
   Hotel: Jawohl. Was für ein Zimmer?
   Guest: Ein Doppelzimmer mit Bad.
   Hotel: Für wie lange?
   Guest: Für zwei Nächte.

4. *Guest*: Haben Sie ein Zimmer frei?
   Hotel: Jawohl. Was für ein Zimmer?
   Guest: Ein Einzelzimmer mit Dusche.
   Hotel: Für wie lange?
   Guest: Für eine Woche.

5. *Guest*: Haben Sie ein Zimmer frei?
   Hotel: Jawohl. Was für ein Zimmer?
   Guest: Ein Zweibettzimmer.
   Hotel: Für wie lange?
   Guest: Für zwei Nächte.

6. *Guest*: Haben Sie ein Zimmer frei?
   Hotel: Jawohl. Was für ein Zimmer?

Guest: Ein Doppelzimmer mit Dusche.
Hotel: Für wie lange?
Guest: Für eine Woche.

7. *Guest*: Haben Sie ein Zimmer frei?
   Hotel: Jawohl. Was für ein Zimmer?
   Guest: Ein Einzelzimmer mit Bad.
   Hotel: Für wie lange?
   Guest: Für drei Nächte.

8. *Guest*: Haben Sie ein Zimmer frei?
   Hotel: Jawohl. Was für ein Zimmer?
   Guest: Ein Doppelzimmer.
   Hotel: Für wie lange?
   Guest: Für vier Nächte.

9. *Guest*: Haben Sie ein Zimmer frei?
   Hotel: Jawohl. Was für ein Zimmer?
   Guest: Ein Einzelzimmer.
   Hotel: Für wie lange?
   Guest: Für drei Nächte.

10. *Guest*: Haben Sie ein Zimmer frei?
    Hotel: Jawohl. Was für ein Zimmer?
    Guest: Ein Einzelzimmer mit Dusche.
    Hotel: Für wie lange?
    Guest: Für zwei Nächte.

Answers to Exercise 2

Schmidt
1. Guten Tag!

3. Haben Sie ein Zimmer frei?

5. Haben Sie ein Einzelzimmer frei?

7. Für eine Nacht.

9. Ich nehme das Zimmer.

Empfang

2. Guten Tag, der Herr!

4. Ja, ein Zimmer habe ich.

6. Für wie lange, bitte?

8. Für eine Nacht.
   Das geht in Ordnung.

10. Tragen Sie sich bitte ein!

Answers to Exercise 3

Müller
1. Guten Tag!

3. Haben Sie ein Zimmer frei?

5. Haben Sie ein Doppelzimmer
   frei? – mit Bad?

Rezeption

2. Grüß Gott!

4. Ja, das ist möglich.

6. Ja, ein Doppelzimmer habe ich
   noch. Für wieviele Nächte,
   bitte?

7. Von heute bis Sonntag.

9. Ich nehme das Zimmer.

8. Ja, das geht.

10. Bitte, tragen Sie sich ein.

Section B

Answers to Exercise 4
1. Haben Sie ein Einzelzimmer?
2. Wie lange bleiben Sie?
3. Ich nehme das Zimmer.
4. Entschuldigen Sie, bitte.
5. Wie komme ich nach Stauting?
6. Fahren Sie hier geradeaus.
7. Er biegt hier nach links ab.
8. Nehmen Sie dann die erste Straße links.
9. Gehen Sie die Marktstraße hoch.
10. Haben Sie einen Tisch für zwei?
11. Ich habe einen Tisch um 8 Uhr.
12. Sie bleiben eine Nacht.
13. Sie kommen zur Adriastraße.

Answers to Exercise 5
1. Der zweite Mai neunzehnhundertachtundsiebzig.
2. Der sechzehnte Juni neunzehnhundertzweiundachtzig.
3. Der einunddreißigste Dezember neunzehnhundertneunundsiebzig.
4. Der elfte August neunzehnhundertzweiundachtzig.
5. Der siebenundzwanzigste März neunzehnhundertdreiundachtzig.
6. Der siebzehnte Mai neunzehnhundertfünfundachtzig.

Chapter 4 Travelling by train

Section A

Answers to Exercise 1
1. Um wieviel Uhr/Wann fährt der Zug nach Nürnberg?
2. Um wieviel Uhr/Wann fährt der Zug nach Würzburg?
3. Um wieviel Uhr/Wann fährt der Zug nach Innsbruck?
4. Um wieviel Uhr/Wann fährt der Zug nach Frankfurt?
5. Um wieviel Uhr/Wann fährt der Zug nach Treuchtlingen?
6. Um wieviel Uhr/Wann fährt der Zug nach Erlangen?
7. Um wieviel Uhr/Wann fährt der Zug nach Ansbach?
8. Um wieviel Uhr/Wann fährt der Zug nach Großhabersdorf?
9. Um wieviel Uhr/Wann fährt der Zug nach Forchheim?
10. Um wieviel Uhr/Wann fährt der Zug nach Schwabach?

Answers to Exercise 2
1. *Reisender*: Zweimal zweiter Klasse nach Hamburg, bitte.
   Angestellte: Hin und zurück?
   Reisender: Nein, einfach.

2. *Reisender*: Einmal zweiter Klasse nach Bremen, bitte.
   Angestellte: Hin und zurück?
   Reisender: Ja, hin und zurück, bitte.

3. *Reisender*: Einmal erster Klasse nach Hamm, bitte.
   Angestellte: Hin und zurück?
   Reisender: Nein, einfach.

4. *Reisender*: Einmal erster Klasse nach Münster, bitte.
   Angestellte: Hin und zurück?
   Reisender: Ja, hin und zurück, bitte.

5. *Reisender*: Dreimal zweiter Klasse nach Dortmund, bitte.
   Angestellte: Hin und zurück?
   Reisender: Nein, einfach.

6. *Reisender*: Zweimal zweiter Klasse nach Düsseldorf, bitte.
   Angestellte: Hin und zurück?
   Reisender: Nein, einfach.

7. *Reisender*: Zweimal zweiter Klasse nach Bonn, bitte.
   Angestellte: Hin und zurück?
   Reisender: Ja, hin und zurück bitte.

8. *Reisender*: Einmal erster Klasse nach Koblenz, bitte.
   Angestellte: Hin und zurück?
   Reisender: Ja, hin und zurück, bitte.

9. *Reisender*: Zweimal zweiter Klasse nach Köln, bitte.
   Angestellte: Hin und zurück?
   Reisender: Nein, einfach.

10. *Reisender*: Dreimal erster Klasse nach München, bitte.
    Angestellte: Hin und zurück?
    Reisender: Ja, hin und zurück, bitte.

Section B

Answers to Exercise 3
1. Oma ruft am Samstag an.
2. Ingrid geht am Dienstag aus.
3. Die Kinder räumen den Laden auf.
4. Mutter räumt die Spielsachen auf.
5. Peter wäscht die Teller ab.
6. Inge kauft Lebensmittel ein.
7. Helmut wäscht am Sonntag ab.
8. Der Chef gibt seine Arbeit auf.
9. Maria schließt den Laden ab.
10. Oma geht am Samstag aus.

Answers to Exercise 4
1. Wann fährt der Zug nach Bonn ab?
2. Wir schließen den Laden ab.
3. Oma geht am Dienstag aus.
4. Peter ruft am Mittwoch an.

5. Der Chef kauft Lebensmittel ein.
6. Mutter wäscht die Teller ab.
7. Die Kinder trocknen die Teller ab.
8. Er kauft Lebensmittel ein.
9. Der Chef gibt seine Arbeit auf.
10. Ich räume die Spielsachen auf.

Chapter 5 Travelling by taxi, bus or tram

Section A

Answers to Exercise 1
Fährt dieser Bus nach Egersdorf?
Fährt dieser Bus nach Steinach?
Fährt dieser Bus zum Stadttheater?
Fährt dieser Bus zum Rathaus?
Fährt dieser Bus zum Flughafen?
Fährt dieser Bus zur Stadtmitte?
Fährt dieser Bus zur Goethestraße?

Fährt diese Straßenbahn nach Egersdorf?
Fährt diese Straßenbahn nach Steinach?
Fährt diese Straßenbahn zum Stadttheater?
Fährt diese Straßenbahn zum Rathaus?
Fährt diese Straßenbahn zum Flughafen?
Fährt diese Straßenbahn zur Stadtmitte?
Fährt diese Straßenbahn zur Goethestraße?

Fährt dieser Zug nach Egersdorf?
Fährt dieser Zug nach Steinach?
Fährt dieser Zug zum Stadttheater?
Fährt dieser Zug zum Rathaus?
Fährt dieser Zug zum Flughafen?
Fährt dieser Zug zur Stadtmitte?
Fährt dieser Zug zur Goethestraße?

Fährt die Nummer 15 nach Egersdorf?
Fährt die Nummer 15 nach Steinach?
Fährt die Nummer 15 zum Stadttheater?
Fährt die Nummer 15 zum Rathaus?
Fährt die Nummer 15 zum Flughafen?
Fährt die Nummer 15 zur Stadtmitte?
Fährt die Nummer 15 zur Goethestraße?

Answers to Exercise 2
1. Fährt die (Nummer) 17 zum Rathaus?
2. Fährt die (Nummer) 17 zur Oper?
3. Fährt die (Nummer) 17 nach Perlach?
4. Fährt die (Nummer) 23 zur Stadtmitte?
5. Fährt die (Nummer) 31 zum Flughafen?
6. Fährt die (Nummer) 1 zum Freibad?

7. Welche Straßenbahn fährt zum Hauptbahnhof?
8. Welcher Bus fährt zur Heidenstraße?
9. Welcher Bus fährt nach Egersdorf?
10. Welcher Bus fährt nach Göttingen?

Answers to Exercise 3
1. Er hat kein Auto.
2. Sie möchte keinen Kaffee.
3. Er ist kein Professor.
4. Sie hat keine Einladung.
5. Wir haben keinen Hund.
6. Das ist nicht der Bahnhof.
7. Der Garten ist nicht groß.
8. Der Vater ist nicht alt.
9. Frau Meier ist nicht jung.
10. Santos ist nicht in Hamburg.

Chapter 6 Illness

Section A

Answers to Exercise 1
1. Ich habe Zahnschmerzen.
2. Ich habe Bauchschmerzen.
3. Ich habe Kopfschmerzen.
4. Ich habe Halsschmerzen.
5. Ich habe Ohrenschmerzen.
6. Ich habe Fieber.
7. Meine Füße tun weh.
8. Ich habe Durchfall.
9. Mein Knie tut weh.
10. Ich habe Fieber.

Answers to Exercise 2

Patient

1. Guten Tag, Herr Doktor.

Arzt

2. Guten Tag. Was fehlt Ihnen?

3. Ich habe Halsschmerzen.

4. Seit wann haben Sie Halsschmerzen?

5. Seit drei Tagen.

6. Ich verschreibe Ihnen etwas für die Halsschmerzen.

Answers to Exercise 3

Mein Kopf tut weh.
Mein Bein tut weh.
Mein Fuß tut weh.
Meine Hand tut weh.
Mein Rücken tut weh.

Mein Arm tut weh.
Mein Bauch tut weh.
Mein Ohr tut weh.
Mein Knie tut weh.
Mein Zahn tut weh.

Section B

Answers to Exercise 4
1. Nein, das ist kein gutes Buch.
2. Nein, das ist keine schöne Frau.
3. Nein, das ist keine ruhige Straße.
4. Nein, das ist kein ruhiges Zimmer.
5. Nein, das war kein schöner Abend.
6. Nein, das war keine gute Reise.
7. Nein, das war keine ruhige Nacht.
8. Nein, das war kein schöner Ausblick.

Answers to Exercise 5
1. Nein, ich habe keine ruhige Frau.
2. Nein, ich habe kein gutes Zimmer.
3. Nein, ich habe keinen schönen Ausblick.
4. Nein, ich habe kein neues Buch.
5. Nein, ich habe keinen neuen Fußball.
6. Nein, ich habe keinen guten Doktor.
7. Nein, ich habe keine nette Schwester.
8. Nein, ich habe keine ruhige Straße.

Chapter 7 Shopping

Section A

Answers to Exercise 1
1. *Verkäuferin*: Was darf es sein?
   Kundin: Ich möchte einen Rock.
   Verkäuferin: Welche Größe brauchen Sie?
   Kundin: Größe 40.
   Verkäuferin: An welches Material hatten Sie gedacht?
   Kundin: Popeline.
   Verkäuferin: Welche Farbe möchten Sie?
   Kundin: Ich möchte dunkelrot, bitte.
   Verkäuferin: Der ist sehr elegant.
   Kundin: Ja, er gefällt mir.
   Was kostet er?

2. *Verkäuferin*: Was darf es sein?
   Kundin: Ich möchte eine Bluse.
   Verkäuferin: Welche Größe brauchen Sie?
   Kundin: Größe 42.
   Verkäuferin: An welches Material hatten Sie gedacht?
   Kundin: Krepp.
   Verkäuferin: Welche Farbe möchten Sie?
   Kundin: Ich möchte rosa, bitte.
   Verkäuferin: Die ist sehr elegant.
   Kundin: Ja, sie gefällt mir.
   Was kostet sie?

3. *Verkäuferin*: Was darf es sein?
   Kunde: Ich möchte ein Hemd.
   Verkäuferin: Welche Größe brauchen Sie?
   Kunde: Größe 38.
   Verkäuferin: An welches Material hatten Sie gedacht?
   Kunde: Seide.
   Verkäuferin: Welche Farbe möchten Sie?
   Kunde: Ich möchte weiß, bitte.
   Verkäuferin: Das ist sehr elegant.
   Kunde: Ja, es gefällt mir.
   Was kostet es?

4. *Verkäuferin*: Was darf es sein?
   Kunde: Ich möchte eine Jacke.
   Verkäuferin: Welche Größe brauchen Sie?
   Kunde: Größe 46.
   Verkäuferin: An welches Material hatten Sie gedacht?
   Kunde: Leder.
   Verkäuferin: Welche Farbe möchten Sie?
   Kunde: Ich möchte dunkelbraun.
   Verkäuferin: Die ist sehr elegant.
   Kunde: Ja, sie gefällt mir.
   Was kostet sie?

Answers to Exercise 2

1. Ja, der gefällt mir. Was kostet er?
2. Ja, die gefällt mir. Was kostet sie?
3. Ja, das gefällt mir. Was kostet es?
4. Ja, die gefällt mir. Was kostet sie?
5. Ja, die gefällt mir. Was kostet sie?
6. Ja, der gefällt mir. Was kostet er?
7. Ja, der gefällt mir. Was kostet er?
8. Ja, die gefällt mir. Was kostet sie?
9. Ja, die gefällt mir. Was kostet sie?
10. Ja, das gefällt mir. Was kostet es?

Section B

Answers to Exercise 3

1. I'm only looking.
2. I'd like a pullover.
3. I don't know exactly.
4. Which material were you thinking of?
5. The blue pullover is certainly very nice.
6. I need a new pair of shoes.
7. I always wear size 40.
8. Can I try it on?
9. Have you any shoes with leather soles?
10. That's too expensive for me.

Answers to Exercise 4

1. Was kosten sie?

2. Die Schuhe gefallen mir gar nicht.
3. Sind die Sohlen aus Leder?
4. Haben Sie diese Art eine Größe kleiner?
5. Was kosten die braunen Schuhe im Schaufenster?
6. Ich möchte ein Nachthemd.
7. Ich schaue mich nur um.
8. Das Hemd ist aus Seide.
9. Was kosten die Schuhe?
10. Der Pullover ist mir zu teuer.

Answers to Exercise 5
1. Das weiße Hemd.
2. Die rote Hose.
3. Die schwarzen Schuhe.
4. Das lange Kleid.
5. Die braune Jacke.
6. Das hellblaue Hemd.
7. Der braune Anzug.
8. Der kurze Regenmantel.
9. Die grüne Bluse.
10. Das kleine schwarze Kleid.

Chapter 8 Families and nationalities

Section A

Answers to Exercise 1
1. *Pfarrer*: Sagen Sie, Herr Schmidt.
   Sind Sie verheiratet?
   Herr Schmidt: Geschieden.
   Pfarrer: Und haben Sie Kinder?
   Herr Schmidt: Nein, ich habe keine Kinder.
   Pfarrer: Es ist besser so.

2. *Pfarrer*: Sagen Sie, Herr Schmidt.
   Sind Sie verheiratet?
   Herr Schmidt: Nein, ich bin verwitwet.
   Pfarrer: Und haben Sie Kinder?
   Herr Schmidt: Ja, ich habe drei Kinder.
   Pfarrer: Ach so!

3. *Pfarrer*: Sagen Sie, Herr Schmidt.
   Sind Sie verheiratet?
   Herr Schmidt: Ja, aber wir leben getrennt.
   Pfarrer: Und haben Sie Kinder?
   Herr Schmidt: Ja, ich habe ein Kind.
   Pfarrer: Ach so!

4. *Pfarrer*: Sagen Sie, Herr Schmidt.
   Sind Sie verheiratet?
   Herr Schmidt: Nein, ich bin nicht verheiratet.

Answers to Exercise 2

1. *Question*: Sind Sie verheiratet?
   Answer: Ja.
   Question: Und haben Sie Kinder?
   Answer: Ja, wir haben ein Baby.

2. *Question*: Sind Sie verheiratet?
   Answer: Ja.
   Question: Und haben Sie Kinder?
   Answer: Ja, wir haben einen Sohn und eine Tochter.

3. *Question*: Sind Sie verheiratet?
   Answer: Ja.
   Question: Und haben Sie Kinder?
   Answer: Ja, wir haben zwei Töchter.

4. *Question*: Sind Sie verheiratet?
   Answer: Ja.
   Question: Und haben Sie Kinder?
   Answer: Ja, wir haben drei Söhne.

5. *Question*: Sind Sie verheiratet?
   Answer: Ja.
   Question: Und haben Sie Kinder?
   Answer: Ja, wir haben vier Söhne und eine Tochter.

Section B

Answers to Exercise 3
1. Ich bin Architekt.
2. Ich bin Lehrerin.
3. Ich bin Polizistin.
4. Ich bin Arzt.
5. Ich bin Studentin.
6. Ich bin Lehrer.
7. Ich bin Verkäufer.
8. Ich bin Verkäuferin.

Chapter 9 Places and weather

Answers to Exercise 1
1. Nicht weit von Bremen.
2. Nicht weit von Hannover.
3. Nicht weit von Bielefeld.
4. Nicht weit von Koblenz.
5. Nicht weit von Frankfurt.
6. Nicht weit von Mannheim.
7. Nicht weit von Nürnberg.
8. Nicht weit von München.
9. Nicht weit von Stuttgart.
10. Nicht weit von Salzburg.

Answers to Exercise 2

1. Kiel ist in Norddeutschland.
2. Passau ist in Süddeutschland.
3. Lübeck ist in Norddeutschland.
4. München ist in Süddeutschland.
5. Hamburg ist in Norddeutschland.
6. Augsburg ist in Süddeutschland.
7. Oldenburg ist in Norddeutschland.
8. Ulm ist in Süddeutschland.
9. Bremen ist in Norddeutschland.
10. Freiburg ist in Süddeutschland.

Answers to Exercise 3

1. Zu Weihnachten.
2. Bei meinen Eltern.
3. Aus diesem Grund.
4. Aus Versehen.
5. Bei diesem Wetter.
6. Mit dem Zug.
7. Zu Fuß.
8. Nach meiner Meinung/Meiner Meinung nach.
9. Bei der Arbeit.
10. Nach einer halben Stunde.

Answers to Exercise 4

1. Sie kommt mit einem eleganten Kleid.
2. Er hat einen süddeutschen Akzent.
3. Es gibt eine schöne Kirche dort.
4. Mein kleiner Bruder wohnt in Hamburg.
5. Bad Reichenhall ist nicht weit von einem hohen Berg.
6. Dort gibt es ein großes Kurhaus.
7. Bei Schaffhausen ist ein großer See.
8. Die Zugspitze ist ein hoher Berg.
9. Er hat ein weißes Hemd.
10. Sie trägt einen blauen Pullover.

Chapter 10 Revision

Answers to Test 1

Das ist meine Frau.
Das ist mein Vater.
Das ist meine Mutter.
Das ist mein Sohn.
Das ist meine Tochter.
Das ist mein Onkel.
Das ist meine Tante.

Answers to Test 2

Das ist unser Garten.
Das ist unsere Küche.

Das ist unser Schlafzimmer.
Das ist unsere Garage.
Das ist unser Hund.
Das ist unsere Katze.

Answers to Test 3
1. Guten Morgen!
2. Prost/Zum Wohl!
3. Entschuldigen Sie bitte!
4. Viel Spaß/Viel Vergnügen!
5. Entschuldigen Sie vielmals!
6. Gute Besserung!
7. Gute Nacht!
8. Entschuldigung!/Entschuldigen Sie!
9. Entschuldigen Sie, bitte!
10. Guten Appetit!

Answers to Test 4
Hiermit bestätige ich meine Reservierung für:
1. ein Doppelzimmer mit Bad
2. ein Einzelzimmer mit Dusche
3. ein Zweibettzimmer mit Dusche
4. ein Einzelzimmer
5. ein Doppelzimmer

für die Zeit vom:
1. 1. August bis zum 13. August einschließlich
2. 4. April bis zum 7. April einschließlich
3. 10. Juni bis zum 12. Juni einschließlich
4. 10. August bis zum 17. August einschließlich
5. 26. Februar bis zum 28. Februar einschließlich
Hochachtungsvoll.

Answers to Test 5
Empfang: Grüß Gott!
You: Grüß Gott!
       Haben Sie ein Zimmer frei, bitte?
Empfang: Möchten Sie ein Einzelzimmer oder ein Doppelzimmer?
You: Ich möchte ein Doppelzimmer bitte.
Empfang: Ja, das ist möglich.
   Fur wieviele Nächte, bitte?
You: Für 3 Nächte bitte.
Empfang: Möchten Sie das Zimmer mit Bad oder mit Dusche?
You: Mit Dusche, bitte.
Empfang: Ja, ein Doppelzimmer mit Dusche habe ich.
   Das geht in Ordnung.
You: Was kostet das Zimmer?
Empfang: Das Zimmer kostet 55 Mark pro Nacht.
You: Ist das mit Frühstück?
Empfang: Jawohl.
You: Ist das mit Mehrwertsteuer?
Empfang: Ja, selbstverständlich.

You:　Ich nehme das Zimmer.
Empfang:　Tragen Sie sich bitte ein.

Answers to Test 6

1. *Reisender*:　Wann fährt der Zug nach Freiburg ab?
   Angestellte:　Er fährt um 9 Uhr 45 ab.
   Reisender:　Wann kommt er in Freiburg an?
   Angestellte:　Er kommt um 17.03 an.
   Reisender:　Muß ich umsteigen?
   Angestellte:　Nein, der Zug fährt direkt.

2. *Reisender*:　Wann fährt der Zug nach Fulda ab?
   Angestellte:　Er fährt um 11 Uhr 14 ab.
   Reisender:　Wann kommt er in Fulda an?
   Angestellte:　Er kommt um 13.36 an.
   Reisender:　Muß ich umsteigen?
   Angestellte:　Nein, der Zug fährt direkt.

3. *Reisender*:　Wann fährt der Zug nach Basel ab?
   Angestellte:　Er fährt um 12.10 ab.
   Reisender:　Wann kommt er in Basel an?
   Angestellte:　Er kommt um 17.46 an.
   Reisender:　Muß ich umsteigen?
   Angestellte:　Nein, der Zug fährt direkt.

4. *Reisender*:　Wann fährt der Zug nach Freiburg ab?
   Angestellte:　Er fährt um 15.34 ab.
   Reisender:　Wann kommt er in Freiburg an?
   Angestellte:　Er kommt um 17.03 an.
   Reisender:　Muß ich umsteigen?
   Angestellte:　Nein, der Zug fährt direkt.

5. *Reisender*:　Wann fährt der Zug nach Karlsruhe ab?
   Angestellte:　Er fährt um 13.37 ab.
   Reisender:　Wann kommt er in Karlsruhe an?
   Angestellte:　Er kommt um 16.02 an.
   Reisender:　Muß ich umsteigen?
   Angestellte:　Nein, der Zug fährt direkt.

6. *Reisender*:　Wann fährt der Zug nach Basel ab?
   Angestellte:　Er fährt um 17.04 ab.
   Reisender:　Wann kommt er in Basel an?
   Angestellte:　Er kommt um 17.46 an.
   Reisender:　Muß ich umsteigen?
   Angestellte:　Nein, der Zug fährt direkt.

7. *Reisender*:　Wann fährt der Zug nach Freiburg ab?
   Angestellte:　Er fährt um 14.42 ab.
   Reisender:　Wann kommt er in Freiburg an?
   Angestellte:　Er kommt um 17.03 an.
   Reisender:　Muß ich umsteigen?
   Angestellte:　Nein, der Zug fährt direkt.

8. *Reisender*: Wann fährt der Zug nach Frankfurt ab?
   Angestellte: Er fährt um 10.00 ab.
   Reisender: Wann kommt er in Frankfurt an?
   Angestellte: Er kommt um 14.36 an.
   Reisender: Muß ich umsteigen?
   Angestellte: Nein, der Zug fährt direkt.

9. *Reisender*: Wann fährt der Zug nach Frankfurt ab?
   Angestellte: Er fährt um 11 Uhr 14 ab.
   Reisender: Wann kommt er in Frankfurt an?
   Angestellte: Er kommt um 14.36 an.
   Reisender: Muß ich umsteigen?
   Angestellte: Nein, der Zug fährt direkt.

10. *Reisender*: Wann fährt der Zug nach Basel ab?
    Angestellte: Er fährt um 16.03 ab.
    Reisender: Wann kommt er in Basel an?
    Angestellte: Er kommt um 17.46 an.
    Reisender: Muß ich umsteigen?
    Angestellte: Nein, der Zug fährt direkt.

Answers to Test 7
1. Oma ruft am Samstag an.
2. Ingrid geht am Dienstag aus.
3. Die Kinder räumen den Laden auf.
4. Mutter räumt die Spielzeuge auf.
5. Peter wäscht die Teller ab.
6. Inge kauft Lebensmittel ein.
7. Helmut wäscht am Sonntag auf.
8. Der Chef gibt seine Arbeit auf.
9. Maria schließt den Laden ab.
10. Oma geht am Samstag aus.

Answers to Test 8
Dialogue A
Müller: Entschuldigen Sie, bitte!
Meier: Ja, bitte?
Müller: Fährt dieser Bus nach Opladen?
Meier: Nach Opladen?
Nein, dieser Bus fährt nach Ludwigshafen.
Müller: Welcher Bus fährt nach Opladen?
Meier: Sie brauchen die Nummer 14.

Dialogue B
Schmidt: Entschuldigen Sie, bitte!
Schüth: Ja. Kann ich Ihnen helfen?
Schmidt: Fährt diese Straßenbahn zum Schauspielhaus?
Schüth: Nein, nicht zum Schauspielhaus.
Sie fährt zum Hofgarten.
Schmidt: Welche Straßenbahn fährt zum Schauspielhaus?
Schüth: Sie brauchen die Nummer 1.

Sie fährt zum Schauspielhaus.
Schmidt: Danke schön.

Answers to Test 9
1. Der Professor heißt Doktor Schmidt.
2. Wo ist die Tasse?
3. Hier ist das Buch.
4. Der Kaffee ist heiß.
5. Hier ist die Frau.
6. Das Auto fährt schnell.
7. Der Mann heißt Herr Müller.
8. Die Einladung kommt heute.
9. Das Schlafzimmer ist groß.
10. Die Küche ist klein.

Answers to Test 10
Arzt

1. Guten Tag.

3. Was fehlt Ihnen denn?

5. Ihr Bein?
   Ist es ein leichter Schmerz?

7. Ach so, stichartig.
   Seit wann tut es weh?

9. So, so. Drei Tage schon.
   Kein Fußball für Sie.

Patient

2. Guten Tag, Herr Doktor.

4. Mein Bein tut weh.

6. Nein, es ist ein stichartiger
   Schmerz.

8. Seit drei Tagen.

10. O weh.

Answers to Test 11
Sepp: Ja, mein Kopf tut weh.
Ja, mein Bein tut weh.
Ja, mein Knie tut weh.
Ja, mein Rücken tut weh.
Ja, mein Hals tut weh.
Ja, mein Ellbogen tut weh.
Ja, mein Ohr tut weh.
Ja, meine Nase tut weh.
Ja, meine Schulter tut weh.
Ja, mein Finger tut weh.

Answers to Test 12
1. Haben Sie dieses Material in blau?
2. Haben Sie diese Art eine Nummer kleiner?
3. Haben Sie diese Farbe in Wolle?
4. Haben Sie diese Farbe eine Nummer größer?
5. Haben Sie dieses Material in hellblau?
6. Haben Sie diese Art in Baumwolle?

7. Haben Sie diese Farbe in Polyester?
8. Haben Sie diese Art in schwarz?
9. Haben Sie diese Art in Velours?
10. Haben Sie diese Größe in weiß?

Answers to Test 13

1. Es ist sehr heiß im Sommer und es regnet im Winter.
2. Es ist sehr heiß im Sommer und es schneit im Winter.
3. Es regnet im Sommer und es regnet im Winter.
4. Es ist sehr heiß im Sommer und es ist sehr kalt im Winter.
5. Es ist sehr heiß im Sommer und es regnet im Winter.

Chapter 11 Eating out

Section A

Answers to Exercise 1

1. *A*: Herr Ober! (Fräulein!)
   Ich möchte bestellen.
   B: Ja, bitte schön?
   A: Einmal Eisbein mit Sauerkraut.
   B: Einmal Eisbein mit Sauerkraut.
   Möchten Sie etwas zu trinken?
   A: Nein, danke.

2. *A*: Herr Ober! (Fräulein!)
   Ich möchte bestellen.
   B: Ja, bitte schön?
   A: Zweimal Austern
   B: Zweimal Austern
   A: Zweimal Seezungenfilet.
   B: Zweimal Seezungenfilet.
   A: Zweimal Zigeunersteak.
   B: Zweimal Zigeunersteak.
   A: Zweimal Ananas.
   B: Zweimal Ananas.
   Möchten Sie etwas zu trinken?
   A: Eine Flasche Rheinwein, bitte.
   B: Jawohl.

3. *A*: Herr Ober! (Fräulein!)
   Ich möchte bestellen.
   B: Ja, bitte schön?
   A: Einmal Rührei mit Schinken.
   B: Einmal Rührei.
   A: Einmal Frankfurter.
   B: Einmal Frankfurter.
   A: Und einmal Forelle.
   B: Einmal Forelle.
   Möchten Sie etwas zu trinken?
   A: Dreimal Mineralwasser, bitte.
   B: Jawohl.

MENU

HORS D'OEUVRES

Prawn cocktail
Jellied eel
Oysters

SOUPS

Chicken soup with noodles
Goulash soup
Onion soup

EGG DISHES

Scrambled egg
Fried eggs with ham
Omelette – various

FISH DISHES

Rollmop herring
Poached trout with green salad and
   boiled potatoes
Fillet of Dover sole with French
   beans and boiled potatoes

MEAT DISHES

Pickled knuckle of pork with
   sauerkraut
'Texas' steak with chips
   and mixed salad
Veal (or pork) escalope garnished
   with mushroom sauce and chips
Veal (or pork) escalope with
   breadcrumbs garnished with fried
   egg, salad and roast potatoes
Veal (or pork) escalope garnished
   with paprika sauce with onions,
   rice and green salad

FOR CHILDREN

Scrambled egg with ham
Two Frankfurters with chips

CHEESE

Emmenthal, butter, bread
Mixed cheese platter, butter, bread

DESSERTS

Mixed cold stewed fruit
Grapefruit
Pancakes
Pineapple flambé with cherry
   brandy

BEVERAGES

Beer   Pils
       Export
Quarter litre Moselle wine
             Rhine wine
Red wine

Sekt (German champagne)
Cognac
German brandy
Mineral water

Cup of coffee or tea
Pot (of coffee or tea)
OUR PRICES INCLUDE SERVICE AND VAT

4. *A*:   Herr Ober! (Fräulein!)
        Ich möchte bestellen.
    B: Ja, bitte schön?
    A: Einmal Rührei.
    B: Einmal Rührei.
    A: Einmal Spiegeleier mit Schinken.
    B: Einmal Spiegeleier.
    A: Einmal die Käseplatte.
    B: Einmal die Käseplatte.
        Möchten Sie etwas zu trinken?
    A: Zweimal Kaffee, bitte.
    B: Jawohl.

Answers to Exercise 2

1. Haben Sie einen Tisch für drei?
2. Fräulein!
3. Ich möchte bestellen.
4. Zweimal Krabbencocktail und einmal Aal in Aspik.
5. Dreimal Texas Steak.
6. Zwei Viertel Rotwein und einen Pils.
7. Zahlen, bitte!

Section B

Answers to Exercise 3

1. Möchten Sie auch eine Vorspeise?
2. Möchten Sie auch ein Mineralwasser?
3. Möchten Sie auch einen Cognac?
4. Möchten Sie auch eine Gulaschsuppe?
5. Möchten Sie auch eine Forelle?
6. Möchten Sie auch Salzkartoffeln?
7. Möchten Sie auch Eisbein?
8. Möchten Sie auch ein Wiener Schnitzel?
9. Möchten Sie auch eine Käseplatte?
10. Möchten Sie auch ein gemischtes Kompott?

Answers to Exercise 4

1. Wieviel Uhr ist es?
   Es ist ein Uhr.
2. Wieviel Uhr ist es?
   Es ist Mittag.
3. Wieviel Uhr ist es?
   Es ist fünf (Minuten) nach neun.
4. Wieviel Uhr ist es?
   Es ist viertel nach sechs.
5. Wieviel Uhr ist es?
   Es ist fünfundzwanzig (Minuten) nach vier.
6. Wieviel Uhr ist es?
   Es ist halb zehn.
7. Wieviel Uhr ist es?
   Es ist zehn (Minuten) nach elf.
8. Wieviel Uhr ist es?
   Es ist zwanzig (Minuten) nach sechs.
9. Wieviel Uhr ist es?
   Es ist halb zehn.
10. Wieviel Uhr ist es?
    Es ist viertel vor drei.

Chapter 12 Asking permission

Answers to Exercise 1

Kann ich Ihr Auto borgen, bitte?
Kann ich Ihre Zahnbürste borgen, bitte?
Kann ich Ihre Zahnpasta borgen, bitte?

Kann ich Ihren Rasierapparat borgen, bitte?
Kann ich Ihre Zeitung borgen, bitte?

Answers to Exercise 2
1. Selbstverständlich
2. Auf keinen Fall
3. Aber natürlich
4. Nein, das ist unmöglich
5. Selbstverständlich
6. Nein, es tut mir leid
7. Auf keinen Fall
8. Auf keinen Fall
9. Aber natürlich
10. Selbstverständlich

Answers to Exercise 3
1. Darf ich hier parken?
2. Kann ich Ihr Fahrrad borgen, bitte?
3. Kann ich etwas Zucker borgen, bitte?
4. Kann ich das Auto nehmen, bitte?
5. Kann ich Ihre Zahnbürste borgen, bitte?

Answers to Exercise 4
1. Kann ich Ihre Zeitung sehen, bitte?
2. Kann ich Ihr Auto borgen, bitte?
3. Kann ich Ihre Lampe haben, bitte, Frau Fiebiger?
4. Kann ich Ihren Fernsehapparat nehmen, bitte?
5. Kann ich Ihr Radio borgen, bitte, Herr Fiebiger?
6. Kann ich bitte Ihren Regenmantel nehmen, Frau Fiebiger?
7. Kann ich bitte Ihren Rasierapparat haben, Herr Fiebiger?
8. Kann ich bitte Ihre Zahnpasta borgen?
9. Kann ich bitte Ihr Buch sehen, Frau Fiebiger?
10. Kann ich bitte Ihren Kamm haben, Herr Fiebiger?

Chapter 13 Jobs and professions

Section A

Answers to Exercise 1
1. Herr Moezer ist Bäcker.
2. Frau Hacker ist Friseuse.
3. Fräulein Siegling ist Studentin.
4. Herr Mader ist Taxifahrer.
5. Frau Meyer ist Hausfrau.
6. Fräulein Bauer ist Sekretärin.
7. Frau Augustin ist Kellnerin.
8. Herr Flohr ist Polizist.
9. Herr Kahle ist Techniker.
10. Herr Löb ist Lehrer (Hauptschullehrer).

Answers to Exercise 2

1. *A*: Was sind Sie von Beruf, Herr Löb?
   B: Ich bin Lehrer.
   A: Wann beginnen Sie mit der Arbeit?
   B: Um acht Uhr.
   A: Wann haben Sie Feierabend?
   B: Ich habe um vierzehn Uhr (zwei Uhr) Feierabend.

2. *A*: Was sind Sie von Beruf, Frau Hacker?
   B: Ich bin Friseuse.
   A: Wann beginnen Sie mit der Arbeit?
   B: Um neun Uhr.
   A: Wann haben Sie Feierabend?
   B: Ich habe um achtzehn Uhr (sechs Uhr) Feierabend.

3. *A*: Was sind Sie von Beruf, Frau Augustin?
   B: Ich bin Kellnerin.
   A: Wann beginnen Sie mit der Arbeit?
   B: Um vierzehn Uhr (zwei Uhr).
   A: Wann haben Sie Feierabend?
   B: Ich habe um zweiundzwanzig Uhr dreißig (halb elf) Feierabend.

4. *A*: Was sind Sie von Beruf, Herr Mader?
   B: Ich bin Taxifahrer.
   A: Wann beginnen Sie mit der Arbeit?
   B: Um fünf Uhr.
   A: Wann haben Sie Feierabend?
   B: Ich habe um dreizehn Uhr (ein Uhr) Feierabend.

5. *A*: Was sind Sie von Beruf, Herr Moezer?
   B: Ich bin Bäcker.
   A: Wann beginnen Sie mit der Arbeit?
   B: Um vier Uhr.
   A: Wann haben Sie Feierabend?
   B: Ich habe um elf Uhr Feierabend.

Section B

Answers to Exercise 3

1. Gefällt Ihnen die Farbe?
2. Gefällt Ihnen die Landschaft?
3. Gefällt Ihnen das Auto?
4. Gefallen Ihnen die Schuhe?
5. Gefällt Ihnen der Wind?
6. Gefällt Ihnen das Material?
7. Gefällt Ihnen das Wetter?
8. Gefällt Ihnen der Schnee?
9. Gefallen Ihnen die Geschäfte?
10. Gefällt Ihnen der Regen?

Chapter 14 Accommodation

Section A

Answers to Exercise 1
1. Ja, ich habe ein Wohnzimmer.
2. Ja, ich habe ein Eßzimmer.
3. Ja, ich habe eine Küche.
4. Ja, ich habe ein Badezimmer.
5. Ja, ich habe ein Schlafzimmer.
6. Ja, ich habe eine Toilette.

Answers to Exercise 2
1. Ja, ich habe ein Wohnzimmer.
2. Nein, eine Garage habe ich nicht.
3. Nein, ein Eßzimmer habe ich nicht.
4. Nein, eine Terrasse habe ich nicht.
5. Ja, ich habe eine Küche.
6. Nein, einen Balkon habe ich nicht.
7. Ja, ich habe ein Badezimmer.
8. Nein, einen Garten habe ich nicht.

Answers to Exercise 3
Winkler: Ich habe ein Schwimmbad.
Helmut: Ich habe auch ein Schwimmbad.
Winkler: Ich habe einen Balkon.
Helmut: Ich habe auch einen Balkon.
Winkler: Ich habe einen Tennisplatz.
Helmut: Ich habe auch einen Tennisplatz.
Winkler: Ich habe eine Terrasse.
Helmut: Ich habe auch eine Terrasse.
Winkler: Ich habe viele Bäume.
Helmut: Ich habe auch viele Bäume.
Winkler: Ich habe viele Sträuche.
Helmut: Ich habe auch viele Sträuche.

Section B

Answers to Exercise 4
1. Ja, er wohnt in München.
2. Nein, er hat eine Einzimmerwohnung.
3. Ja, er hat ein Badezimmer.
4. Ja, er hat eine Küche.
5. Ja, er hat viele Bilder.
6. Antonios Onkel wohnt in Neapel (Napoli).
7. Nein, er hat ein Einzelhaus.
8. Er hat sechs Schlafzimmer.
9. Er hat zwei Gästezimmer.
10. Nein, Antonio hat eine Sozialwohnung.
11. Ja, er hat ein Eßzimmer.
12. Ja, er hat ein Badezimmer.

13. Ja, er hat eine Küche.
14. Nein, er hat einen Balkon.

Chapter 15 Hobbies and Interests

Section A

Answers to Exercise 1
1. Ich tanze gern.
2. Ich wandere sehr gern.
3. Ich male wirklich sehr gern.
4. Ich lese außerordentlich gern.
5. Ich singe furchtbar gern.

Answers to Exercise 2
1. Ich koche nicht gern.
2. Ich bastele gar nicht gern.
3. Ich tanze überhaupt nicht gern.

Answers to Exercise 3
1. Nein, ich tanze nicht gern.
2. Nein, ich wandere nicht gern.
3. Ja, ich male gern.
4. Ja, ich spiele gern Karten.
5. Nein, ich fahre nicht gern Ski.
6. Ja, ich lese gern.
7. Nein, ich singe nicht gern.
8. Nein, ich reite nicht gern.

Section B

Answers to Exercise 4
1. Ja, aber Rumenigge ist größer.
2. Ja, aber Rumenigge ist schneller.
3. Ja, aber Rumenigge ist gesünder.
4. Ja, aber Rumenigge ist stärker.
5. Ja, aber Rumenigge ist jünger.
6. Ja, aber Rumenigge ist klüger.
7. Ja, aber Rumenigge spielt härter.
8. Ja, aber Rumenigge spielt besser.

Chapter 16 'Want' and 'Must'

Answers to Exercise 1
1. Ich muß mein Geld mitnehmen.
2. Ich muß meine Stiefel mitnehmen.
3. Ich muß meinen Tennisschläger mitnehmen.
4. Ich muß meine Landkarte mitnehmen.
5. Ich muß meine Eintrittskarten mitnehmen.

6. Ich muß meine Badehose mitnehmen.
7. Ich muß meinen Reisepaß mitnehmen.
8. Ich muß meine Zahnbürste mitnehmen.
9. Ich muß meinen Regenschirm mitnehmen.

Answers to Exercise 2
1. Er muß Elke besuchen.
2. Er muß die Karten abholen.
3. Er muß nach Nürnberg fahren.
4. Er muß eine Kette für Elke kaufen.
5. Er muß einen Tennisschläger kaufen.
6. Er muß nach Stuttgart fahren.
7. Er muß im Bett bleiben.

Answers to Exercise 3
1. Nein, Sie brauchen Ihre Stiefel nicht mitnehmen.
2. Nein, Sie brauchen Ihre Landkarte nicht mitnehmen.
3. Nein, Sie brauchen Ihre Badehose nicht mitnehmen.
4. Nein, Sie brauchen Ihre Zahnbürste nicht mitnehmen.
5. Nein, Sie brauchen Ihre Schuhe nicht mitnehmen.
6. Nein, Sie brauchen Ihren Smoking nicht mitnehmen.
7. Nein, Sie brauchen Ihren Mantel nicht mitnehmen.
8. Nein, Sie brauchen Ihre Tabletten nicht mitnehmen.
9. Nein, Sie brauchen Ihr Buch nicht mitnehmen.
10. Nein, Sie brauchen Ihren Tennisschläger nicht mitnehmen.

Chapter 17 Suggestions and Proposals

Answers to Exercise 1
1. a) Karlheinz! Wollen wir Fußball spielen?
   b) Ja, gern.
2. a) Karlheinz! Wollen wir reiten?
   b) Nein, ich kann nicht reiten.
3. a) Karlheinz! Wollen wir Karten spielen?
   b) Ja, gern.
4. a) Karlheinz! Wollen wir Tennis spielen?
   b) Nein, ich kann nicht Tennis spielen.
5. a) Karlheinz! Wollen wir schwimmen gehen?
   b) Nein, ich kann nicht schwimmen.
6. a) Gertraute! Wollen wir tanzen gehen.
   b) Ja, gern.
7. a) Gertraute! Wollen wir Ski fahren?
   b) Nein, ich kann nicht Ski fahren.
8. a) Gertraute! Wollen wir einen Spaziergang machen?
   b) Ja, gern.
9. a) Gertraute! Wollen wir Fußball spielen?
   b) Nein, ich kann nicht Fußball spielen.
10. a) Gertraute! Wollen wir Karten spielen?
    b) Nein, ich kann nicht Karten spielen.

Answers to Exercise 2
1. Ja, ausgezeichnet.
2. Nein, nicht sehr gut.
3. Ja, ausgezeichnet.
4. Nein, nicht sehr gut.
5. Nein, nicht sehr gut.
6. Ja, ausgezeichnet.
7. Nein, nicht sehr gut.
8. Nein, nicht sehr gut.
9. Ja, ausgezeichnet.

Answers to Exercise 3
1. Der Junge geht in die Schule.
2. Der Lehrer arbeitet in der Schule.
3. Die Klasse kommt in das Klassenzimmer.
4. Die Mädchen warten in dem Klassenzimmer.
5. Das Radio steht auf dem Tisch.
6. Ich stelle die Milch in den Kühlschrank.
7. Das Bild hängt an der Wand.
8. Ich halte meine Zeitung unter dem Arm.
9. Ich gehe an die Tür.
10. Ich stelle die Tasse auf den Tisch.

Chapter 18 Dreams and Wishes

Answers to Exercise 1
1. Ich möchte ihn reinigen lassen.
2. Ich möchte sie reparieren lassen.
3. Ich möchte ihn reinigen lassen.
4. Ich möchte ihn reparieren lassen.
5. Ich möchte es reinigen lassen.
6. Ich möchte sie reinigen lassen.
7. Ich möchte sie reparieren lassen.

Answers to Exercise 2
1. Ich möchte reisen (die Welt sehen).
2. Ich möchte bezahlen.
3. Ich möchte telefonieren.
4. Ich möchte schlafen.
5. Ich möchte gehen.
6. Ich möchte Peter besuchen.
7. Ich möchte Fräulein Braun sprechen.
8. Ich möchte München sehen.
9. Ich möchte nach Bonn fahren.
10. Ich möchte mein Geld wechseln.

Answers to Exercise 3
1. Ich möchte mir die Haare waschen lassen.
2. Er will seinen Apparat reparieren lassen.

3. Elke will New York besuchen.
4. Ich möchte die Welt sehen.
5. Er möchte nach Hamburg fahren.
6. Wir müssen das Geld wechseln.
7. Wir möchten bezahlen.
8. Sie muß sich ein neues Kleid machen lassen.
9. Kann ich bitte Herrn Schmidt sprechen.
10. Sie will ihren Pelzmantel reinigen lassen.

Chapter 19 Talking about the past

Answers to Exercise 1
Montag – Ich bin nach Solingen gefahren.
Dienstag – Ich habe eine Armbanduhr gekauft.
Mittwoch – Ich habe eine Kette für Inge gesucht.
Donnerstag – Ich bin mit Elke ins Kino gegangen.
Freitag – Ich habe Wein mit Peter getrunken.
Samstag – Ich habe Bayern-München gegen Hamburg gesehen.
Sonntag – Ich bin in die Kirche gegangen.

Answers to Exercise 2
1. Ich war im Büro.
2. Ich war in der Post.
3. Ich war am Marktplatz.
4. Ich war im Gasthaus Bauer.
5. Ich war bei Müller.
6. Ich war im Café.
7. Ich war im Zug.

Answers to Exercise 3
1. Ich habe Bier getrunken.
2. Ich bin in die Stadt gegangen.
3. Er ist nach Bremen gefahren.
4. Wir sind um 8 Uhr gekommen.
5. Sie sind zu lange geblieben.
6. Sie hat ein Hemd gekauft.
7. Wir haben eine Wohnung gesucht.
8. Sie hat ihre Armbanduhr verloren.
9. Ich habe einen guten Film gesehen.
10. Sie haben Herrn Schüth getroffen.

Chapter 20 Revision

Answers to Test 1
Kellner: Guten Abend!
Sie: Guten Abend!
   Haben Sie einen Tisch für zwei?
Kellner: Kommen Sie, bitte.
Sie: Herr Ober!
Kellner: Bitte schön?

Sie: Die Speisekarte, bitte.
Kellner: Die Speisekarte, bitte schön.
Sie: Möchten Sie eine Vorspeise?
Freund(in): Ja, bitte.
Sie: Möchten Sie Austern?
Freund(in): Austern. O ja!
Sie: Zweimal Austern, bitte.
Kellner: Zweimal Austern.
Sie: Möchten Sie das Zigeuner Schnitzel?
Freund(in): Nein, danke. Ich möchte ein Jägerschnitzel.
Sie: Einmal Jägerschnitzel und einmal Wienerschnitzel.
Kellner: Jawohl.
Sie: Möchten Sie etwas zu trinken?
Freund(in): O ja. Ich möchte dein Jägerschnitzel.
Sie: Ich möchte auch einen Rotwein.
   Zwei Viertel Rotwein, bitte.
Kellner: Jawohl, mein Herr.

Answers to Test 2

Customer	*Head waiter*
Guten Abend!	Guten Abend!
Ich möchte einen Tisch	Fur wieviele Personen?
Für zwei	Kommen Sie, bitte.

Answers to Test 3

Customer	*Head waiter*
Guten Tag!	Guten Tag!
Ich möchte einen Tisch	Für wann?
Für heute abend.	Auf welchen Namen?
Schmidt	Für wieviele Personen?
Für zwei	Um wieviel Uhr?
Um acht Uhr	Ist in Ordnung
Auf Wiederhören!	

Answers to Test 4

Einmal Apfelkuchen	Dreimal Matjesfilet
Zweimal Brathähnchen	Zweimal Obstsalat
Ein gekochtes Ei	Einmal Pfeffersteak
Zweimal Ente	Zweimal Traubensaft
Dreimal Leber	Einmal Sauerkraut
Einmal Leberkäs	Dreimal Schweinefleisch

Answers to Test 5

1. Kann ich einen Tisch borgen, bitte?
2. Kann ich ein Kleid borgen, bitte?
3. Kann ich einen Stuhl borgen, bitte?
4. Kann ich einen Pullover borgen, bitte?
5. Kann ich ein Hemd borgen, bitte?
6. Kann ich eine Bluse borgen, bitte?
7. Kann ich eine Jacke borgen, bitte?

8. Kann ich eine Hose borgen, bitte?
9. Kann ich einen Regenmantel borgen, bitte?
10. Kann ich ein Nachthemd borgen, bitte?

Answer to Test 6
(Assume today is Wednesday):
Heute, gestern, vorgestern, morgen, übermorgen.

Answers to Test 7
1. Ja, das Wetter gefällt mir.
2. Ja, der Sonnenschein gefällt mir.
3. Nein, der Regen gefällt mir nicht.
4. Ja, der Schnee gefällt mir.
5. Nein, der Wind gefällt mir nicht.
6. Ja, die Landschaft gefällt mir.
7. Ja, das Meer gefällt mir.
8. Nein, der Nebel gefällt mir nicht.
9. Nein, der Strand gefällt mir nicht.
10. Ja, die Berge gefallen mir.

Answers to Test 8
1. Ich wohne in einem Haus.
2. Ich wohne in einer Eigentumswohnung.
3. Ich wohne in einem Einfamilienhaus.
4. Ich wohne in einem Reihenhaus.
5. Ich wohne in einem Mietshaus.
6. Ich wohne in einem Einzelhaus.
7. Ich wohne in einem Zweifamilienhaus.
8. Ich wohne in einer Wohnung.
9. Ich wohne in einer Sozialwohnung.
10. Ich wohne in einer Mietwohnung.

Answers to Test 9
1. Ja, ich reite gern.
2. Ja, ich fahre gern Ski.
3. Ja, ich fahre gern mit dem Rad.
4. Ja, ich reise gern.
5. Nein, ich spiele nicht gern Klavier.
6. Nein, ich spiele nicht gern Karten.

Answers to Test 10
1. Ich interessiere mich für Musik.
2. Ich interessiere mich für Bilder.
3. Ich interessiere mich für Bücher.
4. Ich interessiere mich für Fotografie.
5. Ich interessiere mich für Fußball.
6. Ich interessiere mich für Leichtathletik.

Answers to Test 11
1. Am Donnerstag muß er einen Tennisschläger kaufen.
2. Am Dienstag muß er nach Nürnberg fahren.

3. Am Sonntag muß er Elke besuchen.
4. Am Mittwoch muß er eine Kette für Elke kaufen.
5. Am Montag muß er die Karten abholen.
6. Am Freitag muß er nach Stuttgart fahren.
7. Am Samstag muß er im Bett bleiben.

Answers to Test 12
1. Können Sie Tennis spielen?
2. Wollen wir spazieren gehen?
3. Können Sie tanzen?
4. Er kann schwimmen.
5. Sie wollen Fußball spielen.
6. Wir können Karten spielen.
7. Wollen wir nach London fahren?
8. Kann sie singen?
9. Er will nicht trinken.
10. Sie können nicht schwimmen.

TRANSLATIONS
OF DIALOGUES

The following translations give equivalents of the German dialogues.

Chapter 1 Greetings and Introductions

Dialogue 1
1   *Secretary*: Ah Professor Hecht! Good Morning (Good Afternoon).
   Professor Hecht: Good morning, Mrs Hausmann.
    Is Mr Kirchhof there?
   Secretary: Yes, just a moment.
5   Mr Kirchhof ...
    Professor Hecht is here.
    ...
   Mr Kirchhof: Good morning, Professor Hecht.
   Prof. Hecht: Good morning, Mr Kirchhof.
   Mr Kirchhof: Please come in.
10 *Prof. Hecht*: Thank you.
    How are you?
   Mr Kirchhof: Very well, thank you.
    Please sit down.
   Prof. Hecht: Thank you.
15 *Mr Kirchhof*: Would you like a cup of coffee?
   Prof. Hecht: Oh yes, please.
   Mr Kirchhof: Mrs Hausmann, two cups of
    coffee, please.
   Mrs Hausmann: Certainly.
20 *Mr Kirchhof*: Now, how is your wife?
   Prof. Hecht: Very well indeed.
   Mr Kirchhof: And how are Andreas and Daniella?
   Prof. Hecht: Very well, too.
   Mr Kirchhof: And here is the catalogue.
25 *Prof. Hecht*: Yes, the catalogue.

Dialogue 2
1   *Elke*: Good evening!
   Doctor Neumann: Elke, good evening!
   Elke: How nice.
    Do come in.

5 *Dr Neumann*:   Thank you.
Can I introduce my wife?
Elke: Good evening, Mrs Neumann.
Welcome!
Mrs Neumann: Good evening
10 Thank you for the invitation.
Elke: Not at all.
That's Fritz.
Fritz: Good evening!
My name is Löb.
15 *Elke*:   Eckhard!
Eckhard: Elke!
Elke: You here!
This is marvellous!
Eckhard: Elke, you are as beautiful as ever.
20 *Elke*:   Oh no.
Eckhard: Yes you are.
Elke: Oh yes.
That's Fritz.
Eckhard: My name is Becker.
25 Pleased to meet you.
Fritz: My name is Löb.
Pleased to meet you.
Elke: Excuse me!

Prof. Hecht: Goodbye.
30 Thank you very much.
Elke: Not at all.
Goodbye.

Chapter 2: Getting about

Dialogue 1
1 *Mrs Meyer*:   Excuse me!
How do I get to the Amalienstraße,
please?
Pedestrian: Sorry?
Mrs Meyer: The Amalienstraße.
5 How do I get to the Amalienstraße?
Pedestrian: Now let me see, the Amalienstraße.
Mrs Meyer: Terrible!
quite terrible!
Pedestrian: Sorry?
10 *Mrs Meyer*:   Everything is new here.
Pedestrian: Yes, that's right.
To the Adriastraße, wasn't it?
Mrs Meyer: No, not the Adriastraße,
to the Amalienstraße.
How do I get to the Amalienstraße?
15 *Pedestrian*:   Oh yes.
go straight on,

> then take the first street on the
> left.

Mrs Meyer: The first street on the left.

Pedestrian: That's Market Street.

20   Go up Market Street,
> then you come to the Amalienstraße.

Mrs Meyer: Thank you.

Pedestrian: That's quite all right.

Dialogue 2

1   *Elke*:   Excuse me!
> How do we get to Mittenwald?

Boy: Sorry?

Elke: To Mittenwald.

5   *Boy*:   I don't know.

Elke: Thank you.
> (Under her breath)
> Silly idiot!
> You, Fritz, ask that girl over there.

Fritz: Excuse me!

10   How do we get to Mittenwald?

Girl: To Mittenwald?
> Go straight on.

Fritz: Straight on.

Girl: To Garmisch.

15   Turn left when you get there.
> That is the B28.

Fritz: Is it far?

Girl: No.
> About twenty kilometres.

20   *Fritz*:   Thank you.

Girl: Keep going towards Innsbruck.

Fritz: Towards Innsbruck.
> Thank you.

Girl: That's all right.

Chapter 3 Staying in hotels

Dialogue 1

1   *Antonio*:   Good evening!

Receptionist: Good evening!

Antonio: I want to reserve a room.

Receptionist: Yes, how long for?

5   *Antonio*:   Five nights
> Monday to Saturday.

Receptionist: A single room or a
> double room?

Antonio: A double room.

Receptionist: With bath or shower?

10   *Antonio*:   With a shower.
> A quiet room.

Receptionist: Yes the room is nice and quiet.

Antonio: Good.

Receptionist: What is the name, please?

15 *Antonio*: Santos. S-A-N-T-O-S.

Receptionist: Thank you very much.

Antonio: How much is the room?

Receptionist: It costs 60 marks a night.

Antonio: Is that with breakfast?

20 *Receptionist*: Yes, that's with breakfast
and VAT.

Antonio: Thank you.

Receptionist: That's all right.

Dialogue 2

1 *Elke*: Good afternoon!

Receptionist: Good afternoon!

Elke: Have you a room, please?

Receptionist: Yes.

5 What sort of room?

Elke: A single room.
With bathroom.

Receptionist: For how many nights?

Elke: I'm staying two nights.

10 *Receptionist*: A single room with a bathroom.
Yes, I can do that.

Elke: What does the room cost?

Receptionist: It costs 95 marks a night
with breakfast.

Elke: I'll take it.

15 *Receptionist*: Would you please sign the register.
. . .
Your room is on the fifth floor.

Elke: Has the room got a view?

Receptionist: Yes, it's got a lovely view
over the Alster.

20 *Elke*: How nice.

Receptionist: Have you any luggage?

Elke: Yes, my luggage is here.

Receptionist: Porter!

Dialogue 3

1 *Receptionist*: Hotel Bayerischer Hof.

Fritz: Good afternoon!
Have you a room available for next
Saturday, please?

Receptionist: For the 12th?

5 *Fritz*: Yes, for Saturday the 12th.

Receptionist: No, I'm sorry,
we're completely booked up.

Fritz: Thank you.

Receptionist: Not at all.

Chapter 4: Travelling by train

Dialogue 1

1   *Mrs Meyer*: Good morning!
    Clerk: Good morning!
    Mrs Meyer: Second class ticket to Augsburg,
     please.
    Clerk: Single or return?
5   *Mrs Meyer*: Return please.
     How much is that?
    Clerk: Thirty-two marks.
    Mrs Meyer: What? As much as that!
    Clerk: Sorry!
10 *Mrs Meyer*: That's terrible!
    Clerk: There's nothing I can do about it.
    Mrs Meyer: Forty marks.
    Clerk: (counts) 33, 34, 35, 40, thank you.
    Mrs Meyer: Thank you.
15 (still grumbling) Thirty two marks.
    That's terrible!

    Mrs Meyer: Excuse me!
    Information: Yes?
    Mrs Meyer: What time is the train to Augsburg?
20 *Information*: Augsburg ... Augsburg ....
    The train leaves at 9.27 a.m.,
    and arrives at 10.13.
    Mrs Meyer: Thank you.
    Do I have to change?
25 *Information*: No. It's a through train.
    Mrs Meyer: Thank you.
    Information: You're welcome.

Dialogue 2

1   *Antonio*: Good morning!
    Clerk: Good morning!
    Antonio: Two second class tickets to Innsbruck.
    please.
    Clerk: Single or return?
5   *Antonio*: Single, please.
    Clerk: Two singles to Innsbruck.
    Ninety-eight marks, please.
    Antonio: Just a minute.
    A ticket to Innsbruck, too.
10 *Clerk*: Single?
    Antonio: No.
    Return.
    Clerk: Two singles.
    One return.
15 Is that right?
    Antonio: Yes, that's right.
    Clerk: That's 196 marks, please.

Antonio: What time does the train leave for
Innsbruck?
Information: At 9.31.
20 *Antonio*: Thank you.
Which platform?
Information: Platform 3.
Antonio: Thank you.
Information: That's OK.

Chapter 5: Travelling by taxi, bus or tram

Dialogue 1
1 *Elke*: I want a taxi,
please.
Clerk: What name?
Elke: Kustmann.
5 *Clerk*: What's your address?
Elke: Fürstenstraße 15.
Clerk: Where do you want to go to?
Elke: To the Nietzschestraße.
Clerk: The taxi will be there in 10 minutes.
10 *Elke*: Thank you.

Taxi Driver: Mrs Kustmann?
Elke: Yes.
Taxi Driver: Your taxi is here.
15 *Elke*: Nietzschestraße,
please.
Number 30.
Taxi Driver: All right.

Here you are.
20 *Elke*: How much is that?
Taxi driver: 6 marks 50.
Elke: Thank you.
That's all right.
25 *Taxi driver*: Thank you.
Goodbye.

Dialogue 2
1 *Mrs Meyer*: Excuse me!
Does the number 23 go to the town hall?
Man: No, not the 23.
Mrs Meyer: Good heavens!
5 Which tram does go to the
town hall then?
Man: You need number 18.
The 18 goes to the town hall.
Mrs Meyer: I see, thank you very much.
The number 18.
10 *Man*: Yes, that goes to the town hall.

> *Mrs Meyer*: (to herself)
> That's unheard of!!
> It was always the 23!!

Chapter 6: Illness

Dialogue 1

1 *Receptionist*: Doctor Storm's surgery.
    Good morning.
    Mrs Meyer: Good morning.
    I'd like to see the doctor.
5 *Receptionist*: Have you got an appointment?
    Mrs Meyer: No.
    Is this morning possible?
    Receptionist: No.
    I'm sorry.
10 There's no time available this morning.
    Mrs Meyer: Oh heavens above!
    Isn't there any time available?
    Receptionist: No.
    I'm sorry.
15 *Mrs Meyer*: Is this afternoon possible?
    Receptionist: Yes. Come at 4 o'clock.
    Mrs Meyer: Thank goodness!
    At 4 o'clock.
    Yes, that's all right.
20 Thank you.
    Receptionist: Goodbye.
    Mrs Meyer: Goodbye.

Dialogue 2

1 *Doctor Storm*: Now, what's the matter?
    Fritz: I've got a headache.
    Doctor Storm: Is that all?
    Fritz: No, doctor.
5 I've got a pain in my stomach and I've got diarrhoea.
    Doctor Storm: How long have you had diarrhoea?
    Fritz: Since yesterday.
    Doctor Storm: I'll prescribe something
    for the diarrhoea.
    Fritz: Thank you, doctor.

Dialogue 3

1 *Doctor Storm*: Now, where does it hurt?
    Antonio: Here,
    It's my back.
    Doctor Storm: Here?
5 *Antonio*: Ow!! Yes!
    Doctor Storm: Is it a sharp pain?
    Antonio: Yes! It's a shooting pain.

Doctor Storm: Is it always a shooting pain?
Antonio: No.
10   In the night it was a dull pain.
Doctor Storm: I see.
No more football for you.
Antonio: Oh dear.

Chapter 7: Shopping

Dialogue 1

1 *Saleswoman*: Can I help you?
Fritz: (speaking by instinct)
I'm just looking round.
Saleswoman: Yes, of course.
Fritz: (clears his throat)
Miss!
5 *Saleswoman*: Yes? Can I help you?
Fritz: I want a pullover.
Saleswoman: Yes. A gentleman's or a lady's pullover?
Fritz: I'm looking for a lady's pullover.
Saleswoman: Yes. What size does the lady take?
10 *Fritz*: Oh I don't know exactly.
Medium size, I think.
Saleswoman: Like me?
Fritz: (embarrassed and trying not to look too closely)
Yes, about like that.
Saleswoman: Yes, that's size 40.
15   What material were you thinking of?
Fritz: Oh yes. The material? Of course.
Saleswoman: Wool? Cotton? Nylon?
Fritz: Wool! Yes, wool.
Saleswoman: I've got a lovely red pullover here.
20   It's made of wool.
Fritz: No. She's already got a˙red pullover.
Have you got this sort of thing in blue?
Saleswoman: Has the lady got blue eyes?
Fritz: Yes, (she has) actually.
25 *Saleswoman*: I've got a blue pullover here.
Fritz: Yes. The blue pullover is really very nice.
What does it cost?
Saleswoman: 65 Marks.
Fritz: I'll take it.

Dialogue 2

1 *Salesman*: Can I help you?
Mrs Meyer: I need some new shoes.
Salesman: Yes, of course.
(looking at Mrs Meyer's shoes)
You take size 4½, I think.
5 *Mrs Meyer*: No. I always take size 4.

Salesman: (sceptically)
Really?
Mrs Meyer: How much do the brown shoes cost in the window?
Salesman: They are size 4½.
10 *Mrs Meyer*: Have you got the brown shoes a size smaller?
Salesman: Yes, I've got the same shoes here.
But they're black.
Mrs Meyer: Can I try them on?
15 *Salesman*: Of course you can try them on.
Mrs Meyer: (taking a few steps)
Ow!!! That hurts!
They're too small.
Salesman: Would you like to try on the brown shoes?
Mrs Meyer: Are the soles made of leather?
20 *Salesman*: No. The brown shoes have got crepe soles.
Mrs Meyer: Crepe soles! That's terrible!
I don't like that at all.
Haven't you got any shoes with leather soles?
25 *Salesman*: Certainly.
Look!
These blue shoes are very elegant.
They are made entirely of leather.
Mrs Meyer: What size are they?
30 *Salesman*: Size 4½.
Mrs Meyer: How much do they cost?
Salesman: They cost 145 marks.
Mrs Meyer: What? That's too expensive!
Goodbye!
35 *Salesman*: Goodbye!
Mrs Meyer: (grumbling to herself) Disgusting! It's
disgusting! 145 marks!

Chapter 8 Families and nationalities

Dialogue 1

1 *Antonio*: Good day!
Owner: Good day!
Antonio: I've come about the job
as a waiter.
Owner: Oh yes.
5 Do you have any experience?
Antonio: No, unfortunately.
Owner: Hmm. Can you speak Italian?
Antonio: Of course.
I am Italian.
10 *Owner*: Oh, you are Italian.
Where do you come from?
Antonio: I come from Naples.
Owner: Naples! Naples!
I come from Benevento.
15 *Antonio*: That's wonderful!

My Aunt Concetta comes from
Benevento.

Owner: No!

Antonio: Yes, she does.

Owner: That's fantastic!

20   When can you begin?

Dialogue 2

1 *Parson*:   The church is very old, Mr
Löb.

Fritz: Yes, one can see that.

Parson: Over three hundred years old.

Fritz: Really?

5 *Parson*:   Yes
Look.
The altar is beautiful, isn't it?

Fritz: That's true.
It's very beautiful.

10 *Parson*:   Riemenschneider.

Fritz: Really.
Tilman Riemenschneider.

Parson: Yes.
Tell me, Mr Löb.

15   What do you do (What are you by profession?)
if I may ask? (If you don't mind my asking?)

Fritz: I'm a teacher.
In Munich.

Parson: Really.
Are you married?

20 *Fritz*:   Yes. That's to say, we're
separated.

Parson: I'm sorry.

Fritz: Thank you.

Parson: Have you got any children?

Fritz: No, I haven't got any children.

25 *Parson*:   Perhaps it's better that way.

Fritz: Yes, it's better that way.
Young children need a father.

Parson: That's right.

Chapter 9: Places and weather

Dialogue 1

1 *Man*:   I beg your pardon!

Elke: Yes?

Man: I just wanted to say ...
that's a very elegant dress.

5 *Elke*:   Oh, thank you.
That's very nice of you.

Man: You have a north German accent.

     Elke: Yes. I come from Mölln.

     Man: Mölln? Where is Mölln?

10 *Elke*: In North Germany.

         Not far from Hamburg.

     Man: Oh yes. Near Hamburg.

     Elke: Yes. Between Hamburg and Lübeck.

     Man: What is the countryside like there?

15 *Elke*: There's a large lake there,

         and a very beautiful church.

     Man: Have you still got any family there?

     Elke: Yes. My brother lives in Mölln,

         with my parents.

     Man: Oh, you've got a brother.

20 *Elke*: Yes. He's coming to Munich next week.

         He's an enthusiastic skier.

     Man: Isn't there any snow in Mölln then?

     Elke: No. It rains a lot in winter.

         But there's not much snow.

25 *Man*: Oh, I see.

Dialogue 2

 1 *Antonio*: Cheers!

     Girl: Cheers!

     Antonio: Are you from Munich

     Girl: No. I come from Bad Reichenhall.

 5 *Antonio*: Where is Bad Reichenhall?

     Girl: Not far from Salzburg.

         And you?

     Antonio: I come from Naples.

         But I'm a 'Münchener' now.

10 *Girl*: Oh, I see.

     Antonio: What is there to see there,

         in Bad Reichenhall?

     Girl: There is a fine pump room,

         and nice shops.

     Antonio: And the countryside?

         What is the countryside like there?

15 *Girl*: Oh the countryside is wonderful!

         There are high mountains.

     Antonio: That's nice.

     Girl: Yes. The Predigtstuhl for example.

         That is a very high mountain.

20 *Antonio*: What's the weather like?

     Girl: It's usually nice.

         There is a lot of snow in winter.

     Antonio: And in summer?

     Girl: It rains sometimes in summer.

25   Unfortunately.

Chapter 11: Eating out

Dialogue 1

1 *Owner*: Blue House Restaurant.
  Good morning (or good afternoon).
  Fritz: Good morning!
  I should like a table for this evening.
5 *Owner*: For how many people?
  Fritz: For two.
  Owner: At what time?
  Fritz: At 8 o'clock.
  Owner: Yes, at 8 o'clock.
10 I have a table for 8 o'clock.
  Fritz: Good.
  Owner: What name please?
  Fritz: Löb (spells his name) L – Ö – B.
  Owner: Mr Löb.
15 That's all right, Mr Löb.
  Fritz: Goodbye.
  Owner: Goodbye.

  Fritz: Good evening!
  Reception: Good evening!
20 *Fritz*: I have reserved a table.
  Reception: For how many people?
  Fritz: For two poeple.
  Reception: What name, please?
  Fritz: Löb.
25 *Reception*: Oh, yes.
  Mr Löb
  This way, please.

Dialogue 2

1 *Fritz*: Would you like a starter?
  Elke: I'd like some soup –
  some onion soup.
  Fritz: And then?
  Elke: A Texas steak.
5 And you?
  What would you like?
  Fritz: I think I'd like some soup, tco –
  some goulash soup.
  And then ... Texas steak as well.
10 *Waiter*: Have you chosen?
  Fritz: One onion soup.
  One goulash soup.
  Waiter: One onion soup.
  One goulash soup.
15 *Fritz*: And then – two Texas steaks.

    Elke: Without chips, please.

    Waiter: Two Texas steaks.

        One with chips.

        One without.

20   Very good.

    Fritz: Would you like something to drink?

    Elke: Yes, I'd like a quarter of red wine, please.

    Fritz: Two quarters of red wine, please.

    Waiter: Two quarters of red wine.

25   Thank you.

Chapter 12: Asking permission

Dialogue 1

1 *Antonio*:   Excuse me!

      (louder) Excuse me!

    Policeman: Yes?

    Antonio: Can I park here?

5 *Policeman*:   No. Sorry.

      You're not allowed to park here.

    Antonio: (pointing) What about over there?

      Can I park over there?

    Policeman: No.

10   You're not allowed to park there either.

    Antonio: Damn!

      Where can I park then?

    Policeman: In the multi-storey car park.

      Drive to the multi-storey car park.

15 *Antonio*:   To the car park! To the car park!

      OK, to the car park.

Dialogue 2

1 *Mrs Meyer*:   Yes?

      Oh, it's you, Mr Löb.

    Fritz: Good morning, Mrs Meyer!

      Excuse me for disturbing you.

5 *Mrs Meyer*:   What can I do for you?

    Fritz: Mrs Meyer, my car won't start.

      The battery has run out, I think.

    Mrs Meyer: I'm sorry.

    Fritz: Can I borrow your bicycle?

10 *Mrs Meyer*:   My bicycle?

      Yes, of course you can.

      It's downstairs in the cellar.

    Fritz: Thank you very much.

      Oh, can I borrow the pump as well?

15 *Mrs Meyer*:   Of course you can.

      You can borrow the pump too.

    Fritz: Thank you very much.

    Mrs Meyer: That's quite all right.

Mind how you go.
20 *Fritz*:   Yes, of course.

Chapter 13: Jobs and professions

Dialogue 1
1 *Mrs Meyer*:   Yes?
        Oh, it's you. Mr Löb.
    Fritz: Good morning, Mrs Meyer.
        Excuse me for disturbing you.
5   Here is your bicycle.
    Mrs Meyer: Thank you very much.
        Was everything all right?
    Fritz: Yes, everything was all right.
        Thank you very much.
10 *Mrs Meyer*:   You are a teacher, aren't you?
    Fritz: Yes, that's right.
    Mrs Meyer: Do you like your work?
    Fritz: Oh yes, very much.
    Mrs Meyer: When do you begin in the morning?
15 *Fritz*:   We begin at eight o'clock.
    Mrs Meyer: Oh, I see.
        And when do you normally come home?
    Fritz: I usually come home about two o'clock.
    Mrs Meyer: How many days do you work a week?
20 *Fritz*:   Only five.
        Thank heavens!
    Mrs Meyer: When I was a schoolgirl,
        we had school on Saturdays too.
    Fritz: Yes, we are better off.
25   Now, thank you very much again for the bicycle.
    Mrs Meyer: That's quite all right, Mr Löb.
        Goodbye.

Dialogue 2
1 *Man*:   What do you do (for a living),
        if you don't mind my asking?
    Elke: I'm a sales assistant.
    Man: Here in Munich?
    Elke: Yes, at Zilling Fashions.
5   In the Leopoldstraße.
    Man: Do you like the work?
    Elke: Oh, yes and no.
        The pay is very good.
    Man: When do you begin work?
10 *Elke*:   At eight o'clock.
    Man: And do you have a midday break?
    Elke: Yes. From twelve to one.
    Man: I have a midday break from twelve to one too.
    Elke: (ironically) Well now!

15   *Man*:   When do you come home in the evening?
     Elke: I'm free at five o'clock.
     Man: Me too.
        Could I pick you up at your shop?
        I have a car.
20   Perhaps we could drive out into the country.
     Elke: Thank you very much.
        But I have my own car.
     Man: Oh, I see.
     Elke: And today my boyfriend is coming at five o'clock.
25   We want to go shopping in the Viktualien Market.
     Man: Oh, that's a pity.
        Some other time perhaps.
     Elke: Perhaps.

Chapter 14: Accommodation

Dialogue 1

1   *Antonio*:   Cheers!
     Fritz: Cheers!
     Antonio: The punch is nice and warm, isn't it?
     Fritz: Yes, nice and warm.
5   *Antonio*:   Do you live here in Munich?
     Fritz: Yes, I live in the Nietzschestraße.
     Antonio: Do you live in a block of flats?
     Fritz: Yes, I have a one-room flat,
        in a large house divided up into flats.
10   *Antonio*:   Have you only got one room?
     Fritz: Well, I have a bathroom,
        and a kitchen.
     Antonio: Anything else?
     Fritz: Apart from that I have a bed-sitting room.
     Antonio: Is the flat nice?
15   *Fritz*:   Yes, it's small but quite nice.
        I have a lot of pictures there.
     Antonio: Pictures?
     Fritz: Yes.
        I collect pictures.
20   *Antonio*:   Hmm, interesting.

Dialogue 2

1   *Antonio*:   My uncle has got lots of pictures too.
     Fritz: Where does he live?
     Antonio: In Naples.
     Fritz: Ah, in Naples.
5   *Antonio*:   He's got a detached house.
     Fritz: That's nice.
     Antonio: He's got six bedrooms
        and two guest-rooms.
     Fritz: Good heavens!

Antonio: Just imagine that!
10   Six bedrooms!
Fritz: Has he got a garden too?
Antonio: I should say so!
He's got trees
and bushes everywhere.
Fritz: Very nice.
15 *Antonio*: As for me ...
I've got a council flat,
in the Kaufmannstraße.
Fritz: How many rooms have you got?
Antonio: I've got a dining-room,
and a bedroom.
Fritz: You've got a bathroom
and a kitchen?
20 *Antonio*: Of course!
And I've got a balcony.
That's nice.

Chapter 15: Hobbies and Interests

Dialogue 1
1 *Fritz*: Won't you come in?
Elke: Thank you.
Fritz: This is my one-room flat.
Elke: It's very nice.
5 *Fritz*: It's unfortunately a bit too small.
Elke: You've got a lot of pictures,
but they are all of churches.
Fritz: Yes, I'm interested in churches.
Elke: Yes, so I see.
10 *Fritz*: You know,
I like photography.
I like taking pictures of churches.
Elke: Yes, so I see.
Fritz: Would you like a cup of coffee?
15 *Elke*: Oh yes, please.
Fritz: Look ...
this church is beautiful, isn't it?
Elke: Hmm.
Fritz: It's Romanesque.
20 *Elke*: Really?
Fritz: Yes. I'm very interested in Romanesque churches.
I like taking photographs of them.
Elke: Yes, so I see.
Fritz: Oh, excuse me.
25   Your coffee.
Do you take sugar?
Elke: No, thank you.

272

Dialogue 2

 1 *Student*: Antonio!
   Antonio: What's the matter?
   Student: Nothing.
     I just wanted to tell you something.
 5 *Antonio*: Well then?
   Student: As you know,
     I'm interested in Italian.
   Antonio: Yes, I know.
   Student: And I like Italian food very much.
10 *Antonio*: Yes, I know that as well.
   Student: Well,
     yesterday I was in an Italian restaurant.
   Antonio: Whereabouts?
   Student: In St Mark's Street.
15   It's called the Trattoria Giovanni.
   Antonio: I don't know it.
     Is it good?
   Student: Well, I like pizza very much
     and the pizza was really good.
20 *Antonio*: Were you alone?
   Student: No, Birgit was there.
     She prefers cannelloni.
   Antonio: Hmm. Was the cannelloni good as well?
   Student: Not bad, I believe.
25 *Antonio*: I must go there too.
     I love pizza.

Chapter 16: 'Want' and 'Must'

Dialogue 1

 1 *Elke*: Fritz! Do you know what?
   Fritz: No.
   Elke: Herr Zilling has got tickets for Parsifal
     and he can't go.
 5 *Fritz*: That's bad luck
   Elke: For him
     but not for us.
   Fritz: How's that?
   Elke: Shall we take the tickets?
   Fritz: What do they cost?
10 *Elke*: Sixty marks each.
   Fritz: That's expensive.
   Elke: It is Bayreuth, you know.
   Fritz: Yes.
     Must I put on my evening dress (i.e. dinner jacket)?
15 *Elke*: Well, that is normal.
     I want to put on my new dress.
   Fritz: Nice!
   Elke: I want to wear my mink coat, too.

Fritz: Aha!
20 *Elke:* And of course my pearl necklace.
Fritz: When must we decide?
Elke: Oh, immediately.
We do want to go, don't we?
Fritz: Oh yes, of course we do.
25 When must we pick up the tickets?

Dialogue 2

1 *Doctor Bauer:* Now, Mrs Meyer,
what's the matter with you?
Mrs Meyer: It's my head, doctor.
I keep on getting giddy.
Doctor Bauer: How old are you, Mrs Meyer?
5 *Mrs Meyer:* I'm 75 years old.
Doctor Bauer: And where do you live?
Mrs Meyer: In the Nietzschestraße.
Doctor Bauer: Where is your flat?
On the ground floor?
10 *Mrs Meyer:* No, doctor.
On the third floor.
Doctor Bauer: And you go shopping every day?
Mrs Meyer: Yes, and I fetch little Sandra from school.
15 *Doctor Bauer:* Yes, yes. Now Mrs Meyer,
You must run about a little bit less.
When do you get up in the morning?
Mrs Meyer: At six o'clock.
Doctor Bauer: You must stay in bed a bit longer,
20 and you must lie down for an hour every afternoon.
Mrs Meyer: Must I stay at home, doctor?
Doctor Bauer: No, you don't need to stay at home,
but you must take these tablets.
Mrs Meyer: Must I take them in the evening?
25 I shan't go to sleep.
Doctor Bauer: No, you don't need to take them in the evening.
Mrs Meyer: Thank heavens!

Chapter 17: Suggestions and Proposals

Dialogue 1

1 *Antonio:* Is this seat free?
Girl: Yes.
Antonio: Nice weather, isn't it?
Girl: Yes. Very nice.
5 *Antonio:* My name is Antonio.
Girl: Hmm.
Antonio: Antonio Santos.
. . .
Antonio: What's your name?
If you don't mind my asking?

10 *Girl*: Claudia.
   Antonio: Claudia. A nice name.
   Girl: Thank you.
   . . .
   Antonio: Tell me, Claudia.
   Can you play tennis?
15 *Girl*: Yes.
   Antonio: Good. Shall we play tennis?
   Girl: When?
   Antonio: Tomorrow, perhaps?
   Girl: Yes, I'd like to.
20 *Antonio*: Do you play often?
   Girl: Fairly often.
   Four or five times a week.
   Antonio: Where do you play?
   Girl: In the Carlton Club.
25 *Antonio*: Oh?
   Do you play well?
   Girl: Hmm, quite well.
   And you?
   Antonio: No, not very well.
   That's marvellous!!! (spoken ironically)

Dialogue 2

1 *Fritz*: Hello, Elke!
   Elke: It's you, Fritz!
   Come in!
   Fritz: Thank you.
5   How are you?
   Elke: Fine!
   Fritz: Elke . . . .
   Shall we go away at the weekend?
   Elke: Oh yes! Where to?
10 *Fritz*: I know a very pretty church
   near Rosenheim.
   Elke: Oh no, Fritz!
   Another church!
   Fritz: What's the matter?
15 *Elke*: Every time a church!
   Fritz: I'm interested in churches.
   You know that.
   Elke: But you have a different church every week.
   That's just too much.
20 *Fritz*: I'm sorry.
   Elke: Shall we go to Kufstein?
   We can go ski-ing there.
   Fritz: But I can't ski.
   Elke: But I can ski very well.
25 *Fritz*: All right.
   Let's go to Kufstein.
   Elke: Yes, you can learn
   (on the nursery slopes).

Chapter 18: Dreams and Wishes

Dialogue 1

1   *Elke*:   Fritz?
    Fritz: Yes?
    Elke: It's nice here, isn't it?
    Fritz: Yes. Lovely.
5   *Elke*:   You are really nice, you know.
    Fritz: Yes?
      . . .
    Elke: Fritz?
    Fritz: Yes?
    Elke: Do you know what?
10 *Fritz*:   No.
    Elke: I should like to go to America.
    Fritz: Really?
    Elke: Yes. I should like to see Hollywood.
    Fritz: Hollywood?
15 *Elke*:   Yes. And I should like to visit New York.
    Fritz: Oh, New York isn't nice.
    Elke: Yes, it is!
      And I should like to go on a tramcar in San Francisco.
20 *Fritz*:   Why do you want to go on a tramcar?
      You can do that in Munich.
    Elke: Oh, you don't understand.
      It's so romantic in San Francisco.
    Fritz: But expensive.
25 *Elke*:   That's typically male!!
      You only think about money.
      I want to travel.
      I want to see the world.

Dialogue 2

1   *Mrs Meyer*:   Leni?   Do you know what?
      Inge is going to have a baby!
    Leni: No. That's wonderful!
      Where is she?
5   *Mrs Meyer*:   In Liverpool.
    Leni: Oh yes, that's right.
      In England.
    Mrs Meyer: Of course I shall go to Liverpool.
    Leni: Yes, of course.
10 *Mrs Meyer*:   I must have my fur coat cleaned.
    Leni: Yes, of course.
    Mrs Meyer: And I must have a new dress made.
    Leni: Yes, of course.
    Mrs Meyer: And then I shall need a camera.
15   I must have my old camera repaired.
    Leni: Of course.
    Mrs Meyer: Then I must get some money changed too.
    Leni: Yes, of course.
    Mrs Meyer: What sort of money do they have in England?

20   Dollars, isn't it?
      Leni: No. They have pounds and pennies.
      Mrs Meyer: Oh yes. Of course.
      Then I must have my hair washed.
      Leni: Wait a minute, Irmgard.
25   When is Inge expecting her child?
      Mrs Meyer: Next year.
      In March.
      Leni: Look, Irmgard.
      You have got a lot of time.

Chapter 19: Talking about the past

Dialogue 1
1   *Fritz*: Good heavens!
     Where have you been?
     Elke: What's the matter?
     My bus was late.
5   *Fritz*: It was late yesterday.
     And today it was late again.
     Elke: My bus wasn't late yesterday.
     Fritz: Yes, it was!
     It was thirty minutes late.
10   *Elke*: That's not true.
     Fritz: Yes, it is true.
     I was at the cinema at seven o'clock.
     And you weren't there until seven thirty.
     Elke: I was there on time.
15   You were simply at the cinema too early.
     Fritz: And why weren't you on time the day before yesterday?
     Elke: I was in the shop.
     Fritz: What? Until eight o'clock?
     I don't believe it!
20   *Elke*: I had a lot to do.
     Fritz: And the boss was there too, wasn't he?
     Elke: Of course.
     He had a lot to do, too.
     Fritz: Ah hah. Now I understand ... !

Dialogue 2
1   *Antonio*: Can I help you?
     Mrs Meyer: Oh, I have lost my wristwatch.
     Antonio: Here on the street?
     Mrs Meyer: Yes, I think so,
5   I went into town.
     And I had some coffee there.
     Antonio: Do you think you have lost your watch in town?
     Mrs Meyer: No.
     I saw it in the tram.
10   *Antonio*: Have you looked at the tram stop?
     Mrs Meyer: Yes, of course.

I met Mrs Moezer there.

I went to the Post Office with her.

Antonio: Do you think you have lost the watch in the post office?

15 *Mrs Meyer*: No, I don't think so.

Antonio: Have you come here straight from the post office?

Mrs Meyer: No. I bought some apples first.

At Schötz's.

Antonio: I see. At Schötz's.

20 How long did you stay at Schötz's?

Mrs Meyer: Oh, not long.

Five minutes perhaps.

Antonio: Have you looked in your bag?

Mrs Meyer: What?

25 *Antonio*: Have you looked in your bag?

Mrs Meyer: Good Lord!

There it is!

GRAMMATICAL SUMMARY

SECTION A – WORD FAMILIES

1. Cardinal numbers
The cardinal numbers are as follows:

1	ein(s)	14	vierzehn	70	siebzig
2	zwei	15	fünfzehn	80	achtzig
3	drei	16	sechzehn	90	neunzig
4	vier	17	siebzehn	100	hundert
5	fünf	18	achtzehn	120	hundert(und) zwanzig
6	sechs	19	neunzehn	221	zweihundert- einundzwanzig
7	sieben	20	zwanzig	1,000	tausend
8	acht	21	einundzwanzig	1,101	eintausendein hundertundeins
9	neun	22	zweiundzwanzig	1,000,000	eine Million
10	zehn	30	dreißig	2,000,000	zwei Millionen
11	elf	40	vierzig		
12	zwölf	50	fünfzig		
13	dreizehn	60	sechzig		

Tausend is not generally used in dates: das Jahr neunzehnhundertzweiundachtzig, 'the year 1982'.

Slight irregularities are to be noticed in the numbers 16, 17, 30, 60 and 70.

Compound numbers of hundreds, tens and units (e.g. zweihunderteinundzwanzig) are usually written as one word.

2. Ordinal numbers
The ordinal numbers below 20 (except those meaning first, third and eighth) are formed by adding -t to the corresponding cardinal number; from 20 onwards they are formed by adding -st. When the number is a compound one, only the last part of the cardinal is changed into an ordinal:

1st	der erste	8th	der achte
2nd	der zweite	9th	der neunte
3rd	der dritte	10th	der zehnte

4th	der vierte		20th	der zwanzigste
5th	der fünfte		100th	der hundertste
6th	der sechste		101st	der hundert(und)erste
7th	der siebente/siebte		120th	der hundert(und)zwanzigste
			221st	der zweihunderteinund-zwanzigste

Der siebente is better than der siebte, which is sometimes used.

3. Days of the week

Sonntag	Sunday
Montag	Monday
Dienstag	Tuesday
Mittwoch	Wednesday
Donnerstag	Thursday
Freitag	Friday
Samstag/Sonnabend	Saturday

4. Parts of the body (Plural forms are given where relevant)

der Arm (-e)	arm	das Knie (-n)	knee
der Fuß (-̈e)	foot	das Auge (-n)	eye
die Lippe (-n)	lip	das Bein (-e)	leg
die Hand (-̈e)	hand	das Ohr (-en)	ear
der Zahn (-̈e)	tooth	der Finger (-)	finger
der Kopf (-̈e)	head	der Zeh (-en)	toe
die Schulter (-n)	shoulder	der Ellbogen (-)	elbow

der Mund	mouth
die Nase	nose
der Bauch	stomach
der Hals	neck

5. Nouns of nationality

Nouns of nationality make their feminine form in two ways:

(i) Nouns of nationality which end in e make their feminine form by changing the e into in. Here are some examples:

der Franzose	die Französin
der Däne	die Dänin
der Ire	die Irin
der Finne	die Finnin
der Grieche	die Griechin
der Nordire	die Nordirin
der Rumäne	die Rumänin
der Schotte	die Schottin
der Russe	die Russin
der Brite	die Britin
der Schwede	die Schwedin

(ii) Other nouns which end in er make their feminine form by adding in. Here are some examples:

der Engländer	die Engländerin
der Österreicher	die Österreicherin
der Belgier	die Belgierin
der Amerikaner	die Amerikanerin
der Holländer	die Holländerin
der Italiener	die Italienerin
der Norweger	die Norwegerin
der Spanier	die Spanierin
der Schweizer	die Schweizerin
der Waliser	die Waliserin

(iii) German nationality is the only exception:

der Deutsche	die Deutsche	Plural: die Deutschen
but:		
ein Deutscher	eine Deutsche	Plural: Deutsche

6. Sprechen Sie Deutsch?

The German for the most common European languages is as follows:

Bulgarisch
Dänisch
Deutsch
Englisch
Finnisch
Französisch
Griechisch
Holländisch
Italienisch
Norwegisch
Portugiesisch
Russisch
Schwedisch
Spanisch

7. The seasons

der Frühling/im Frühling
der Sommer/im Sommer
der Herbst/im Herbst
der Winter/im Winter

8. The months

Januar	Juli
Februar	August
März	September
April	Oktober
Mai	November
Juni	Dezember

SECTION B – VERBS

Important points to remember:

(i) All the infinitives end in -en or -n.

(ii) German does not distinguish between simple forms (I go), and continuous forms (I am going).

(iii) The questioning, or interrogative, form is made by putting the verb first and the subject second. There is no 'do' or 'does' in German.

9. Some important regular verbs used in *Mastering German*

These verbs are given in the present tense.

The verb KOMMEN – to come

ich komme	I come
du kommst	you come (familiar)
er kommt	he comes
sie kommt	she comes
wir kommen	we come
ihr kommt	you come (familiar plural)
Sie kommen	you come (formal or polite)
sie kommen	they come

The verb GEHEN – to go

ich gehe	I go
du gehst	you go (familiar)
er geht	he goes
sie geht	she goes
wir gehen	we go
ihr geht	you go (familiar plural)
Sie gehen	you go (formal or polite)
sie gehen	they go

The verb BLEIBEN – to stay/remain

ich bleibe	I stay/remain
du bleibst	you stay/remain (familiar)
er bleibt	he stays/remains
sie bleibt	she stays/remains
wir bleiben	we stay/remain
ihr bleibt	you stay/remain (familiar plural)
Sie bleiben	you stay/remain (formal or polite)
sie bleiben	they stay/remain

The verb SUCHEN – to seek/look for

ich suche	I'm looking for
du suchst	you're looking for (familiar)
er sucht	he's looking for
sie sucht	she's looking for
wir suchen	we're looking for
ihr sucht	you're looking for (familiar plural)
Sie suchen	you're looking for (formal or polite)
sie suchen	they're looking for

The verb GLAUBEN – to believe/think

ich glaube	I believe/think
du glaubst	you believe (familiar)
er glaubt	he believes
sie glaubt	she believes
wir glauben	we believe
ihr glaubt	you believe (familiar plural)
Sie glauben	you believe (formal or polite)
sie glauben	they believe

The verb BRAUCHEN – to need

ich brauche	I need
du brauchst	you need (familiar)
er braucht	he needs
sie braucht	she needs
wir brauchen	we need
ihr braucht	you need (familiar plural)
Sie brauchen	you need (formal or polite)
sie brauchen	they need

10. Some important irregular verbs used in *Mastering German*

The verb FAHREN – to go (by vehicle)

ich fahre	I go
du fährst	you go (familiar)
er fährt	he goes
sie fährt	she goes
wir fahren	we go
ihr fahrt	you go (familiar plural)
Sie fahren	you go (formal or polite)
sie fahren	they go

The verb NEHMEN – to take

ich nehme	I take
du nimmst	you take (familiar)
er nimmt	he takes
sie nimmt	she takes
wir nehmen	we take
ihr nehmt	you take (familiar plural)
Sie nehmen	you take (formal or polite)
sie nehmen	they take

The verb HABEN – to have

ich habe	I have
du hast	you have (familiar)
er hat	he has
sie hat	she has
wir haben	we have
ihr habt	you have (familiar plural)
Sie haben	you have (formal or polite)
sie haben	they have

The verb TRAGEN — to wear

ich trage	I wear
du trägst	you wear (familiar)
er trägt	he wears
sie trägt	she wears
wir tragen	we wear
ihr tragt	you wear (familiar plural)
Sie tragen	you wear (formal or polite)
sie tragen	they wear

11. The *modal* verbs

The verb KÖNNEN — to 'can'/to be able to

ich kann	I can
du kannst	you can (familiar)
er kann	he can
sie kann	she can
wir können	we can
ihr könnt	you can (familiar plural)
Sie können	you can (formal or polite)
sie können	they can

The verb DÜRFEN — to 'may'/be allowed to

ich darf	I may
du darfst	you may (familiar)
er darf	he may
sie darf	she may
wir dürfen	we may
ihr dürft	you may (familiar plural)
Sie dürfen	you may (formal or polite)
sie dürfen	they may

The verb WOLLEN — to want to

ich will	I want to
du willst	you want to (familiar)
er will	he wants to
sie will	she wants to
wir wollen	we want to
ihr wollt	you want to (familiar plural)
Sie wollen	you want to (formal or polite)
sie wollen	they want to

The verb MÜSSEN — to 'must'/have to

ich muß	I must/have to
du mußt	you must/have to (familiar)
er muß	he must/has to
sie muß	she must/has to
wir müssen	we must/have to
ihr müßt	you must/have to (familiar plural)
Sie müssen	you must/have to (formal or polite)
sie müssen	they must/have to

The verb BRAUCHEN NICHT – to don't have to/don't need to

ich brauche nicht	I don't have to/need to
du brauchst nicht	you don't have to/need to (familiar)
er braucht nicht	he doesn't have to/need to
sie braucht nicht	she doesn't have to/need to
wir brauchen nicht	we don't have to/need to
ihr braucht nicht	you don't have to/need to (familiar plural)
Sie brauchen nicht	you don't have to/need to (formal or polite)
sie brauchen nicht	they don't have to/need to

A very important part of the verb MÖGEN – to like

ich möchte	I would like (also: I should like, etc.)
du möchtest	you would like (familiar)
er möchte	he would like
sie möchte	she would like
wir möchten	we would like
ihr möchtet	you would like (familiar plural)
Sie möchten	you would like (formal or polite)
sie möchten	they would like

12. The Compound Past tense, or Perfect tense, and general reference list of verbs

This contains the verbs used in *Mastering German*, and includes the fifty most frequently occurring verbs in spoken German.

The past participles of most of these verbs begin with ge-,
end with   -en.

Some of them change the vowel sound in the du and er form of the Present tense. This is indicated.

Some of them change the vowel sound in the past participle.

Some make their Perfect tense with haben, others with sein.

Group A

INFINITIVE	VOWEL CHANGE in present tense	PAST PARTICIPLE	MEANING
bleiben		geblieben (sein)	to stay; remain
bringen		gebracht	to bring
denken		gedacht	to think
essen	i	gegessen	to eat
fahren	ä	gefahren (sein)	to go; drive
finden		gefunden	to find
geben	i	gegeben	to give
*gefallen	ä	gefallen	to like; to please
gehen		gegangen (sein)	to go
halten	ie	gehalten	to hold
heißen		geheißen	to be called
†helfen	i	geholfen	to help
kennen		gekannt	to know someone

Group A cont.

INFINITIVE	VOWEL CHANGE in present tense	PAST PARTICIPLE	MEANING
kommen		gekommen (sein)	to come
laufen	ä	gelaufen (sein)	to run
lesen	ie	gelesen	to read
liegen		gelegen	to lie; recline
nehmen	i	genommen	to take
nennen		gennant	to name
reisen		gereist (sein)	to travel
reiten		geritten	to ride
schlafen	ä	geschlafen	to sleep
schwimmen		geschwommen (sein/haben)	to swim
sehen	ie	gesehen	to see
singen		gesungen	to sing
sitzen		gesessen	to sit
sprechen	i	gesprochen	to speak
stehen		gestanden	to stand
tragen	ä	getragen	to wear; carry
treffen	i	getroffen	to meet
trinken		getrunken	to drink
tun		getan	to do
verlieren		verloren	to lose
waschen	ä	gewaschen	to wash
werden	i	geworden (sein)	to become
wiegen		gewogen	to weigh
wissen	weiß	gewußt	to know something

*The verb gefallen (to like) operates in a special way. In order to render 'I like it', one must say es gefällt mir, literally 'it pleases me'. Note that 'me' is rendered by mir (dative case).

† The verb helfen (to help) has an object in the dative case. 'He helps me' is rendered by er hilft mir.

Group B
All these verbs make their past participle by dropping the -en at the end of the infinitive, and adding -t (or -et). They are all conjugated with haben.

INFINITIVE	PAST PARTICIPLE	MEANING
arbeiten	gearbeitet	to work
basteln	gebastelt	to make things as a hobby
bauen	gebaut	to build
borgen	geborgt	to borrow
brauchen	gebraucht	to need
fragen	gefragt	to ask

Group B cont.

INFINITIVE	PAST PARTICIPLE	MEANING
gehören	gehört	to belong
glauben	geglaubt	to believe
hören	gehört	to hear
kaufen	gekauft	to buy
kochen	gekocht	to cook
kriegen	gekriegt	to get
lernen	gelernt	to learn
malen	gemalt	to paint
machen	gemacht	to make, do
parken	geparkt	to park
rauchen	geraucht	to smoke
regnen (es)	geregnet	to rain
reinigen	gereinigt	to clean
sagen	gesagt	to say; tell
sammeln	gesammelt	to collect
schauen	geschaut	to look; see
spielen	gespielt	to play
starten	gestartet	to start
stecken	gesteckt	to put
stellen	gestellt	to put; lay
suchen	gesucht	to look for
tanzen	getanzt	to dance
träumen	geträumt	to dream
trennen	getrennt	to separate
wandern	gewandert	to go walking
wählen	gewählt	to choose
wechseln	gewechselt	to change (money)
wohnen	gewohnt	to live
zahlen	gezahlt	to pay
zittern	gezittert	to shiver

Group C

These verbs have separable affixes, and form their past participle by placing the -ge between affix and stem.

INFINITIVE	VOWEL CHANGE in present tense	PAST PARTICIPLE	MEANING
abfahren	ä	abgefahren (sein)	to leave; depart
abholen		abgeholt	to fetch
abschließen		abgeschlossen	to lock up
abtrocknen		abgetrocknet	to dry up
abwaschen	ä	abgewaschen	to wash up
anfangen	ä	angefangen	to begin
ankommen		angekommen (sein)	to arrive
anrufen		angerufen	to telephone
anziehen		angezogen	to put on (clothes)

Group C cont.

INFINITIVE	VOWEL CHANGE in present tense	PAST PARTICIPLE	MEANING
aufgeben		aufgegeben	to give up
aufräumen		aufgeräumt	to tidy up
aufstehen		aufgestanden	to get up
ausgehen		ausgegangen (sein)	to go out
einkaufen		eingekauft	to do the shopping
einschlafen	ä	einschlafen	to go to sleep
sich hinlegen		sich hingelegt	to lie down
umsteigen		umgestiegen (sein)	to change (trains)
wegfahren	ä	weggefahren (sein)	to go away
vorstellen		vorgestellt	to introduce

Group D

These verbs have no ge- in the past participle. They are all conjugated with haben.

INFINITIVE	PAST PARTICIPLE	MEANING
anprobieren	anprobiert	to try on
beginnen	begonnen	to begin
bekommen	bekommen	to get
besuchen	besucht	to visit
erwarten	erwartet	to expect
erzählen	erzählt	to tell (a story)
sich interessieren (für)	interessiert	to be interested in
reparieren	repariert	to repair
reservieren	reserviert	to reserve
telefonieren	telefoniert	to telephone
verdienen	verdient	to earn
verschreiben	verschrieben	to prescribe
verstehen	verstanden	to understand
wiederholen	wiederholt	to repeat

The four groups of verbs given above indicate how to form the Compound Past tense. This is the tense which you should learn to use when you want to speak or write German. There is, however, another past tense: the Simple Past tense. Some Germans use this instead of the Compound Past. At this stage of learning German it is only necessary to know how to use the Simple Past tense of the verbs haben, sein, sagen, fragen and the 'modal' verbs. It will, however, be useful for you to recognise the Simple Past tense of other verbs, if and when they are used by native speakers of German.

Simple Past of MALEN – to paint
ich mal – TE
du mal – TEST
er mal – TE
sie mal – TE
wir mal – TEN
ihr mal – TET
Sie mal – TEN
sie mal – TEN

The Simple Past tense is made by adding t to the stem of the verb, e.g.
fragen – fragte (to ask).

Verbs which make their Simple Past tense in an irregular way are given as follows:

INFINITIVE	SIMPLE PAST TENSE
bleiben	blieb
bringen	brachte
denken	dachte
essen	aß
fahren	fuhr
finden	fand
geben	gab
gehen	ging
halten	hielt
heißen	hieß
kennen	kannte
kommen	kam
laufen	lief
lesen	las
liegen	lag
nehmen	nahm
nennen	nannte
reisen	reiste
reiten	ritt
schlafen	schlief
schwimmen	schwamm
sehen	sah
singen	sang
sitzen	saß
sprechen	sprach
stehen	stand
tragen	trug
treffen	traf
trinken	trank
tun	tat
verlieren	verlor
waschen	wusch
werden	wurde
wiegen	wog
wissen	wußte

Simple Past of HABEN – to have

ich hatte	I had
du hattest	you had (familiar)
er hatte	he had
sie hatte	she had
es hatte	it had
wir hatten	we had
ihr hattet	you had (familiar plural)
Sie hatten	you had (formal or polite)
sie hatten	they had

Simple Past of SEIN – to be

ich war	I was
du warst	you were (familiar)
er war	he was
sie war	she was
es war	it was
wir waren	we were
ihr ward	you were (familiar plural)
Sie waren	you were (formal or polite)
sie waren	they were

Simple Past of SAGEN – to say

ich sagte	I said
du sagtest	you said (familiar)
er sagte	he said
sie sagte	she said
es sagte	it said
wir sagten	we said
ihr sagtet	you said (familiar plural)
Sie sagten	you said (formal or polite)
sie sagten	they said

Simple Past of FRAGEN – to ask

ich fragte	I asked
du fragtest	you asked (familiar)
er fragte	he asked
sie fragte	she asked
es fragte	it asked
wir fragten	we asked
ihr fragtet	you asked (familiar plural)
Sie fragten	you asked (formal or polite)
sie fragten	they asked

Simple Past of KÖNNEN – to be able to

ich konnte	I could
du konntest	you could (familiar)
er konnte	he could
sie konnte	she could
es konnte	it could
wir konnten	we could
ihr konntet	you could (familiar plural)
Sie konnten	you could (formal or polite)
sie konnten	they could

Simple Past of WOLLEN – to want to

ich wollte	I wanted to
du wolltest	you wanted to (familiar)
er wollte	he wanted to
sie wollte	she wanted to
es wollte	it wanted to
wir wollten	we wanted to
ihr wolltet	you wanted to (familiar plural)
Sie wollten	you wanted to (formal or polite)
sie wollten	they wanted to

Simple Past of MÜSSEN – to have to

ich mußte	I had to
du mußtest	you had to (familiar)
er mußte	he had to
sie mußte	she had to
es mußte	it had to
wir mußten	we had to
ihr mußtet	you had to (familiar plural)
Sie mußten	you had to (formal or polite)
sie mußten	they had to

Simple Past of DÜRFEN – to be allowed to

ich durfte	I was allowed to
du durftest	you were allowed to (familiar)
er durfte	he was allowed to
sie durfte	she was allowed to
es durfte	it was allowed to
wir durften	we were allowed to
ihr durftet	you were allowed to (familiar plural)
Sie durften	you were allowed to (formal or polite)
sie durften	they were allowed to

SECTION C – WORD ORDER

Many sentences in this course are short phrases consisting of one or two words only. In this respect German resembles English.

When a sentence contains a verb, however, there are certain differences. Below, you will find a list of the principal sentence types used in *Mastering German*.

14. Statements

subject	verb	
Das	ist	Fritz
Ich	bleibe	zwei Nächte
Ich	habe	Kopfschmerzen
Ich	weiß	es nicht genau
Sie	hat	schon einen Pullover
Ich	nehme	ihn
Diese blauen Schuhe	sind	sehr elegant

15. Questions

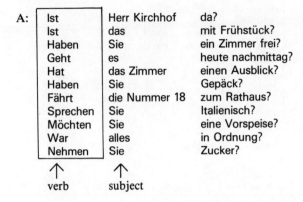

A:	Ist	Herr Kirchhof	da?
	Ist	das	mit Frühstück?
	Haben	Sie	ein Zimmer frei?
	Geht	es	heute nachmittag?
	Hat	das Zimmer	einen Ausblick?
	Haben	Sie	Gepäck?
	Fährt	die Nummer 18	zum Rathaus?
	Sprechen	Sie	Italienisch?
	Möchten	Sie	eine Vorspeise?
	War	alles	in Ordnung?
	Nehmen	Sie	Zucker?
	↑	↑	
	verb	subject	

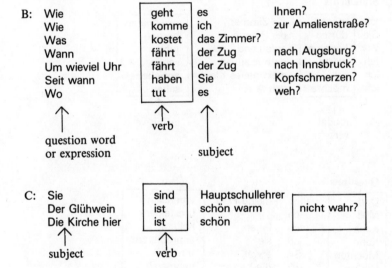

B:	Wie	geht	es	Ihnen?
	Wie	komme	ich	zur Amalienstraße?
	Was	kostet	das Zimmer?	
	Wann	fährt	der Zug	nach Augsburg?
	Um wieviel Uhr	fährt	der Zug	nach Innsbruck?
	Seit wann	haben	Sie	Kopfschmerzen?
	Wo	tut	es	weh?
	↑	↑	↑	
	question word or expression	verb	subject	

C:	Sie	sind	Hauptschullehrer	nicht wahr?
	Der Glühwein	ist	schön warm	
	Die Kirche hier	ist	schön	
	↑	↑		
	subject	verb		

16. Orders or commands

Kommen	Sie	herein
Nehmen	Sie	Platz
Nehmen	Sie	die erste Straße links
Gehen	Sie	die Marktstraße hoch
Fahren	Sie	Richtung Innsbruck
Tragen	Sie	sich ein
Entschuldigen	Sie	die Störung
↑	↑	
verb	subject	

17. Emphasis

Hier	ist	alles	neu
Dann	kommen	Sie	zur Amalienstraße
Heute vormittag	ist	nichts	mehr frei
In der Nacht	war	es	ein dumpfer Schmerz
Einen Damenpullover	suche	ich	
Das	sehe	ich	
Gestern	war	ich	in einem italienischen Restaurant
Giovanni	heißt	es	
↑	↑	↑	
element to be emphasised	verb	subject	

18. Modal verbs

A: Statements

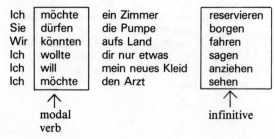

Ich	möchte	ein Zimmer	reservieren
Sie	dürfen	die Pumpe	borgen
Wir	könnten	aufs Land	fahren
Ich	wollte	dir nur etwas	sagen
Ich	will	mein neues Kleid	anziehen
Ich	möchte	den Arzt	sehen
	↑		↑
	modal verb		infinitive

B: Questions

(i)

Darf	ich	meine Frau	vorstellen?
Muß	ich	–	umsteigen?
Kann	ich	Ihnen	helfen?
Kann	ich	sie	anprobieren?
Möchten	Sie	etwas	trinken?
Wollen	wir	die Karten	nehmen?
↑			↑
modal verb			infinitive

(ii)

Was	darf	es	sein?
Wo	kann	ich denn hier	parken?
Warum	möchtest	du mit einer Straßenbahn	fahren?
↑	↑		↑
question word	modal verb		infinitive

C: Emphasis

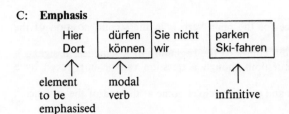

Hier	**dürfen** Sie nicht	**parken**
Dort	**können** wir	**Ski-fahren**

element
to be
emphasised

modal
verb

infinitive

19. Verbs with separable affixes

Der Zug	**fährt**		**ab**
Der Zug	**kommt**		**an**
Sie	**steigen**	in Koblenz	**um**
Ich	**schaue**	mich	**um**
Er	**wäscht**	die Teller	**ab**
Sie	**geht**	am Samstag	**aus**

verb

affix

20. Compound Past (Perfect) tense

A: Statements

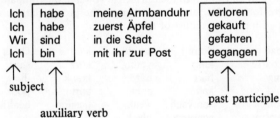

Ich	**habe**	meine Armbanduhr	**verloren**
Ich	**habe**	zuerst Äpfel	**gekauft**
Wir	**sind**	in die Stadt	**gefahren**
Ich	**bin**	mit ihr zur Post	**gegangen**

subject

auxiliary verb

past participle

B: Questions

(i)

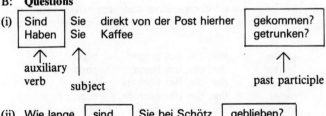

Sind	Sie	direkt von der Post hierher	**gekommen?**
Haben	Sie	Kaffee	**getrunken?**

auxiliary
verb

subject

past participle

(ii)

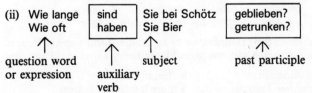

Wie lange	**sind**	Sie bei Schötz	**geblieben?**
Wie oft	**haben**	Sie Bier	**getrunken?**

question word
or expression

auxiliary
verb

subject

past participle

SUMMARY

(a) The 'normal' place for the main verb is in the second position of the sentence.

(b) When the main verb comes to the beginning of a sentence, it signals a command, or a question (though a question can be introduced by a 'question word').

(c) Infinitives, affixes and past participles come at the end of the sentence.

SECTION D – COMPARISONS

21. Comparison of adjectives

Adjectives usually make their comparative form by adding -er. The superlative form of the adjective is usually made by adding -st.

(a) Some adjectives, which end in the letters -el, -en, -er, usually drop the -e in the comparative form.

 edel edler der, die, das edelste noble

(b) Adjectives which end in -d, -t, or a sibilant (i.e. -s) add -est in the superlative form.

 heiß heißer der, die, das heißeste hot

(c) Many adjectives add an Umlaut to their principal vowel in the comparative and the superlative form. This, of course, changes the pronunciation: e.g. groß – größer, alt – älter. Here is a list of them:

arg	bad	dumm	stupid	klug	clever
grob	coarse	jung	young	kurz	short
groß	big	hart	hard	krank	ill
alt	old	kalt	cold	arm	poor
lang	long	schwach	weak	gesund	healthy
warm	warm	schwarz	black		
stark	strong	scharf	sharp		

(d) Some adjectives make their comparative and superlative form in an irregular way. Unfortunately, they are very popular adjectives. Here is a list of them:

groß	größer	der, die, das größte	big
gut	besser	der, die, das beste	good
hoch	höher	der, die, das höchste	high
nah(e)	näher	der, die, das nächste	near
viel	mehr	der, die, das meiste	much
wenig	weniger	der, die, das wenigste	little

(e) When adjectives in their comparative or superlative form come in front of a noun, they have to agree with the noun like ordinary adjectives. Examples:

eine klarere Aussicht	a clearer view
eine intelligentere Frau	a more intelligent woman
ein intelligenterer Mann	a more intelligent man

(f) Sometimes the superlative form of the adjective is made by using -am. Here are some examples:

Im Januar ist das Wetter am kältesten	The weather is coldest in January
Im Juni ist das Wetter am wärmsten	The weather is warmest in June
Im Juni sind die Tage am längsten	In June the days are longest

(g) This is how you can translate the word 'most':

die meisten Bücher	most (of the) books

(h) Notice the way that you repeat adjectives in German:

Die Tage werden immer länger	The days are getting longer and longer
Die Nächte werden immer kühler	The nights are getting cooler and cooler

(i) Here are some important expressions for making comparisons:

Peter ist (eben) so groß wie Klaus	Peter is just as big as Klaus
Klaus ist nicht so groß wie Peter	Klaus is not as big as Peter

22. Adverbs

Most adjectives in German can be used as *adverbs*. Here is a normal regular comparison of adverbs.

scharf	schärfer	am schärfsten	sharply
deutlich	deutlicher	am deutlichsten	clearly
klar	klarer	am klarsten	clearly

Er spricht deutlicher als sie	He speaks more clearly than she does
Ich spreche am deutlichsten	I speak most clearly (of all)

Here are some irregular comparisons of adverbs:

bald	früher	am frühesten	soon
gut	besser	am besten	well

SECTION E – THE CASES

23. The nominative case – the case of the *subject* of a sentence

	Masc.		Fem.	Neut.	Plur.
(a) **The indefinite article**	ein	– a	eine	ein	–
(b) **The negative article**	kein	– not a	keine	kein	keine

(c) **The possessive**	mein	– my	meine	mein	meine
adjectives	dein	– your	deine	dein	deine
	sein	– his	seine	sein	seine
	ihr	– her	ihre	ihr	ihre
	sein	– its	seine	sein	seine
	unser	– our	unsere	unser	unsere
	euer	– your	euere	euer	euere
	Ihr	– your	Ihre	Ihr	Ihre
	ihr	– their	ihre	ihr	ihre

(d) **The definite**	der	– the	die	das	die
article					

(e) Adjective endings

(i) After ein/mein, etc.:

ein—er + NOUN   eine—e + NOUN   ein—es + NOUN

meine—en + NOUN

(ii) After der/dieser, etc.:

der—e + NOUN   die—e + NOUN   das—e + NOUN

die—en + NOUN

(f) The personal pronouns

Sing.			Plur.		
ich	–	I	wir	–	we
du	–	you	ihr	–	you
Sie	–	you	Sie	–	you
er	–	he			
sie	–	she	sie	–	they
es	–	it			

24. The accusative case – the case of the *direct object* of a sentence

	Masc.		**Fem.**	**Neut.**	**Plur.**
(a) **The indefinite article**	einen	– a	eine	ein	–
(b) **The negative article**	keinen	– not a	keine	kein	keine
(c) **The possessive adjectives**	meinen	– my	meine	mein	meine
	deinen	– your	deine	dein	deine
	seinen	– his	seine	sein	seine
	ihren	– her	ihre	ihr	ihre
	seinen	– its	seine	sein	seine
	unseren	– our	unsere	unser	unsere
	eueren	– your	euere	euer	euere
	Ihren	– your	Ihre	Ihr	Ihre
	ihren	– their	ihre	ihr	ihre
(d) **The definite article**	den	– the	die	das	die

(e) Adjective endings

(i) After ein/mein, etc.:
einen—en + NOUN   eine—e + NOUN   ein—es + NOUN
                     meine—en + NOUN

(ii) After der/dieser, etc.:
den—en + NOUN   die—e + NOUN   das—e + NOUN
                   die—en + NOUN

(f) The personal pronouns

Sing.		Plur.	
mich	– me	uns	– us
dich	– you	euch	– you
Sie	– you	Sie	– you
ihn	– him		
sie	– her	sie	– them
es	– it		

25. The dative case – the case of the *indirect object* of a sentence

	Masc.	Fem.	Neut.	Plur.
(a) The indefinite article	einem – a	einer	einem	–
(b) The negative article	keinem – not a	keiner	keinem	keinen
(c) The possessive adjectives	meinem – my	meiner	meinem	meinen
	deinem – your	deiner	deinem	deinen
	seinem – his	seiner	seinem	seinen
	ihrem – her	ihrer	ihrem	ihren
	seinem – its	seiner	seinem	seinen
	unserem – our	unserer	unserem	unseren
	euerem – your	euerer	euerem	eueren
	Ihrem – your	Ihrer	Ihrem	Ihren
	ihrem – their	ihrer	ihrem	ihren
(d) The definite article	dem – the	der	dem	den

(e) Adjective endings

(i) After ein/mein, etc.:
einem—en + NOUN   einer—en + NOUN   einem—en + NOUN
                     meinen—en + NOUN

(ii) After der/dieser, etc.:
dem—en + NOUN   der—en + NOUN   dem—en + NOUN
                   den—en + NOUN

(f) The personal pronouns

Sing.			Plur.		
mir	–	me	uns	–	us
dir	–	you	euch	–	you
Ihnen	–	you	Ihnen	–	you
ihm	–	him			
ihr	–	her	ihnen	–	them
ihm	–	it			

26. Possessive adjectives

Mein Mann
Meine Frau

The following are the possessive adjectives with the corresponding personal pronouns:

ich	I	mein	my
du	you (familiar)	dein	your (familiar)
er	he	sein	his
sie	she	ihr	her
es	it	sein	its
wir	we	unser	our
ihr	you (familiar)	euer	your (familiar)
Sie	you (polite)	ihr	your (polite)
sie	they	ihr	their

This is how *possessive adjectives* agree with *nouns*.

Masc.

mein Mann	–	my husband
dein Mann	–	your husband
sein Garten	–	his garden
ihr Mann	–	her husband
sein Garten	–	its garden
unser Garten	–	our garden
euer Garten	–	your garden
Ihr Mann	–	your husband
ihr Garten	–	their garden

Fem.

meine Frau	–	my wife
deine Frau	–	your wife
seine Frau	–	his wife
ihre Zeitung	–	her newspaper
seine Küche	–	its kitchen
unsere Küche	–	our kitchen
euere Küche	–	your kitchen
Ihre Zeitung	–	your newspaper
ihre Straße	–	their street

Neut.

mein Auto	–	my car
dein Auto	–	your car
sein Auto	–	his car
ihr Auto	–	her car
sein Fenster	–	its window
unser Haus	–	our house
euer Haus	–	your house
Ihr Haus	–	your house
ihr Haus	–	their house

Plur.

meine Schuhe	–	my shoes
deine Schuhe	–	your shoes
seine Schuhe	–	his shoes
ihre Schuhe	–	her shoes
seine Zimmer	–	its rooms
unsere Autos	–	our cars
euere Freunde	–	your friends
Ihre Freunde	–	your friends
ihre Freunde	–	their friends

27. The indefinite article

	Masc.	Fem.	Neut.
NOMINATIVE	ein	eine	ein
ACCUSATIVE	einen	eine	ein
DATIVE	einem	einer	einem

All these words mean 'a' or 'an'. The 'nominative case' is used for the subject of the sentence, and the 'accusative case' is used for the direct object of the sentence.

Examples of direct objects:

| Haben Sie ein Zimmer? (das Zimmer) | Have you got a room? |
| Ich möchte einen Kaffee (der Kaffee) | I'd like a coffee |

You do not use the indefinite article when you want to indicate somebody's profession:

| Er ist Professor | He is a professor |
| Sie ist Sekretärin | She is a secretary |

There is no direct object after the verb sein: 'to be'.

28. Negative ('not a ... ')

The negative form of ein, meaning 'not a' is kein.

| Er ist kein Freund | He is not a friend |
| Nein, sie ist keine Sekretärin | No, she is not a secretary |

Schmidt: Eine Tasse Kaffee?
Müller: Ja, bitte.
Schmidt: Ugh! Das ist kein Kaffee. Das ist Tee!

29. The definite article

	Masc.	Fem.	Neut.	Plur.
NOMINATIVE	der	die	das	die
ACCUSATIVE	den	die	das	die
DATIVE	dem	der	dem	den

The nominative case is used for the subject of the sentence and the accusative case is used for the direct object of the sentence.

The dative case is used for the indirect object of a sentence.

(a) Contractions of the definite article

The definite article is often contracted with certain prepositions. E.g. an das – ans, auf das – aufs, in das – ins, um das – ums.

(b) Definite article with countries, geographical features and streets

Die Schweiz	Switzerland
Der Rhein	the Rhine
Die Donau	the Danube

Die Weser	the Weser
Die Elbe	the Elbe
Die Mozartstraße	Mozart Street

(c) **The definite article is not used when two nouns are closely connected in one idea**

Stadt und Land	town and country
Hand in Hand	hand in hand
Wind und Wetter	wind and weather

30. Adjective endings (1)

Agreement of the adjective after the words der, die or das (also after dieser, diese, dieses – *nominative case*. The adjective is part of the subject of the sentence:

Der blaue Pullover ist sehr schön
Die blauen Schuhe sind sehr elegant

Agreement of the adjective after the words der, die or das (also after dieser, diese, dieses – *accusative case*:

Haben Sie die blauen Schuhe?
Ich habe die gleichen Schuhe

Agreement of the adjective in a phrase introduced by a preposition governing the *dative case*:

Er kommt aus der schönen Stadt Bonn
Wir fahren mit dem alten Taxi

Sing.

	Masc.	Fem.	Neut.
NOMINATIVE	der rote Rock	die schöne Bluse	das weiße Hemd
ACCUSATIVE	den roten Rock	die schöne Bluse	das weiße Hemd
DATIVE	dem roten Rock	der schönen Bluse	dem weißen Hemd

Plur.

NOMINATIVE	die roten Röcke	die schönen Blusen	die weißen Hemde
ACCUSATIVE	die roten Röcke	die schönen Blusen	die weißen Hemde
DATIVE	den roten Röcken	der schönen Blusen	den weißen Hemden

Nouns in the dative plural end in -n or -en, except those which end in -s.

31. Adjective endings (2)

Agreement of the adjective after the words ein, kein, mein, unser, etc. – *nominative case*. The adjective is part of the subject of the sentence:

Ein *guter* Wein kostet viel Geld
Mein *altes* Fahrrad ist kaputt

The adjective is part of the direct object of a sentence, or agrees with a preposition governing the *accusative case*:

Ich habe einen *neuen* Mantel gekauft
Wir gehen eine *alte* Straße entlang

The adjective is part of the indirect object of a sentence, or agrees with a preposition governing the *dative case*:

Er gibt seiner *schönen* Sekretärin eine Kette
Er kommt mit seinem *alten* Koffer

	Sing.		
	Masc.	**Fem.**	**Neut.**
NOMINATIVE	ein guter Wein	eine schöne Kette	ein altes Auto
ACCUSATIVE	einen guten Wein	eine schöne Kette	ein altes Auto
DATIVE	einem guten Wein	einer schönen Kette	einem alten Auto

	Plur.		
NOMINATIVE	meine alten Schuhe	meine schönen Blusen	unsere alten Autos
ACCUSATIVE	meine alten Schuhe	meine schönen Blusen	unsere alten Autos
DATIVE	meinen alten Schuhen	meinen schönen Blusen	unseren alten Autos

Most nouns in the dative plural end in -n or -en.

32. Adjective endings (3)
Sometimes adjectives occur by themselves. That is to say, they are not preceded by the words der or dieser, or by the words ein, mein, kein, etc. In these cases the adjective is declined somewhat differently. The endings are set out for you below:

	Sing.		
	Masc.	**Fem.**	**Neut.**
	good wine	good milk	good beer
NOMINATIVE	gut*er* Wein	gut*e* Milch	gut*es* Bier
ACCUSATIVE	gut*en* Wein	gut*e* Milch	gut*es* Bier
DATIVE	gut*em* Wein	gut*er* Milch	gut*em* Bier

	Plur.		
NOMINATIVE	gut*e* Weine	schön*e* Blusen	rot*e* Hemde
ACCUSATIVE	gut*e* Weine	schön*e* Blusen	rot*e* Hemde
DATIVE	gut*en* Wein*en*	schön*en* Blus*en*	rot*en* Hemd*en*

33. Prepositions governing the accusative case
The following prepositions make the definite or indefinite article occur in the accusative case:

bis	as far as
durch	through
entlang	along
für	for
ohne	without
um	round

Bis

Er kommt bis an die Tür	He comes as far as (i.e. up to) the door
Wir bleiben bis Sonntag	We are staying till Sunday

Durch

Der Fußball geht durch das Fenster	The football goes through the window
Sie geht durch den Zug	She goes through the train

Entlang

Wir gehen die Straße entlang	We go along the street
Er kommt den Korridor entlang	He comes along the corridor

Note that the word entlang comes after the noun.

Für

Hier ist ein Brief für den Chef	Here is a letter for the boss
Ich kaufe einen Pullover für das Kind	I buy a pullover for the child

Ohne

Ich komme ohne meinen Mantel	I'm coming without my coat
Sie schwimmt ohne eine Bademütze	She is swimming without a bathing cap

Um

Wir sitzen um den Tisch	We're sitting round the table
Er geht um das Rathaus	He goes round the town hall

34. Prepositions governing the dative case

The following *prepositions* govern the dative case

aus	out of/from
außer	beside/except
bei	near/with/among
mit	with
nach	to/after/according to
seit	since
von	about
zu	to/at
gegenüber	opposite

Aus

generally means 'out of', 'from':

(a) to express movement from a place

Er kommt aus dem Zimmer	He comes out of the room

(b) to express origin referring to time, place or material

Glas aus der Römerzeit	Glass from Roman times
Er kommt aus Hamburg	He comes from Hamburg
Das Haus ist aus Stein	The house is made of stone

(c) to express a cause – special phrases

Aus diesem Grund	For that reason
Aus Versehen	By mistake

Außer

generally means 'outside', 'out of', 'beyond':

Außer Gefahr	Out of danger
Außer Frage	Out of the question
Außer sich	Beside oneself (e.g. for joy)
Außer Zweifel	Beyond doubt
Außer Kontrolle	Beyond control

Bei

generally means 'by', 'near', beside:

(a) Mölln bei Hamburg   Mölln near Hamburg

(b) it means 'at the house of' or 'living with'

    Er wohnt bei seinen Eltern   He lives with his parents

(c) it means 'with' or 'on', referring to persons

    Ich habe kein Geld bei mir   I have no money with me, or on me

(d) other phrases

Beim Frühstück	At breakfast
Beim Mittagessen	At lunch
Bei Tisch	At table
Bei diesem Wetter	In this weather
Bei dieser Gelegenheit	On this occasion
Bei der Arbeit	At work

Mit

generally means 'with', 'by'

(a) Kommen Sie mit?   Are you coming (with me or without)?

(b) it means 'by', referring to means of transport

Mit dem Zug	By train
Mit dem Auto	By car
Mit dem Rad	By bicycle

Nach

(a) it means 'to' with the names of places

Nach Berlin	To Berlin
Nach Deutschland	To Germany

(b) it means 'after'

Nach 10 Minuten	After 10 minutes
Nach einer halben Stunde	After half an hour

(c) it means 'according to'

Nach seinem Brief ist er krank	According to his letter he is ill
Nach meiner Meinung (or meiner Meinung nach)	In my opinion
Nach Belieben	As desired

(d) other phrases

Nach Hause gehen (fahren)	To go home
Nach oben	To go upwards or upstairs
Nach außen	To go outwards or outside

Seit
generally means 'since'
(a) Seit Weihnachten   Since Christmas
     Seit Ostern   Since Easter
(b) it also means 'for'
     Seit 10 Jahren   For 10 years
     Ich wohne seit 10 Jahren in   I have been living in Hamburg for
       Hamburg   10 years

Note that the Present tense is used. And note that the expression of time comes *before* that of place.

Von
(a) it means 'of', or 'about', or 'concerning'
     Ich spreche von ihm   I'm speaking about him
     Ich spreche von ihr   I'm speaking about her
(b) it means 'by', e.g. written by
     Hamlet von Shakespeare   Hamlet by Shakespeare
(c) it means 'from'
     von Jahr zu Jahr   From year to year
     von Zeit zu Zeit   From time to time

Note that the English word 'of' is sometimes omitted in German:
     Zwei Glas Milch   Two glasses of milk
     Eine Menge Leute   A crowd of people
     Eine Tasse Tee   A cup of tea
     Die Stadt London   The town of London
     Die Firma Schmidt   The firm of Smith
     Der Monat Januar   The month of January

Zu
(a) it means 'to', when used with the names of places, or buildings in a town
     Ich gehe zum Rathaus   I'm going to the town hall
     Er geht zur Haltestelle   He's going to the bus stop
(b) it means 'at' with the names of seasons
     Zu Weihnachten   At Christmas
     Zu Ostern   At Easter
(c) it means 'at' referring to prices
     Fleisch zu 11 Mark das Pfund   Meat at 11 marks a pound
(d) it means 'for' referring to purpose
     Zu diesem Zweck   For this purpose
     Zum Beispiel   For example
(e) other phrases
     Zu Fuß   On foot
     Zum zweiten Mal   For the second time
     Zum dritten Mal   For the third time
     Zu Ende   At an end
     Zu Hause   At home

Gegenüber
     Das Rathaus ist gegenüber   The town hall is opposite the
       dem Theater   theatre
     Wir sind gegenüber der Post   We're opposite the post office

35. Prepositions governing either the accusative or the dative case

an	by/on/at/to
auf	on
hinter	behind
in	in
neben	beside/near
über	over/above
unter	under
vor	in front of/before
zwischen	between

When they occur with a verb which indicates *position*, they govern the dative.

When they occur with a verb which indicates *movement towards* something, they govern the accusative.

An with the dative
generally means 'at', 'near', by the side of

Er sitzt an dem Tisch	He is sitting at the table
Das Bild hängt an der Wand	The picture is hanging on the wall
Er steht an dem Fenster	He is standing at the window

An with the accusative
generally means 'at', 'to'

Er setzt sich an den Tisch	He sits down at the table
Er hängt das Bild an die Wand	He hangs the picture on the wall
Er geht an das Fenster	He goes to the window

Auf with the dative
generally means 'on', 'on top of'

Das Buch liegt auf dem Tisch	The book is on the desk

In a number of idioms, auf means 'in' or 'at'

Auf der Straße	In the street
Auf dem Markt	At the market
Auf dem Land	In the country

Auf with the accusative
generally means 'on', 'on top of'

Er stellt die Tasse auf den Tisch	He puts the cup on the table
Er stellt das Radio auf den Stuhl	He puts the radio on the chair

Auf also means 'for' when it refers to future time

Er fährt auf drei Tage nach Hamburg	He is going to Hamburg for three days

Hinter means 'behind'

Er steht hinter der Tür	He is standing behind the door
Er geht hinter die Tür	He goes behind the door

In with the dative
generally means 'in', referring to time or place.

Das Geld ist in meiner Tasche	The money is in my pocket
Das Radio ist im Wohnzimmer	The radio is in the living room

In also has a number of other meanings

In der Schule	At school
In der Kirche	At church
Im Alter von ...	At the age of ...
Im ersten Stock	On the first floor
Im großen und ganzen	On the whole
Im Gegenteil	On the contrary
Heute in acht Tagen	Today week

In with the accusative
generally means 'into'

Er steckt das Geld in seine Tasche	He puts the money into his pocket
Er fährt das Auto in die Garage	He drives the car into the garage

Other meanings of in

Er geht in die Kirche	He goes to church
Sie fährt in die Stadt	She drives to town
Wir gehen ins Theater	We go to the theatre

Neben generally means 'besides', 'by', 'at the side of'

Er steht neben der Tür	He is standing by the door
Er stellt den Stuhl neben die Tür	He puts the chair beside the door

Über with the dative
generally means 'over', 'above'

Über dem Berg sind Wolken	There are clouds over the mountain

Über with the accusative
generally means 'over', 'across'

Er geht über die Straße	He goes across the street
Sie schwimmt über den Fluß	She swims across the river

Other meanings of *über*

Das Päckchen wiegt über 500 Gramm	The packet weighs more than 500 grams
Der Zug fährt über München	The train goes via Munich

Unter with the dative
generally means 'under', 'among', 'amid'

Öl ist unter dem Auto	There is oil under the car
Du bist unter Freunden	You are among friends

Other meanings of *unter*

Das Päckchen wiegt unter 500 Gramm	The packet weighs less than 500 grams
Unter dieser Bedingung	On this condition
Unter diesen Umständen	Under these circumstances

Unter with the accusative
generally means 'under', 'among'

Der Ball rollt unter das Auto	The ball rolls underneath the car
Die Katze läuft unter den Tisch	The cat runs under the table

Vor with the dative
generally means 'before' (referring to time or place), 'in front of'

Vor dem Krieg	Before the war
Er steht vor dem Haus	He stands in front of the house

Other meanings of *Vor*

Vor zwei Tagen	Two days ago
Vor langer Zeit	A long time ago
Sie zittert vor Kälte	She is shivering with cold

Vor with the accusative
generally means 'before', 'in front of'

Sie kommt vor die Klasse	She comes in front of the class
Er springt vor das Auto	He jumps in front of the car

Zwischen means 'between'

Das Fahrrad ist zwischen dem Bus und dem Auto	The bicycle is between the bus and the car
Er fährt das Auto zwischen die Polizisten	He drives the car between the policemen

MONEY, WEIGHTS
AND MEASURES

WEST GERMAN, AUSTRIAN, SWISS AND EAST GERMAN MONEY

West German currency
Marks = DM; Pfennigs = Pf; DM1 = 100Pf.
DM 2,72 = zwei Mark zweiundsiebzig Pfennig.

COINS (Münzen)		NOTES (Banknotes)	
DM – ,1	ein Pfennig	DM 5, –	fünf Mark
DM – ,5	fünf Pfennig	DM 10, –	zehn Mark
DM – ,10	zehn Pfennig	DM 20, –	zwanzig Mark
DM – ,50	fünfzig Pfennig	DM 50, –	fünfzig Mark
DM 1, –	eine Mark	DM 100, –	hundert Mark
DM 2, –	zwei Mark	DM 500, –	fünfhundert Mark
DM 5, –	fünf Mark		

Currency in East Germany consists of the same coins and banknotes as in West Germany. The value and purchasing power are, however, different.

Austrian currency
100 Groschen = 1 Schilling.

COINS	NOTES
2 Groschen	20 Schillinge
5 Groschen	50 Schillinge
10 Groschen	100 Schillinge
50 Groschen	500 Schillinge
1 Schilling	1000 Schillinge
5 Schillinge	
10 Schillinge	

Swiss currency
100 Centimes = 1 Franc.
In German you say Rappen for centimes and Franken for francs.

COINS	NOTES
5 Rappen	10 Franken
10 Rappen	20 Franken
20 Rappen	50 Franken

½ Franke   100 Franken
1 Franke   1000 Franken
2 Franken
5 Franken

DISTANCES

1 mile = 1.6 kilometres   1.6 Kilometer = 1 Meile

Miles	10	20	30	40	50	60	70	80	90	100	Meilen
Kilometres	16	32	48	64	80	97	113	128	145	160	Kilometer

LENGTHS AND SIZES

General clothes sizes (including chest/hip measurements)

GB	USA	Germany	Europe	ins	cms
8	6	34	36	30/32	76/81
10	8	36	38	32/34	81/86
12	10	38	40	34/36	86/91
14	12	40	42	36/38	91/97
16	14	42	44	38/40	97/102
18	16	44	46	40/42	102/107
20	18	46	48	42/44	107/112
22	20	48	50	44/46	112/117
24	22	50	52	46/48	117/122
26	24	52	54	48/50	122/127

Waist measurements

(ins)   GB/USA

22	24	26	28	30	32	34	36	38	40	42	44	46	48	50

(cms)   Europe

56	61	66	71	76	81	86	91	97	102	107	112	117	122	127

Shoes

GB

3	3½	4	4½	5	5½	6	6½	7	7½	8	8½	9	10	11	12

USA

4½	5	5½	6	6½	7	7½	8	8½	9	9½	10	10½	11½	12½	13½
36		37		38		39		40		41		42	43	44	45

WEIGHTS

Some approximate equivalents – Gramm (g) (grams) and Kilogramm (Kg) (kilograms):

1000 Gramm (1000g)	=	1 Kilogramm (1 Kilo/kg)
1 oz	=	25 Gramm (g)
4 oz	=	100/125 Gramm
8 oz	=	225 Gramm
1 pound (16 oz)	=	450 Gramm
1 pound 2 oz	=	500 Gramm (½ Kilogramm)
2 pounds 4 oz	=	1 Kilogram (1 Kilo/kg)
1 stone	=	6 Kilogram

Body weight
Body weight in Europe is measured in kilograms (Kilogramm). Some approximate equivalents:

POUNDS	STONES	KILOGRAMS
28	2	12½
42	3	19
56	4	25
70	5	32
84	6	38
98	7	45
112	8	51
126	9	57½
140	10	63
154	11	70
168	12	76
182	13	83
196	14	90

LIQUID MEASURES

Petrol and oil are measured in litres (Liter), so are most other liquids, including milk. Wine is sometimes sold in litre bottles, but more frequently in bottles containing ¾ litre.

Some approximate equivalents:
1 pint = 0.57 Liter (litres)　　　1 gallon = 4.55 litres

GB measures	Liter (litres)	GB measures	Liter (litres)
1 pint	= 0.57		
		4.4 gallons	= 20
		5.5 gallons	= 25
1.7 pints	= 1	6.6 gallons	= 30
1.1 gallons	= 5	7.7 gallons	= 35
2.2 gallons	= 10	8.8 gallons	= 40
3.3 gallons	= 15	9.9 gallons	= 45

TEMPERATURE

	FAHRENHEIT (F)	GRAD CELSIUS (C) CENTIGRADE
Boiling point	212°	100°
	104°	40°
Body temperature	98.4°	36.9°
	86°	30°
	68°	20°
	59°	15°
	50°	10°
Freezing point	32°	0°
	23°	−5°
	0°	−18°

(Convert Fahrenheit to Celsius by subtracting 32 and multiplying by 5/9. Convert Celsius to Fahrenheit by multiplying by 9/5 and adding 32.)

SOME USEFUL HINTS AND TIPS

Visiting a German speaking country means going into a different culture with different ways of doing things. This can sometimes be a problem, even if you know German quite well. You might like to know, therefore, of two publications which are specially prepared for prospective visitors to Germany. One is called Treffpunkt Deutschland, and the other is called Glückliche Ferientage in Deutschland. This second publication appears in English under the title *Happy Days in Germany*. Both can be obtained by sending a postcard to the German Tourist Office in Frankfurt, Beethoven Straße 69, or from its nearest branch. Many large towns also prepare brochures with useful tips and town plans, specially designed for young people who wish to visit Germany. Frankfurt produces a brochure called 16 bis 36 and Munich produces a brochure called *Young People's Guide to Munich*. These and similar brochures can be obtained by writing to the local tourist office. You should write to the Verkehrsamt der Stadt (plus name of town).

TELEPHONING

In a public telephone box you need to put in two 10-Pfennig coins for a local call, and larger coins for trunk calls. You can make international telephone calls from many public call boxes. You should watch out for the notice on the door Auslandsgespräche.

STAMPS

Generally speaking you can buy stamps only in post offices. They are not usually available in souvenir shops.

SHOPPING HOURS

Shops, chemists and also travel agencies are usually open from Monday to Friday from 9 a.m. until 6 or 6.30 p.m. On Saturdays they are usually open only until midday or 2 o'clock.

BANKING HOURS

Banks are open from 9 to 12 a.m. and from 2 until 4 p.m. They are closed on Saturdays. You can sometimes find currency-exchange kiosks in stations and airports. After 6.30 in the evening, you can buy certain things in petrol stations and newspaper kiosks.

PUBLIC TRANSPORT

Most towns have a comprehensive system of trams, buses, underground railways and suburban railways. It is worthwhile making enquiries about tickets. Frequently you can travel right through a whole city with one ticket. Note that taxis are fairly expensive.

REDUCTIONS

If you have an international pupils' or students' card, there are often special reductions for the theatre, museums, mountain railways and city sightseeing tours.

HOW TO EAT CHEAPLY

Look out for snack bars. They will be called Imbiß or Imbißstube. It's worth noting that many butchers' shops often have a small table and chair where you can go to eat freshly cooked sausage. You can eat fairly cheaply in the cafeterias of large department stores, and you can go into university restaurants to eat. You simply have to buy a meal ticket as German students do. If you are in country areas, it's worth while looking out for small guest-houses. Don't forget to ask for German specialities.

TRAVELLING

You can hitchhike in Germany, but not on the motorway. If you wish to travel long distances, you must take care to find a car before it reaches the motorway. It is allowed, however, to thumb a lift at the entries and exits to motorways. Girls are advised not to go hitchhiking alone. It is interesting to note that the first letter or letters of German registration numbers indicate the town where that car is registered.

There is a system in Germany of arranging to travel with somebody who is proposing to make a motorway journey. You give your name to a central office, and say where you want to travel to, and the office puts you in touch with someone who is going to make a journey. You often have to wait one or two days until your name comes to the top of the list, but it is cheap and safe. You should look up Mitfahrer-Zentrale in the telephone directory.

RAIL TRAVEL

Inter Rail available up to the age of 26 years. The ticket is valid for one month in twenty-one different countries of Europe, and costs 360 Marks.

Tramper-Monats-Ticket available up to the age of 26 years, and valid for one month in the Federal Republic of Germany. Costs 198 Marks, and allows you to travel throughout Germany.

Junior-Paß available up to the age of 26 years, and is valid for one year in the Federal Republic. The ticket costs 98 Marks and allows you to buy rail tickets at half price.

CAR RENTAL

You have to be over 21 to hire a car, and it will cost from 300 Marks a week. It is also possible to rent bicycles at more than 200 railway stations. You can leave your bicycle at the station of your destination. The cost is about 7 Marks a day, including insurance.

LIVING IN GERMANY

There are about 600 Youth Hostels (JH) in Germany. You need a valid international Youth Hostel Membership Card, which you can obtain either in your own country or by writing to the Deutscher Jugendherbergsverband (DJH) in Detmold. The price for young people up to the age of 27 years is between 3 and 4 Marks a night. For the high season it's advisable to make a booking as early as possible. In the most popular tourist areas it's even necessary to book up a year in advance. Information about German Youth Hostels can be obtained from DJH, Bülowstraße 26, 4930 Detmold.

You can also stay at the YMCA (CVJM-Jugendheim); guest-houses for young people (Jugendgästehäuser, Jugendhotels); small overnight huts in the alps (Hütten der Alpenvereine). There are camping sites (Camping Plätze), and many private rooms and small guest-houses (Pensionen). Information about all these places can best be obtained by writing to the Verkehrsamt of the town you wish to visit.

EMERGENCIES

If you are ill and cannot find a hospital, go to the nearest telephone kiosk or telephone directory and look for Ärztlicher Notdienst. This service is manned around the clock. In an emergency you could also try the Red Cross (Rotes Kreuz), or the Social Assistance Centre at railway stations (Bahnhofsmission). However, the best thing to do is to insure yourself against illness before travelling abroad.

If you lose your money or passport, you should report the matter to the nearest police station (Polizeirevier) or to the British Embassy or Consulate. Directory enquiries in the German telephone system is found by dialling 118 or 0118. In large cities, the police can be contacted by dialling 110. If you break down on the motorway, there are yellow emergency telephones at the roadside.

A FEW THINGS TO SEE

Here are one or two ideas to whet your appetite. They are the sort of things which many tourists would not think of doing:

Berlin – a stroll through the artists' quarter in Kreuzberg.

Munich – visit the fruit and vegetable market (Viktualienmarkt) in the early morning; or go for a journey on a raft on the river Isar.

Hamburg – visit the fish market at 4 o'clock in the morning.

See some of the beautiful old towns, which have retained their ancient appearance, or been beautifully restored. For example: Freiburg with its cathedral, Bamberg with its cathedral, Passau with its three rivers, the Danube, the Inn and the Ilz, Nürnberg with its medieval castle.

Parts of Germany are already well-known for their beautiful landscapes, such as Bavaria, the Black Forest, the Rhine and the Bodensee (Lake Constance). There are, however, many other beautiful parts of Germany which are less well-known, such as the Bavarian Forest (der Bayerische Wald) with its virgin forest, or the Valley of the river Tauber in Franconia or the Hohenloher Land in Würtemberg with its many castles. Then there are the beautiful areas of the Odenwald, the Spessart, the Rhön, the Eiffel, the Lüneburg Heath and the North Sea islands (Halligen). Instead of doing a boat trip on the Rhine, why not try the river Weser? Instead of visiting Heidelberg and Rothenberg ob der Tauber, why not go to see Schwäbisch Hall, Bad Windsen on the river Nekkar, or the tiny forgotten town of Wolframs Eschenbach in Franconia, with its old town wall still intact? Celle on the Lüneburge Heide and Regensburg on the Danube are well worth a visit, both for their beauty and for their historic interest.

These are, of course, only one or two of the many attractive places you could visit in Germany. The experienced and adventurous traveller, equipped with his copy of *Mastering German* cannot fail to have a delightful holiday by taking the byroads and discovering the beautiful sights which Germany has to offer. Always try to speak a few words of German, and you will instantly make friends.

SIGNS ON PUBLIC DISPLAY

ABFAHRT	Departures
ABTEILUNG	Department
ACHTUNG	Take care
ADAC	German equivalent of AA RAC
AN	On (switches, etc.)
ANKUNFT	Admissions Arrivals
ANLIEGER FREI	Access only (i.e. only if your destination is in this street)
AN SONN- UND FEIERTAGEN FREI	No charge Sundays and Bank Holidays
APOTHEKE	Dispensing chemist
ARZT	Doctor
AUFZUG	Lift
AUS	Off (switches, etc.)
AUSFAHRT	Exit
AUSGANG	Exit
AUSKUNFT	Enquiries
AUßER BETRIEB	Not in use
AUSVERKAUF	Sale
AUTOBAHN	Motorway
AUTOBAHNKREUZ	Motorways merge
BAHNSTEIG	Platform
BAUSTELLE	Building site; road works ahead
BEI VERSAGEN KNOPF DRÜCKEN	Press button to get money back
BESETZT	Engaged; no vacancies; occupied
BETRETEN VERBOTEN	Keep out; no trepassing
BITTE MOTOR ABSCHALTEN	Please switch engine off
DAMEN	Ladies; Ladies' Room
DURCHGEHEND	Continuously
EIN	In
EINBAHNSTRAßE	One-way street
EINFAHRT	Way in
EINFAHRT FREIHALTEN	Do not obstruct entrance
EINGANG	Entrance
EINORDNEN	Get in lane
EINTRITT	Admission

EMPFANG	Reception
ERDGESCHOß	Ground floor
ERSATZTEILE	Spare parts
FAHRPLAN	Timetable
FAHRSPUR GESPERRT	Lane closed
FAHRSTUHL	Lift
FAMILIENNAME	Last name
FESTHALTEN	Hold tight
FLUG	Flight
FRAUEN	Women
FREI	Vacant
FREMDENZIMMER	Room to let (Bed and breakfast)
FUNDBÜRO	Lost property office
GASTHAUS	Inn; pub
GASTHOF	Inn; pub
GEFAHR	Danger
GEPÄCKABGABE	Left Luggage
GESCHLOSSEN	Closed
GRENZÜBERGANG	Frontier
HABEN SIE IHREN SCHLÜSSEL ABGEGEBEN?	Have you handed in your key?
HAUPTBAHNHOF	Main station (in a city)
HEIßE GETRÄNKE	Hot drinks
HERREN	Gentlemen; Gents
KASSE	Cash desk; till
KEIN AUSGANG	No way out
KEINE DURCHFAHRT	No thoroughfare
KEINE EINFAHRT	No access
KEIN EINGANG	Exit only; No entry
KEIN TRINKWASSER	Not drinking water
KOSTENPFLICHTIG	At owner's expense
LANGSAM	Slow
LEBENSGEFAHR	Danger
LKW	Lorries
MÄNNER	Men
MOTOR ABSTELLEN	Switch off engine
MÜNZEINWURF	Insert coin
MÜNZEN	Coins
MÜNZRÜCKGABE	Reject coins
MÜNZWECHSLER	Coin change
NICHT ANGREIFEN	Do not touch
NICHT BERÜHREN	Do not touch
NICHT RAUCHEN	Do not smoke
NICHTRAUCHER	Non-smoker
NICHT RESERVIERT	Unreserved
NICHT ÜBERHOLEN	No overtaking
NOTAUSGANG	Emergency exit; fire exit
NUR FÜR RASIERAPPARATE	Shavers only
NUR MIT SONDERGENEHMIGUNG	Permit holders only
OBEN/UNTEN	(This side) up; down
OFFEN (TÄGLICH) (BIS)	Open (daily) (till)
ÖFFNUNGSZEITEN	Opening hours

PARKPLATZ	Parking
PARKZEIT 30 MINUTEN	Waiting limited to 30 minutes
PKW	Cars
PLATZ	Seat
PLATZRESERVIERUNG	Seat reservations
POLIZEI	Police
POSTAMT	Post Office
PRAKT. ARZT	Doctor
PRIVATPARKPLATZ	Private parking only
RASTPLATZ	Lay-by
RASTSTÄTTE	Services (on the motorway)
REINIGUNG	Cleaners
REISEBÜRO	Travel office
REISEFÜHRER	Guide
REPARATUREN	Repairs
RESERVIERT	Reserved
RESERVIERUNGEN	Reservations
ROLLSPLITT	Loose chippings
RÜCKGABEKNOPF	Press to reject
RUHETAG	Rest day
RUNDFAHRT	Tour
SB-TANKSTELLE	Self-service petrol station
SCHLÜSSELFÄCHER	Left luggage lockers
SCHNELLDIENST	While you wait
SCHWIMMBAD	Swimming pool
SCHWIMMEN UND BADEN VERBOTEN	No bathing; swimming
SELBSTBEDIENUNG	Self-service
SELBST TANKEN	Self-service (petrol)
SONDERANGEBOTE	Bargains; special offers
SPARKASSE	Bank
SPEISEKARTE	Menu
SPRECHSTUNDEN	Surgery hours
SPRECHZEITEN	Surgery hours
STADTMITTE	Town centre
TAGESAUSFLÜGE	Day excursions
TANKSTELLE	Petrol station; service area
TREPPE	Stairs
TRINKWASSER	Drinking water
TÜRE SCHLIEẞEN	Close doors (firmly)
ÜBERNACHTUNG UND FRÜHSTÜCK	Bed and breakfast
UMKLEIDERAUM	Changing room
UMLEITUNG	Diversion
UNFALL	Accident
UNTERFÜHRUNG	Subway
UNTERKUNFT	Accommodation
VERBOTEN	Prohibited
VERKAUFS- UND KUNDENDIENST	Sales and service
VERKEHRSAMT	Tourist office
VORFAHRT BEACHTEN	Give way: major road ahead
VORSICHT	Caution
WARME KÜCHE (DURCHGEHEND)	Hot meals served all day
WARNUNG	Warning

WARTERAUM	Waiting area
WARTEZIMMER	Waiting room
WECHSEL	Exchange
ZAHNARZT	Dentist
ZEITUNGEN	Newspapers
ZENTRUM	Town centre
ZIMMER FREI	Room to let
ZIMMERNACHWEIS	Accommodation bureau
ZIMMER ZU VERMIETEN	Rooms to let
ZUBEHÖR	Accessories
ZUFAHRT	Access
ZUSCHLAG	Additional charge

BIBLIOGRAPHY

Books recommended for improving your spoken German
1. *Get by in German*, BBC Publications, 35 Marylebone High Street, London W1M 4AA.
2. *BBC German Kit* (based on BBC television and radio course Kontakte), BBC Publications, 35 Marylebone High Street, London W1M 4AA.

A small book with lots of useful vocabulary
3. *Survive in German*, Longman.

Grammars
4. A. E. Hammer, *German Grammar and Usage* (Edward Arnold, 1971). A thorough and valuable book for the advanced student.
5. *Harrap's New German Grammar*, C. B. Johnson, Harrap, 1971. Thorough and clear.
6. *A Grammar of Contemporary German* (Deutsch 2000), Hueber, 1976. Adapted from the original German.

Hints and tips about Germany
7. *Treffpunkt Deutschland*, German Tourist Office, Frankfurt, Beethoven Straße 69.
8. *Glückliche Ferientage in Deutschland* (*Happy Days in Germany*), German Tourist Office, Frankfurt, Beethoven Straße 69.

Dictionaries
9. Collins *German Dictionary* (German – English, English – German, in one volume).
10. Harrap's *Standard German and English Dictionary*.
11. Langenscheidt's *New Muret-Sanders Encyclopaedic Dictionary* (four volumes).

Further information about learning German may be obtained from the Centre for Information on Language Teaching and Research, 20 Carlton House Terrace, London SW1Y 5AP